SINGULAR PATHS: OLD MEN LIVING ALONE

COLUMBIA STUDIES OF SOCIAL GERONTOLOGY
AND AGING
Abraham Monk, General Editor

The Political Economy of Aging: The State, Private Power, and Social Welfare. Laura Katz Olson. 1982.

Resolving Grievances in the Nursing Home: A Study of the Ombudsman Program. Abraham Monk, Lenard W. Kaye, and Howard Litwin. 1983.

Old Homes—New Families: Shared Living for the Elderly. Gordon F. Streib, W. Edward Folts, and Mary Anne Hilker. 1984.

Ages in Conflict: A Cross-Cultural Perspective on Inequality Between Old and Young. Nancy Foner. 1984.

A Place to Grow Old: The Meaning of Environment in Old Age. Stephen M. Golant. 1984.

A Will and a Way: What the United States Can Learn from Canada About Caring for the Elderly. Robert L. Kane and Rosalie A. Kane. 1985.

ROBERT L. RUBINSTEIN

Singular Paths:
Old Men Living Alone

COLUMBIA UNIVERSITY PRESS
NEW YORK 1986

Columbia University Press
New York   Guildford, Surrey
Copyright © 1986 Columbia University Press
All rights reserved

Printed in the United States of America

Library of Congress Cataloging-in-Publication Data

Rubinstein, Robert L.
  Singular paths.

  (Columbia studies of social gerontology and aging)
  Bibliography: p.
  Includes index.
  1. Aged men—United States. 2. Widowers—United
States. 3. Single men—United States. 4. Living Alone
—United States. 5. Loneliness. I. Title. II. Series.
HQ1064.U5R82   1986   305.3'1   85-19063
ISBN 0-231-06206-0

Book design by Ken Venezio

Contents

Preface

Since aging is a phenomenon which affects all of us, it is surprising how little we know about the daily lives of older people. This is especially true for older men, who form a minority of the population of Americans age 65 and older. Indeed, the situations, experiences, and feelings of older men are often overlooked and may even be overlooked by those individuals with a special interest in the elderly. This report is a description of aspects of the lives of some older men who live alone and offers a glimpse at some of these feelings and experiences.

In undertaking a project of this sort an investigator finds himself in debt to many persons. I wish to thank all those who have helped me with this project.

The work could not have been undertaken without the generous support of the Frederick and Amelia Schimper Foundation.

The professional staffs at several Philadelphia-area senior centers, senior programs, and housing projects helped with referrals and introductions. I cannot thank these individuals here by name (since Philadelphia is just a big small-town, a name may be associated with a particular center and a center with a particular pseudonymous person discussed below), but I would like to say here that every time I approached a center, center personnel were uniformly helpful and professional, and I am grateful for this.

The Behavioral Research Department at the Philadelphia Geriatric Center provided an ideal environment in which to conduct the research. I especially wish to thank Dr. M. Powell Lawton for his interest, encouragement, and support. Dr. Lawton designed the research upon which this report is based and hired me to carry it out. My debt to him is a very large one indeed. In addition, I wish to thank Miriam Moss for her support, her help with the research, and many hours of conversation. Miriam Moss, Silvia Yaffee, Elizabeth Moles, and Susan Gravatt Crowe aided with the interviewing. The manuscript was typed by Anita Roffman, Sonia Lowenthal, and Bernice Albert; my debt to them is great.

Dr. Sharon Kaufman read and commented on parts of the manuscript, for which I am grateful.

A large debt remains to those men who were interviewed for the project. It is my sincere hope that I have done justice to them and their concerns. My dedication of this book is to the memory of two of these men, H. K. and W. N., now deceased. What these men told me about themselves and their lives touched me deeply.

NOTE

In order to insure their confidentiality, the names of all informants described and discussed in this book have been changed. In addition, the locations of many events have been changed or fictionalized.

CHAPTER 1

Background

This report is a detailed look at the lives of a sample of older men who live alone. It is based on research done by me and others at the Philadelphia Geriatric Center in 1981. The presentation of our research findings is designed to inform both the public and professionals in social gerontology about the lives of older men in general and older men living alone in particular. Men, as a group, are a minority among the elderly. Within this group, older men living alone are themselves a smaller minority. It is our hope that this report serves to give voice to some of the issues and concerns of these older men.

Men in the residentially based category we discuss here—older men who live alone—do not have a consciousness of themselves as a naturally existing group whose members share a mutuality of interests and an identity. While men in the sample are persons of similar sex, age, and residential pattern, such characteristics are not sufficient to lead to the formation of a distinctive group similar to ethnic or interest groups in self-consciousness.

Essentially, the men we interviewed were known to us as individuals: what emerged in our research were a number of memorable persons, each with a distinctive style, worldview, social world, and "slant" on life. We feel it is important here at the beginning to note the uniqueness of each of these men. What emerged in our analysis of our research findings were a variety of issues, themes, ideas, and experiences had by all of the men in common or by groups of the men. These form the central topics of the following chapters.

While most of this report is a presentation of such generalized patterns and themes arranged topically, we note here, and later we argue for, the importance of each individual's own system of meaning and understanding as a significant referent for each individual's behavior and thus for general behavior. We stress the importance of the individual throughout. We rely heavily on individual case material to explain and narrate our findings.

Research findings in the social sciences are strongly influenced by those concerns which led to the undertaking of the research. The reasons we undertook our research on older men living alone are detailed below. This is followed by a discussion of the plan of this report and the manner in which our findings are to be presented.

REASONS FOR THE RESEARCH

In 1981 the Philadelphia Geriatric Center undertook an investigation of the lives of older men living alone. It was drawn up with several specific and general reasons in mind.

1. In many ways the aged male is the "forgotten" man because he is a minority. In 1980 there were about 25.5 million Americans age 65 or older, slightly more than 10 percent of our total population. Of these, about 15 million were women, while about 10 million were men (U.S. Senate 1982). Thus only 4 out of every 10 older persons is a man. Moreover, the disparity between male and female increases with age. Thus in 1975 there were about 77 males per 100 females between the ages of 65 and 74, while between the ages of 75 and 84 there were 62 males per 100 females (National Council on the Aging 1978:13). As men grow older, they become even more of a minority.

2. The reasons by which old men come to live alone are varied, and the influence of a prior life-style on living alone uncertain. About three-quarters of old men are married; about 75 percent of men age 65 to 74 and about 66 percent of men age 75 and over live with a spouse. The 1.5 million older men who live alone (about 15% of the 10 million older men) are made up of individuals from three groups. They derive from the 14 percent of older men who are

widowers (all widowers, of course, do not necessarily live alone); from the approximately 6 percent of older men who are separated or divorced; and from the 5 percent of men over 65 who never married (U.S. Senate 1982).

There are considerable experiential and situational differences among these men in old age. Widowers have gone through the painful experience of the loss of a spouse. The never-married men are not likely to have gone through a similar experience. Elderly widowers are much more likely to have children on whom they can rely in old age. Children—especially daughters—are generally recognized as the primary care giver to a surviving parent in old age (Brody 1981; Shanas 1979a, 1979b). In actuality, while the never married of both sexes make up about but 5 percent of the elderly population, some 20 percent of the elderly have no living children (Johnson and Catalano 1981). Never-married older men and widowers therefore may have different sorts of support systems. While widowers may rely on "natural" (i.e., kin) supports, the never married—especially those without other kin ties—may be forced to construct networks of support or else do without.

3. Despite the small percentages of older persons who make up the group designated as "older men living alone," this is, in fact, a numerically large group. In 1982 there were 1.5 million older men who lived alone (U.S. Senate 1982).

4. Because older men are a minority, they have been neglected by gerontological researchers and practitioners, and activity and service programs may be implicitly tailored to the majority, women. Little research has focused on the problems and situations of older men as a group or on the sometimes severe problems of elderly widowers. The lives of elderly never-married men have rarely figured in gerontological research.

Here we are dealing with what is essentially a double bias. It is true that in old age men represent the minority, and this status is itself represented in gerontological research and in the allocation of social service resources for the elderly. But it is also true that, to a certain extent, the gender-related values espoused by the generations of men over age 65 tend to shape and influence male behavior in a particular way. Gender-based differences in group characteristics, while not the property of all individuals in a group, illustrate tend-

encies of individual class members. In general, elderly men tend to
be accepting of and express satisfaction with their situations in life.
They tend to be less vocal than women about problems, emotions,
and concerns. They may be less gregarious than women of the same
age group. They may have fewer social instrumental skills than
women. Thus not only are elderly men in the minority but they are
less likely to volunteer to participate in research projects which seek
to explain, describe, or understand aspects of their lives. Men are
also less likely to join activity programs or senior centers not only
because the content of the programs may be female-oriented and
viewed as inherently alienating, but also because they tend less to
place a value on "joining in."

5. Older men are often known by others primarily through stereotypes, anecdotes, and impressions.

Stereotypically, old men may be viewed as "old-timers," "Pops,"
and "dirty old men." While stereotypes may be viewed as either
pejorative or nonpejorative, they often serve to reduce dramatically
the complexity of individual motivations and the context of an
individual's life. These three stereotypes evoke a variety of images.
The "old-timer" is the oldest member of a work or a social group
who, despite decreasing physical faculties, maintains some sort of
continuing participation in the group. He is the *emeritus* member.
The "old-timer" may be respected or merely put up with. A "Pops"
is a man above retirement age who continues to work at a job which
requires primarily presence, such as a bank guard or a school crossing
guard. A "Pops" is usually viewed as a kindly, indulgent figure, a
kind of universal grandfather who may demonstrate a special fondness for children. The "dirty old man" is significantly different from
the warm stereotypes of the "Pops" and the "old-timer." The "dirty
old man" is a more complicated figure, evoking images from several
domains; he is an elderly person with an interest in sex, and the
interest spans the generations (younger women, girls). This stereotype
is an imprisoning one because it indicates that any interest in younger
women by older men is to be labeled as perverse. It also supports
the notion that interest in sexuality on the part of the elderly is bad
and that cross-generation relations are improper. Behind the buf-
foonish surface image of the "dirty old man" is a more serious

image of the elderly: that aging is a mysterious process and that the relationship of aging and sexuality is cause for uneasiness.

Some bits of information about older men exist anecdotally and impressionistically. They make up elements of a "popular notion" about older men and may represent ideas held by the average person. These may be a step closer to fact than are stereotypes in that they may actually be based on firsthand or secondhand knowledge of a particular individual or on firsthand impression. Old men living alone are often viewed as not having learned to shop, cook, or perform household tasks. Such jobs may never have been performed by a man or may have been performed by a now-deceased spouse but were never learned following the spouse's death. This is a kind of learned helplessness. Older men may not know how to take care of a house (Lawton 1981). Despite an association of maintenance proficiency with the male gender, an older woman might be more likely to "get someone" to perform a maintenance task than a man would be to do it himself. Older men may be more socially isolated than women. Older men may tend to be less vocal than women, especially in regard to social relations and the expression of emotions. Older men who live alone may be more socially isolated than older men who live with others. It is women who, in general, monitor and maintain ties to kinsmen and others. After a man's wife has died, he may be unable to undertake the responsibility for keeping up relations with kinsmen. Men tend to draw friends from the group of people with whom they work, so, upon retirement, they may lose contact with former co-workers. A woman, if she has never worked, may draw friends from the neighborhood in which she and her husband reside. A married man may be able to switch friendships from former co-workers to neighborhood men under the influence of his wife. A never-married man may not have such opportunities and may become even more isolated upon retirement.

In old age, activities and groups may be "female-dominated." Today's older generation may not be accustomed to opposite-sex friendships. Similarly, after years of marriage to one person, the single life may be viewed by a widower as alien or inappropriate. One may then try to do away with the problems of late-life singlehood by rejecting an active social life, rather than by remarrying. One popular impression is that elderly widowers generally remarry. This is not true. In fact, the rate of remarriage for both elderly widows and widowers is quite low, although it is significantly higher for widowers than it is for widows. Only about 25 percent of men widowed after the age of 65 will ever marry (Cleveland and Gianturco 1976).

Several groups of older men are publicly visible and therefore provide images and impressions for observers. Some of these men fall under the rubrics of "loners," "transients," "center city hotel residents," "roomers," "rooming-house residents," "single-room oc-cupancy (SRO) tenants," and the like. These are men who are viewed as living in *de facto* communities in run-down and nondescript areas of large cities. In fact, social relations in these communities are more complicated than has been imagined (Cohen and Sokolovsky 1980; Eckert 1980; Bohannon 1981).

Similarly, older men are visible in other sorts of informal group-ings. Many neighborhoods have "tavern groups" of retired men who come together informally at a tavern to drink, socialize, reminisce, and discuss events. Other, similar groups congregate around street benches, at street corners, or in public parks.

6. An increasing number of elderly persons are living alone. In fact, about 30 percent of the 25 million or so older Americans live alone (U.S. Senate 1982:14). The experience of living alone is not an uncommon one for the elderly, and it is one which shows no sign of decreasing in frequency. Although living alone is an experience shared by some 7 million older Americans, there is almost no information about what this large group of older persons think, if anything, about their lives. We have no idea, for example, how "the experience of living alone" as a phenomenon *sui generis* is viewed by widowers as opposed to never-married older men. Some evidence (Helsing, Szklo, and Comstock 1981) indicates that living alone is correlated with a statistically significant higher rate of death for widowers of all ages. For all older men living alone, does the experience of living alone itself act to make life more similar for diverse individuals despite a difference in individual lifelong patterns?

7. All in all, not very much is known about the lives of older men in general or older men living alone in particular. The research project described here therefore focused on the lives of older men living alone not only to find out about this minority within a minority

but also as a representation of all elderly men, a group in which problems of isolation, loneliness, and loss may be seen to occur.

While our general purpose was to find out more about older men living alone, this topic was related to a number of specific areas of investigation. Both our general and specific tasks focused around a central methodological and theoretical approach: the discovery of what is meaningful to each individual and the understanding of activity in the context of the meaning life has as a whole for each individual.

Three specific goals we wished to achieve are as follows:

1. To learn more about how some men living alone find enjoyment in life and how they would like to live if they had more choice.
2. To learn how some activity centers have designed successful programs that have engaged the interest and participation of older men.
3. To put the knowledge learned from the older men themselves and from existing activity programs into a guide for programming for older men (Lawton n.d.).

Our findings concerning the first of these topics appear throughout the text, but primarily in chapter 5. Our findings concerning the second and third of these areas are presented in appendix 2.

METHODS AND SAMPLE

Our research design called for us to interview a group of Philadelphia-area older men who lived alone. This group was made of half "nonisolates" and half "isolates." Included in the former were those individuals who were regular attenders at a senior center or who were residents in senior-only housing units. By isolates, we meant older men living alone not so connected. We interviewed 47 men, of whom 17 were regular senior center attenders, 8 resided in senior-only housing, and only 1 man lived in housing for the elderly and also attended a center (making a total of 26 nonisolates), while 21 men were isolates. Our sample is thus what may be called a graded convenience sample, representing no natural universe, other than those demarcated by the criterion of isolation and the context of a particular type of living arrangement.

It was hoped that each informant would be interviewed for about ten hours and that the interviews would be, to a large extent, open-ended, thus enabling the interviewer to come to know the informant in some depth. Thus the information gathered on living alone, activities, loneliness, and social relations could be placed in the context of personal meaning and significance. As it turned out, about 42 of the 47 men we interviewed were seen at considerable length, usually for about nine to twelve hours; 5 of the 47 men were interviewed more briefly. These men discontinued participation primarily due to health problems.

A more complete discussion of methods used in this study is given in appendix 1.

The men we interviewed represented a very diverse collection in almost every way, with the exception of their current living status. In the following discussion, we outline the outstanding characteristics of the sample.

Age. The average age of the men was about 78. The range was from 65 to 98, as follows:

Age	Number
65–69	9
70–74	8
75–79	12
80–84	11
85–89	3
90+	4
	47

Residence. Patterns of residence were diverse: 14 men owned and resided in their own homes—this is below the national average for 65 and older in owner-occupied, single-person dwelling units (51%); 9 men (19%) lived in senior housing units:

Type of Housing	Number
Residence in house owned by self	14
Apartment in senior-only housing unit	9
Apartment in mixed-age public housing	2

Type of Housing	Number
Renter of an apartment or house	16
Renter of a room in a hotel, rooming house, or private home	6
	47

Later, we take up aspects of the residential environment in our discussion of "The Meaning of Living Alone."

Religious and ethnic background. Nineteen men (40%) were Catholics and 13 men each (28%) were Protestant and Jewish. Two men did not identify with a particular religion. Ethnically, the sample was diverse, with the following representation: Jewish (German and Eastern European origins), 13 men (28%); Irish, 7 men (15%); Afro-American, 5 men (11%); German, 4 men (9%); "mixed" (English-Dutch, English-Irish, Scots-Irish, German-Irish), 5 men (11%); and "others" (English, Polish, Dutch, Scottish, Italian, Lithuanian, Swedish).

For many of the men we saw, the participation in formal religion played a very important role in their lives. Several expressed the notion that as one grows older, one becomes more involved with religion whether one really wants to or not. Religion was important both as a central focus in the content of daily life for many men and as a mechanism for the daily and weekly scheduling and structuring of events.

Income. The sample included a variety of income levels:

Monthly Income Range	Number
0–333	10
334–500	17
501–833	6
833+	10
No data	4
	47

Marital status. In this significant attribute again there was considerable diversity.

Status	Number	Percent
Widowed	29	62
Widowed in excess of 50 years	1	2
Never married	11	23
Divorced, wife living	4	9
Divorced, wife dead	1	2
Divorced, wife's status unknown	1	2
	47	100

Most of the widowers were married but once, had lengthy marriages, survived their spouse, and had never remarried. Several of the widowers had original marriages which ended in the death of or divorce from the wife. One of the widowers was married three times, being divorced twice and then finally widowed, and had his strongest attachment to his last wife. One man was married twice and widowed twice, with a seemingly equal attachment to both wives. Two men were married twice: divorced once and widowed once, with a strong attachment to the deceased (second) wife. One man was widowed in excess of fifty years, after a short marriage, and was classified for most purposes with the never-married men. There were 6 divorced men. The living status of the former spouse had some meaning to most of the divorced men.

As far as we could determine, about 5 of the men currently had close or peripheral relationships with women which included sexual intercourse, while another 7 had close but nonsexual relations with nonkin women.

Physical health. Most of the men we interviewed were generally in fair or good health:

Health Condition	Number
1. Very active, with no history of severe health problems	18
2. Very active, with history of some health problems, but not reporting major symptoms at present	7
3. Active, with current health problem a slight limit on behavior	5

Health Condition	Number
4. Active, with current health problem a moderate limit on behavior	5
5. Active, but with current health problem a major limit on behavior	3
6. Less active, generally housebound, or currently ill, with reduced activity	8
7. Deceased during course of interviews	1

It was clear that a majority of these men were well enough not only to function adequately but also to participate in a variety of activities.

The importance of health as an influence on a variety of domains should not be underestimated.

In the year or less that has passed since the completion of interviews to this writing, we have learned that 4 of the men have died.

Children. A large group of the men had no living children, while those with children had diversity in their relationships with them:

No children or stepchildren	(18)
1. Men with no children or stepchildren:	15
2. Men whose children were all deceased:	3

With children	(29)
1. In general, men with close relations with some or all children, some or all of whom lived in vicinity:	17
2. Men with children all of whom lived at least 100 miles away; relationship may be close or distant:	7
3. Men estranged from their children (who lived in general vicinity):	5

It was not only the 11 never-married men who had no living children; rather 7 of the ever-married men had no living children either, and these men also had problems in finding "support" in old age.

Most men with children lived close to at least one of their children and generally had good relations with them, although several reported that they wished to see more of them. Seven men with children lived at least 100 miles away from all of their children, and their emotional relationships varied from close to distant. Finally, 5 men were more or less estranged from their children, although their children were geographically close by. For example, one man had not seen his children in ten years; another had two children who had never been in his apartment.

Employment. Most men in the survey were currently fully retired. Only a handful had employment: 2 worked part-time, 1 was on leave of absence from a job due to temporary illness, 1 ran his own business part-time, 3 did odd jobs for cash. Several men did volunteer work.

Prior employment histories were extremely varied, with blue-collar and white-collar occupations both well represented. Seven men were involved in mechanical, electrical, or machinist trades; 3 were painters. Eight were involved in sales. Other professions represented include police and fire, engineering, barber, office work, driver, food industry, guard. Several were marginally employed.

PLAN OF THIS WORK

Each of the six chapters which follow treats a specific part of our research and findings.

As part of the process of aging, as it is experienced socially, culturally, and psychologically, all men undergo a series of changes and transitions. Chapter 2 is a discussion of some of these changes. The chapter has two purposes. It places the experiences of the men we interviewed into the context of an evolving pattern of life and also presents material pertinent to the lives of most, if not all, men, not only those we interviewed. We discuss events such as retirement, elderhood, changes in gender-related behavior, changes in social networks, and family relations. We found that the transitions in late life are differentially experienced by individuals and are variously experienced as problems.

We found, however, that no life transition was as important to many of these men as was widowhood in late life to those who had been married. For so many of the widowers we interviewed, widowhood was *the* salient event of late life. In so many cases, it "set up" and strongly influenced the life of the surviving man for many years after the death of the wife. In chapter 3, we discuss widowhood in detail. We begin by reviewing the literature which has appeared to date on this life transition and note what appear to be the weaknesses and strengths of the work done so far. We discuss our need to introduce the notions of successful and unsuccessful life reorganization after the death of a spouse in late life. The bulk of the chapter presents case material which illustrates adaptations to widowhood and describes their various aspects. This is done on the basis of data collected from some 25 elderly widowers we interviewed.

In chapter 4 we describe some late-life experiences of the never-married men we interviewed, and we do so in the light of the very little which has been written about them. Our own findings stand in disagreement with this previous work. We note a particular kind of late-life devastation distinctive, to be sure, from that of widowhood, experienced by some never-married elderly men.

Chapter 5 treats some of the activities performed by men in the sample from two perspectives: an etic one which deals with general levels of activity and activity characteristics, and an emic one in which we describe the issues and personal themes which give meaning to the activities which are performed by the men. Extensive case material is provided in our descriptions of the lives of 3 of the men.

We discuss the loneliness experienced by the men in chapter 6. While some of the older men living alone may be relatively lonely, the experience of loneliness by some of these men is tied directly to the experience of widowhood and to an inability to achieve a successful life reorganization after the death of a spouse.

Finally, in chapter 7 we conclude and summarize by discussing the meaning of living alone. The chapter draws together material we had previously presented and places it within a wider context while focusing on what it means to live alone for the men in the sample.

CHAPTER 2

Transitions

Much of what has been written about old age emphasizes its ambiguous nature. On the one hand, old age is a time when people see their plans come to fruition; they may gain a degree of independence from some responsibilities, and observe and take satisfaction in what they have created in life, while continuing to create. On the other hand, old age may bring with it a number of frequently encountered problems. Changes in social roles and activities may be problematic. Reduction of income after retirement can be a problem. Health troubles of various kinds may occur. The loss of a loved one can be devastating.

As individuals age and change they may make a number of transitions from one state of being to another. Most familiar are the *social* role transitions, as people move from the role of worker to that of retiree, from married person to widow or widower, from active parent to elder parent or grandparent, from middle-aged person to "elder." At any age, people possess notions of what properly should go into making up a person based on *cultural* ideas of gender and personhood. For example, "young men" are typically to behave in a way dissimilar to "old men." Finally, in terms of *personal* dynamics, individuals may make transitions from one life stage or sequence of events to another.

Each type of transition, as we have listed them here, represents a thread of a person's life. While understanding the effects of a single change on a life can be a difficult task, it is an easy one in comparison with understanding the aggregate of changes. Continuing changes reveal a mutual influence on one another. One question we can raise, then, is this: Is there any one late-life change in particular which seems to be the most significant or salient for these men?

In this chapter we discuss a number of late-life transitions experienced by the men we interviewed. We do this for two reasons. First, the notion of change in late life and its technical incarnations as transitions, role change, late-life adaptation, late-life development, and adjustment have received considerable attention from gerontologists and others (George 1980; Clark and Anderson 1967). We hope to contribute to this discussion. Also, this topic will further enable us to provide a frame of reference for events which are going on in the lives of the men we interviewed, providing a context for issues we wish to discuss. Our selection of these transitions as a starting point is dictated by our research findings. If successful aging is any one thing, it is the successful management of change based on each individual's recognition of needs and realities.

We divide various transitions into those which may be considered social, cultural, or personal in nature. While social transitions derive their meaning from the cultural context in which they occur, we intend the notion of cultural transition here to apply to the most basic aspects of sociocultural meaning, specifically to issues of gender and personhood, and not social roles per se. By personal transitions, we mean those elements of experience which are primarily internal to an individual such as individual feelings and unique experiences, although similar experiences may be had in common.

SOCIAL CHANGES

Worker to Retiree

Retirement represents a profound change of status for a man. Many of the men to whom we talked had been working from their teens to at least their middle or late 60s. It is indeed difficult to imagine that terminating work—in actuality, completing work—can occur without important ramifications, since it had been a form of endeavor and orientation for so many years.

Nevertheless, the surprising thing about the experience of retirement (or the cessation of work for those marginally employed) is that few of these men regretted retirement or ending full-time work at all. Almost all of the men, when queried, maintained that they did not have a difficult overall time adjusting to the retired life. Several mentioned, however, that if they could find adequate part-time work now, they would take it. The primary reasons cited for the continued desire to work were increasing income and "something to do." Most men who indicated their desire for part-time work wished to work half a day or a full day a few times a week.

While a few men looked to retirement with trepidation, particularly in regards to financial circumstances, most felt retirement would be acceptable, regardless of finances, that they would always "manage somehow."

Several men who had spent careers of mostly marginal employment—these primarily never-married men—did not experience a retirement as such. Some of these men continued to pick up odd jobs into their 70s.

Of the 29 widowers (excluding the 1 man widowed in excess of fifty years), 17 terminated full-time work while the spouse was still alive (we have no data on 4 men). Thus for a majority, each was able to spend some years with his wife prior to her death after retirement from a full-time job. For 8 men, retirement occurred after the death of their spouses.

Twenty-five of the 45 men (no data on 2) spent a lengthy period of time (at least six months) unemployed or underemployed, most often when they were young.

Of the 40 men who were not marginally employed and about whom we have data, 20 are still *in contact* with persons they knew from work, but contact may range from a regular meeting to an infrequent greeting card or chance meeting. Another 6 men remained in contact after their retirement with former co-workers who were either retired or continuing to work, although these former co-workers have since died. Among all men, however, the continuing contacts were close or regular in only a few cases.

Some men were candid about their joy at the arrival of retirement. "I had enough of having the bell go off every day," as one man said. The few professional men we interviewed still try to follow developments and events in their field, although as one professional man put it, "I'd never go back there now, even if they paid me a million dollars." After the passage of years, several men remembered painful disputes at work which still rankled.

Men spontaneously used another measurement to describe their current retired state in comparison with their former employed state of being, by posing the question "Could I still do it?" For salesmen and office workers, the answer was generally yes, but for manual workers, the answer was often no. A great injustice was felt by one former painter when he had to hire someone to paint the front of his house because he could no longer get up the ladders. Another said, "The thing that makes me the most frustrated is that I *know* my house needs to be painted, but I can't do it." To some men, a great satisfaction came from being able to do physical work, for example, to get on the roof to make repairs. There was a kind of defiant and joyful attitude when speaking of this.

The relation of personal identity to former occupation was often direct and still the object of pride. One man, describing the position he had reached, said of his job, "I was a master mechanic. They came to me with *hard* jobs." One man became a fireman because "it's a man's work . . . it's something a man does," while another took up painting because "a man saw I was good at it and invited me down to try out" (at a firm).

These feelings about what one was in one's working career are often part of a person's current identity, part of one's pride of accomplishment. This does not mean that the men now missed the work they had performed. Many continued to reap the glory, but without the daily grind.

After retirement, men can continue aspects of their working career in two ways. They continue to use many of the talents they have, if they are able, be it for odd jobs, volunteer work, or just "living." For example, one bachelor, who spent many years in the military, self-consciously allowed the "army style" of living to continue to influence his life in his interests and personal habits. Second, the manner in which a day was organized while at work is often continued, with some variation, after retirement. For many, the basic structure of the weekday workday is present, although it may be modified for various ends (see chapter 5).

Most men were happy to retire from work, although men generally voiced concern about loss of income and a loss of friends. Work provided a powerful *context* for relating to others. One developed friendships at work around the affairs of work. Such friendships did not usually fare well once they were taken out of the work context. For most men, loss of friends and an opportunity for comradeship was stated to be an especially heartfelt loss.

Nevertheless, the transition from worker to retiree did not seem to be an especially severe one in retrospect for these men. In so many cases, men were able to take away a considerable amount of pride in what they had done upon their retirement. That which was carried away in many cases led to a degree of self-esteem in retirement.

From Income Earner to Pensioner

Besides retirement per se another role transition related to retirement is that occurring when a "breadwinner" becomes a Social Security recipient. While the men we interviewed had little trouble in dealing with retirement, no one enjoyed the loss of income that retirement brings. Of the 29 widowers, 19 had been the sole or major support of their families, while 5 had wives who worked for some time during their marriage (no data on 5 men). For the never-married men, 9 worked so as to support others (a parent or sibling) for some or much of their adult lives. In the case of the never-married men, however, the person who was being supported died prior to retirement of these men in all except 1 case. For the widowers, however, in many cases the person who was primarily being supported (the wife) continued to be supported after retirement.

Faced with a loss of instrumental abilities and reduced income, the typical response on the part of the men we saw depended to a large degree on income received. For all, the view on survival was one conditioned by the notion of "no matter what, we'll make it." Yet for those of lower incomes, ownership of a home became important because it represented a tangible place to which a person belonged. Several poorer men adopted strategies of taking part-time work between their 65th and 75th birthdays, or to a point when they felt they could no longer carry on. After the wife's death, several of the poorer widowers desired to exist with a minimum amount of fuss and could cut back expenses by no longer taking shopping trips downtown or going out to eat.

For those with a greater income, the ability to get by was not severely threatened (with the exception, of course, of the incalculable effects of inflation). For these men, income often came from two or more sources—Social Security, a pension, some investments.

For most widowers, the loss of a spouse meant increased income in the sense that there was now only one person to feed. For most of the men, there was little in the way of financial planning. One gets the impression that the change from income earner to pensioner brings with it, for many, considerably lowered expectations and at the same time a "wait and see" attitude: there is a tendency to adjust one's sights extremely low and then correct them higher as real circumstances dictate.

Parent to Grandparent

Many of the men we interviewed added the role of grandfather to that of father.

Twenty-six of the 47 men were grandparents although the quality of these men's relationships with their grandchildren varied. Of the 26, 6 were especially close to their grandchildren, seeing some of them frequently (at least once a month). Most of the remainder of these men spoke of their grandchildren as more distant persons, people who were important to them but who were not especially close. Unlike the situation between the older men and their children, there was only 1 instance of reported hostility between grandchild and grandfather. In 1 instance, a man had never seen some of his grandchildren due to the hostility between him and the grandchildren's parents.

In the 6 instances where relations between grandfather and grandchildren were especially close, the grandfathers took pride in the accomplishments of the grandchildren or took pride in the closeness of the relationship between themselves and the grandchildren.

Parent of Young Children to Parent of Middle-Aged Children

Twenty-nine men had adult children. The relationships of these men with their children were varied. Seventeen of the 29 men with children had generally close relationships with all or some of their children.

Seven of the 29 lived at least 100 miles away from all of their children, although the relationships could be close or strained. Five of them were estranged from all or most of their children although they lived in the same general area.

Of the 17 with generally close relations with their children, each had at least one daughter. Whatever strain was reported was between elderly father and middle-aged son. Most of these men were in a position to receive instrumental help and emotional support from their children, and about 8 had received instrumental support (help with shopping, meals, transport) in the last three months. Most of these men felt themselves to be part of a family and to be contributing to the family in some way.

Among the 7 older men whose children lived in excess of 100 miles away, relations were generally cordial, although relations were not usually on a day-to-day basis. Four of these men did not need or receive help from others, while the 3 who did received help from friends, a sister, and formal services.

Five men had strained relations with children. Interestingly, in 4 of the 5 cases, the men had sons exclusively.

Men with No Children

While it is often said that one's children are one's insurance in old age, 20 percent of the elderly have no living children (Johnson and Catalano 1981). It is easy to imagine that being young and without children is intrinsically different from being old without children. For the 18 men in the sample without children, supportive relations and instrumental help came from other sources. In this regard, the question of whether an older person living alone has any close family is significant, because such relatives as siblings, nieces, and nephews can also provide support. Twelve of the 18 men with no children (either never married or widowers) had no close family at all. The reaction of 5 of the 12 was to construct elaborate social networks in place of family ties. Seven of the 12 had few individuals on whom they could rely. In contrast to the 12 with no family, 6 of the 18 had some localized family (siblings, nieces, nephews). Four of the 6 could and did receive instrumental help and emotional support from their relatives. Two of the 6, however, had ongoing disputes with family members which precluded them from receiving help.

The Experience of "Role Loss"

Much has been made in the social gerontology literature of the notion of role loss. The idea is that the older person, having passed through various juvenile and adult age-grades for which there are appropriate roles, enters a period, old age, in which there are few, if any, appropriate roles and for which an individual is not prepared. Such a point is elaborated by Rosow (1974). A similar point of view is taken by Kuypers and Bengtson (1973), who suggest that role loss, lack of socialization procedures, and the end of ideas about appropriateness lead to a negative reorganization in late life, making a person more vulnerable to negative social labeling and dependent on external cues for behavior (George 1980).

The notion of role loss is linked to several other ideas, namely, that there are fewer opportunities in American society for the elderly and that being old is a social reality to which a stigma is attached (Matthews 1979). No one seriously debates the real existence of these negative social evaluations and phenomena. Depending on personal style and on specific situations, however, older people perceive role loss or change and the negative realities in a variety of ways.

Most of the men interviewed made some attempt to size up and analyze their own lives, not only in reaction to the interview questions, but also, it appears, as part of their own process of growing older. As part of this sizing up, the men we interviewed may be characterized in terms of their personal style of reaction to the situations of older people in American society. While these styles of reflecting on the place of the elderly in American society are distinctive, they are, of course, exaggerations and caricatures necessary for the purpose of discussion; individuals may mix these styles and they may exist in conflict within individuals. Nevertheless, for each individual, one adaptive style seems to predominate. (These bear some relation to the styles of personal adjustment among older men outlined by Reichard, Livson, and Peterson [1980]).

It should be pointed out that what is behind these attempts to size up and understand the role of "the elderly" in modern day American life is a general level of reflection about or reflexivity upon one's life, a task in which many of the men engaged. As the result of the process of reflecting on their lives, most men could make statements about the kind of person they felt they were, which for them seemed to condense and explain large amounts of what happened in their lives. Thus in one sense the sizing up of the role of the elderly in American life is nothing more than personal issues writ large; on another level it is an attempt to understand and state clearly what are believed to be the inner workings of life in America for the old.

First, several men believed that they had fully "sized up" the social realities of aging in America, these being almost exclusively negative. They found that older people did have decreased opportunities and fewer effective and positive roles available to them. They believed that society had no interest in the elderly and that one of society's major goals was to remove the elderly as a source of *paid* labor and then to warehouse them; or to involve them in unpaid—and therefore unsatisfactory, undignified, and rather juvenile—volunteer work. One important correlate to this point of view is that society—by plan or by chance—sought to spiritually alienate the elderly. Beside Social Security (which is old age insurance paid by an employee and employer and held and administered by the government), several men believed the amount spent by the government on the elderly is a pittance. One man complained forcefully about the notion of "age 65," that moment which, once passed, arbitrarily marks a person as finished. Several men painted an image of the elderly in America as a group of lost sheep, people with no purpose or calling, completely preoccupied by relatively trivial personal problems.

The solutions presented by most of the men who felt this way were moral and political solutions. One must be an individual to the fullest and do what one truly wanted, while trying to ignore the way society regulated the elderly. Further, one must try to be politically aware. One must try to derive pleasure from life, despite the negative situation.

Second, while several other men recognized that roles, especially work roles, changed with age and that in fact one must adjust to change, these men did not see society as necessarily set up in a way that naturally limited the elderly. That is, some men believed that society was not intrinsically against the old. Roles do not really decrease; they change, based on biological realities (some people really do tend to slow up, it is believed). Upon retirement, several such men continued careers of volunteer work or continued on in part-time work. However, in doing this there was a significant change of emphasis. Prior to retirement, emphasis in life had been on earning a living for a family or saving money for retirement. These are affairs of private life, of the domestic sphere. Upon retirement, these men entered the public sphere through volunteer work or other activities, believing that the individual—even through the smallest of contributions—can make a difference to society. Society is thus not viewed mechanistically or deterministically; individual action could make a difference. While these men did not see the powerful political forces known to the men described above, both groups of men placed emphasis on individual action.

Third, for another group of men, health problems and troublesome personal situations (often intertwined) were extremely absorbing so that a person could not direct attention away from himself for long periods of time. Role loss or change was not viewed by these men as social phenomena per se, but as a product of individual history and life conditions. Illness or bereavement, not social forces, prevented a person from doing more. These men often felt shamefully dependent on others to help them and attributed their dependence to individual weakness. The combination of self-absorption and a feeling of guilt led these men to view society (when they did talk about other people in general) as basically hostile and alienating. Despite individual sources of help and aid—neighbors, family, friends, social workers—the self-absorbed sometimes viewed others as a nameless mass of people by and large out for themselves.

Fourth, several other men felt the need for reduced action with age and further felt this need to be an appropriate response to aging. Change, role loss, and a self-definition as old appeared to be accepted gracefully. Wants were meshed with perceived actualities, and when a level of action or a sphere of activity was reduced, this was sometimes viewed as quite acceptable or even desirable. Some of these men tended to live "one day at a time." The future did not seem to be a real concern, and planning for the future did not seem to be an important theme among them. These men came closest to the image of passive disengagement. The relationship between an individual and society may be unclear to these men but the two appear to have little to do with one another. One attitude here is that "things" are just fine the way they are. While it is true that role loss is an intrinsic characteristic of late life for these men, this is not an upsetting happening.

Fifth and finally, another style of reaction to role loss and change for some of these men was to view it as the arrival of freedom from social restrictions and the unwanted responsibilities of earlier life. The ending of a job or career, the maturation of children, and newly gained time may permit the expression of a "true" personality and interests, allowing one to act in new and inventive ways; for some, reduced income seems a bargain to pay for increased freedom. The loss of some roles and activities is a small price for the gaining of one's true self.

Changes in Marital Relations

The relationship of a husband and wife in a marriage changes as both individuals change and as family members depart. Certainly, the evolving nature of this relationship is an important one as it had affected the lives of the widowers we interviewed. Unfortunately, we do not have much information about this topic and we did not inquire systematically about it. Of the 29 widowers, 14 saw the wife decline, in a terminal illness, over a period of greater than six months; 6 men saw the wife die in a period of illness lasting less than six months. We have no data on 9 men. Reports on changes in relationships came primarily from men who witnessed a gradual decline in the health of their wives; negative changes in the relationship were viewed by these men as relating to a wife's illness. Particularly troublesome were profound changes in the wife's personality related to illnesses (senility, terminal cancer affecting the brain). In such cases, profound personal conflicts might have arisen, or conflicts which had long been settled were reopened and left unresolved at the death of the wife. We have little systematic information about changes in sexuality with age, about the long-term ramifications of the "empty nest syndrome," and about sources of recommitment in late life, if any, to the marriage.

Widowhood

Widowhood may be viewed as both a social and an intrapsychic phenomenon. *Widowhood* is a social role, produced by the transition from the married status to the nonmarried status by the death of a spouse. The transition to widowhood as a purely social role can be painful and awkward, with inadequate role modeling and little direction. Intrapsychically, the adjustment to any loss is extraordinarily painful and stressful.

We found that for most of the widowers we interviewed, the loss of one's spouse in late life was *the* most important issue in late life. Because widowhood is so important to these men, the next chapter is devoted to an extensive presentation of material on this topic. In listening to these men talk about loss and their lives since the loss we hear a great depth of sorrow. We are able to see that for many men this loss is a crucial event which has had a profound, enduring effect on their lives. There exists a broad contrast between those men who have recovered from a loss and successfully reorganized their lives and those who have not.

Socially, what is at stake in the transition to the widower role is also profound. Heretofore one's identity has been derived from membership in the "married couple," a fundamental adult social unit. Upon a spouse's death, the survivor no longer has such an identity nor can he participate in couple-oriented events. A male survivor does not necessarily know how appropriately to "handle" his grief in public and therefore may avoid the public until he can master it. For a marriage in which a strongly marked sexual division of labor once existed, the surviving male must find some way of getting things done which were once done by his wife. And if the survivor wishes to date or to remarry, an entirely new set of issues must be confronted.

In examining widowhood as a social phenomenon, we do not applaud the tendency to view the role of widowhood as a unitary "thing," a single, uniform social role or status. As Lopata (1973a, 1979) notes, the age of the wife at the death of her husband is very significant for her experience of widowhood. The idea is absurd that there is something fundamentally similar among a 21-year-old woman who has lost her husband after one year of marriage and has no children, a 55-year-old woman with five children who has lost her husband after thirty-five years of marriage, and a 78-year-old woman who has lost her husband after fifty years of marriage. We would suggest that age, life stage, amount and quality of time spent together, personality, and individual interpretation of meaning account for a lot more. Many of the widowers we interviewed were in their late 60s and 70s when the spouse died. For these men it is *both* the social status of widowhood and the individual and social meaning of age which are the keys to the performance of the social role of widower. Age often overrides social status. Townsend (1968) noted this when he wrote that time "heals" the wounds of loss for younger persons in the sense that there is a greater chance they will be able to replace what has been lost, but that for older persons healing occurs less rapidly and replacements tend to be not as satisfactory as that which has been lost.

Widowhood may also be a mechanism of temporary or permanent disengagement. Widowhood may permanently change the experience of life by the survivor. A measure of reengagement may never be attained by the survivor.

CULTURAL TRANSITIONS

Next we turn to changes in late life which may be described as cultural, that is, pertaining to the basic, axiomatic meanings of things shared by individuals in society. Here, then, we deal with notions of *gender* and *personhood*. Personhood refers to the quality of being a person and therefore to those things which go into making up a person—all those attributes deemed essential in the makeup of a full, adult individual.

These two are closely related, gender appropriateness being an important component of personhood. In old age, defining and maintaining an adequate sense of personhood is a crucial task, as is continuing gender-appropriate behavior. Many problems in adjusting to changes in the life course have a strong gender component. In the "empty nest syndrome," for example, a woman may become anxious and fearful when she can no longer play the role of an active mother because all of her children have moved out of her home and have started homes and careers of their own. Or, in the male mid-life crises, a man may acquire a sense of panic or doom at the loss of the possibility of no longer cutting the youthful and successful male image which had been the goal of so much of his life.

The men we interviewed expressed a considerable number of thoughts about how to maintain their personal integrity and how to continue being "a man." Such ideas can be grouped into four areas: the emotions, activities, social relations, and instrumental functions. We discuss each in turn.

The Emotions

A common attitude to emotions was summed up by one man who poignantly said, "Men are supposed to be strong on the outside but inside you're crying."

There is perhaps no area which is as clearly marked for men as the need to be tough, to be strong so as to resist pain, and to control one's emotions. This is a commonly held notion of idealized masculine behavior, the things that a man should do.

This "should" is an internalized value held by many men in American society regardless of age, but considerable variation exists in its actual working out. For example, the notion that a man should not cry or express emotion may be primarily applied to the expression of emotion on public occasions, while more variation may be acceptable in other situations. For some, a funeral may be considered too public an affair for the expression of emotion, while others find it appropriate. For example, as one man put it about himself (and some others), "Italians always cry at funerals." Most informants were asked if they ever cry nowadays and if so what about. Twenty-three reported that they did cry at times, 18 reported that they did not, while there is no data on 6 men. A majority of the 23 cried when thinking about a departed wife, a few about a deceased mother, 1 about a pet, and several about "sad" television shows. There is considerable variation here, then.

Many men had experienced events which were emotionally devastating, and which had enduring effects—recognized as continuing into the present— although men could also talk about having "passed through" the events.

One informant was in a concentration camp and pointed to this experience as one which profoundly affected the rest of his life, although he also said that he was now "over it." Another man was 13 when he was responsible for attending to the body of his father who had been decapitated in an industrial accident. One man was beaten frequently by his father when he was a child. There were several other cases of similarly severe brutality.

Each of these men still had difficulty in talking about these events which continued to play an important part in their lives today. Such events had a way of resonating with the current state of affairs.

While the ability to control emotions is generally considered an attribute of manhood, this ability was undermined for many of the widowers by the death of a spouse. For several of the men, the spouse's death unleashed a torrent of emotion which was uncontrollable and seemed to never let up. In most cases this eventually subsided, but several men were left shattered by the experience. Some felt as if their lifelong striving to be a man went for nothing. During this period the emotions compel one to recognize them.

For some of the never-married men, a major emotional focus was a feeling of having been abandoned by a parent or sibling. Particularly poignant was the way in which several never-married men described the severity of the blow of the loss of their mother. We discuss this in more detail below.

By and large, men wished to tame those emotions which they felt made them appear weak, needy, or vulnerable, or awkward in the eyes of others. "Being able to take it" is an important notion for many men. This consists of maintaining an even demeanor, of resisting displays of unwanted emotion, and of being able to withstand whatever "life dishes out." "Being able to take it" can also consist of fighting back and using one's cunning to get ahead, as well as resisting taunts. Statements such as "I was always able to get a job, even during the Depression" are examples of "being able to take" what life dishes out. It was not uncommon for men to describe periods of their lives as primarily concerned with "getting through" hardships. Not rarely was the last hardship—the death of one's wife—described as an insurmountable hardship.

Common channels of emotion for the men in their adult life, aside from family life, were male camaraderie and flirting. All-male social groups were common in adulthood and even into late life, and emphasized drinking, card playing, athletic events, etc.

In regard to drinking in youth, several of these men saw aging as a process of maturation. Among the men we interviewed were 4 former alcoholics and 1 current one, as well as several other formerly heavy drinkers. While they were young, "drinking" seemed to be an appropriate behavior, and as it was described it was not solitary drinking, but contextualized in the social atmosphere of taverns or clubs. As men aged, the drinking stopped. What is most remarkable is that in 3 instances the drinking was described as stopping spontaneously in later life. One man put it this way. "I came home from the club where I had been drinking and I thought, 'This is stupid. Why am I doing this?' The next day, I was planning to go again. I took one step down the front porch, and thought, 'I'm just not going to go.' So I didn't. I just stopped it, and I haven't been drinking since."

A complementary activity here is flirting. Many of the men—especially at senior centers—flirt. Several men felt free enough to describe flirting and attachments they had during the course of their marriages. These activities come under the rubric of male camaraderie: all-male social groups, drinking, interest in sports, and flirting form a complex of activities which most men enjoyed in life, which some looked back on with happiness, and which many men continued to enjoy.

As we have mentioned, one positive thing noted by several men in regard to aging is an increasing emotional maturity. This can pertain to the "hotheadedness" said to be a personal attribute by several men in their youth. The ability to be calm was achieved by several men. One man said that he had quite a reputation as a fighter in his neighborhood when he was young. He couldn't explain why he fought. When he was older, he "just changed," and no longer sought out fights. He added that this calming trend continued, and that he was "very satisfied" with life now and at peace with himself.

Men who discussed relationships with their fathers often described them as strained; few described complete and happy relations with their fathers. For most men, their closest relationships with men were with brothers or friends.

In general, the men we interviewed were given the considerable burden of trying to cover up and manage emotions. They were asked to deeply internalize standards for the suppression of pain and rage and to measure up to these. Many were deeply hurt and scarred by the events around them. Regardless of these events, they were expected to act in a rather unbending way. The depth of these conflicts should not be underestimated. One informant, in his 80s, who had suffered from considerable emotional and physical pain in his life, was asked if there was any advice given to him by members of his family when he was young which he carried with him till today. He replied, "Well, the only thing I can think about is, years and years ago I got hurt and my brother picked me up and said, 'Indians don't cry.' He said, 'You know, whenever they get hurt, they don't show it.' I always remembered that and whenever I got hurt, I tried not to show it. . . ."

To be hard in the face of physical and emotional pain, to be unbending, and to be strong are difficult goals to achieve. In a sense, one must admire those men who achieve their goals, as well as feel sorry for them. What a hard lot this seems.

Activities

In American culture activities are generally associated with one or another gender. In the public domain there are a variety of commonly recognized masculine activities and activity domains. Leadership or responsibility in a group may be recognized as typically masculine, although this is changing. Activities such as golfing and fishing may be viewed as masculine but are engaged in by both men and women. One key masculine front of leisure activities is that they are performed in all-male groups. In this sense the major difference between the gals' bridge club and the boys' poker game is not so much one of content, but of gender style.

Of the men we interviewed, a few engaged in vigorous activities such as bicycling or skiing, but the majority did not. The most common modes of physical activity were walking and doing odd jobs around the house.

For some men whose physical capacities had diminished, the diminution was viewed as emasculation. Such men viewed themselves as "cut down."

Of all activities mentioned by men, one which appeared consistently as a favorite activity was walking. For many men, it took on a meaning beyond the physical.

Walking can be viewed as a major metaphor in the lives of so many of these men, representing a continued ability to live independently, to control events, and to be active. Despite any lessening in abilities or options, a continued ability to walk relatively long distances on a regular basis was seen as a major expression of competence. Joy at "still" being able to walk was expressed spontaneously and independently by several men. More interestingly, many men told stories of walks they had taken, either recently, or years in the past, which were recalled vividly and with pleasure and were offered as examples of what "I could/can do." Several men volunteered that they (literally) prayed that their legs would hold out.

For some men, work—paid or volunteer work—continued to be an important activity contributing to personal integrity. While in fact there was a transition to retirement from a particular job or career, for a few men work continued, as part of continuity-in-change. For a majority, however, continued work was not viewed as a necessity for personal integrity in late life.

Social Relations

The need for personal integrity led many men to seek social relations with women in late life. As we have mentioned, flirting was commonplace. At senior centers especially, sexual bantering, discussions of "boyfriends" and "girlfriends," and good-natured kidding were common occurrences. Most of the men admitted that they still had "the eye" for young, good-looking women and took pleasure from a fine female form. Several men had successful platonic or nonplatonic relationships with women. Some of these are detailed in chapter 3.

For widowers, a flirtatious interest in women had antecedents in earlier life, even when the widowers were married. Several men talked about attending "smokers," male-only sessions at which pornographic movies are shown. At least a half dozen men talked about their going to the "tenderloin" area in downtown Philadelphia to see movies or shows.

Several men freely discussed what appeared to them to be the difficulties in getting remarried (if a widower) or getting married (if a bachelor). Provided one wanted to get married and found the right person, obstacles could be serious. Among the most frequently mentioned obstacles were as follows. First, the growing inability with age to change one's set ways and manner of doing things and therefore an inability to get along with a new mate. Second, a desire not to be saddled with the chore of taking care of another potentially terminally ill person. Third, conflicting property claims of children and new spouse. To whom should one leave one's legacy? Should it stay in the family (go to one's children) or go out of the family (go to one's new spouse)?

Instrumental Activities

In the domestic domain the division of labor by sex is usually well marked. Certain activities may be strictly "male," others strictly "female." Most elderly widowers came from couples who tended to follow a more or less traditional division of labor by sex.

For widowers, a question exists of how to adjust to the loss of the instrumental functions performed formerly by the wife. One stereotype of elderly widowers indicates that they do not adequately adjust to this instrumental loss. What does the evidence from the 29 widowers indicate?

First, concerning the marriages of the men about whom we have fullest data (25 of the 29), there was a fairly strict domestic division of labor in which the wife primarily took care of cooking, cleaning, washing and ironing, sewing, and marketing, while the man worked. Only a few mentioned sharing any of these five tasks on a regular basis. A handful of men regularly shopped with their wives, a few helped with the cleaning, and 2 said they enjoyed cooking on a regular basis.

However, a clearer picture emerges in a subgroup of these men who had to take care of a terminally ill wife. The men reported for the most part the "taking on" of domestic responsibilities during the period for which care of their wife was ongoing. Sometimes these men were aided or instructed in performing domestic tasks by their daughters. For these men, the period of taking on domestic duties which can no longer be performed by a wife is the only "socialization for old age" they have. For most men, it is the only time they had to prepare for living alone.

For those men who were unskilled in domestic routines, such tasks had to be learned later. For example, one man whose wife died suddenly described asking a neighbor in his apartment building to instruct him in using the commercial washing machine in the basement of the building.

Of the five instrumental tasks mentioned above, the greatest amount of help is currently received by men with sewing, but not for one particular reason. Most men do not care to learn how to sew because they perceive it as a relatively minor task best left to experts. Nor do they necessarily have the eyes and hands to do it. Some men have always sent their clothes to a tailor for mending and continue to do this. Only 6 of the 25 widowers can take care of some of the sewing jobs they have.

Men receive the next most frequent amount of help with shopping for groceries: 8 of the 25 receive help with this task on a regular basis. Here disability is a problem (1 man is blind, another has lost a leg). One man cannot enter the nearby supermarket because he finds it confusing and because his beloved wife always did the shopping. Generally, grocery shopping is well handled individually but may be done with others in groups as a kind of social outing.

Five men regularly receive help with laundry. Here again disability is the primary reason. Nevertheless, the majority of the men manage to handle the laundry well. Four men receive help on a regular basis with household cleaning (again, because of disabilities). The question is, of course, not whether people say they do the cleaning, but is the house generally clean by common standards? Of the 25 widowers, only 4 men live in homes which are generally not clean.

All of the 25 learned to cook after a fashion. But, as many men noted, "There's Cooking and then there's cooking." Most cooking was done "fry pan style" or by "opening cans." In this way men could fry eggs or cook beef, chicken, or fish. Little in the way of more adventuresome cooking was done. At one point during the interviews, it became apparent that the cutoff point between "fry pan cooking" and more complex cooking was the ability to roast a chicken in the oven. Only a few of the men could do this.

How did the men learn to cook? Most knew of "fry pan cooking" from their younger days, from camping out, or they learned from having the opportunity to observe others, especially their wives, make simple things. Few men were challenged by the desire to improve their level of cooking ability. Cooking was something they had to do, knew how to do to a certain degree, and were satisfied with. Few men could match the experience of one of the more masterful of the widowers who described learning to cook after his wife died this way: "It was nothing! What's there to learn? You just do it. In fact, a year after my wife died I served a full dinner to six people and they were amazed at my ability to do it." This, however, was a far from typical case.

The never-married men also had someone else perform many instrumental tasks for them for the majority of their lives (see chapter 4). While there is some degree of flexibility here too, it appears to be less than for the widowers.

Most of the 11 never-married men do their own laundry, although their clothes tend to be dirtier than those worn by the widowers. Only about half of these men do their own sewing repairs. Five of the 11 men eat out on a regular basis, while others eat out frequently. Only 4 cook for themselves regularly. Among these men there is less reliance on supermarket shopping and a greater reliance on small neighborhood food stores for minor food items. The degree to which these men clean their homes is considerably less than that of the widowers. Five of the 11 men do not seem to clean their homes at all and have permitted them to become filthy. This differential in the sense of residential order is one striking difference between the widowers and the never-married men.

PERSONAL TRANSITIONS

While social role transitions have a personal side, here we will deal with transitions which are more strictly individual in character. Some of the topics we discuss are "the personal journey," an individual's sense of time, elderhood, loss, and entering the senior milieu.

The Personal Journey

Interestingly, many of the men we interviewed used metaphors of travel and passage, particularly the notion of "passing through" events and times, to describe their lives or segments of their lives. Terms such as "passing through," "getting through," "going through," or "living through" relate to this metaphor of a personal journey. The notion of a personal journey is in many ways a reflexive, autobiographical usage, used in order to *talk* to others about one's life but not necessarily to think about or naturally experience one's own life.

"Passing through" is an important theme in several ways. It is very important in connection with the experiences surrounding the death of one's spouse and with the steps that are taken to reorganize one's life thereafter. In particular, trouble may be said to be passed through: for example, one Jewish man felt he had lived to see the end of rabid anti-Semitism in America. He had "passed through" this, he said. Illnesses, bereavement, various problems, were also "passed through." Several men indicated that they had outlived all of their problems. Not only were "hotheadedness" and alcoholism examples of this, but more mundane problems were also cited as no longer being troublesome.

The use of the metaphor of "passing through" indicates that individuals have conceptualized "here and now" viewed as in contrast with some moment or state in the past. Passing through implies both distance and survival and is implicitly positive: one is no longer tied to an unfortunate event.

The notion of a personal journey is also related to concern with the future and with religious issues. Individuals may desire to anticipate a continuing personal journey. About one-third of the group said that old age had brought with it an increased interest in and involvement with religion, not only because of real questions and concerns about an afterlife but also as a philosophical mode which could accompany and complement an enlarged and more accepting worldview which these men felt they had gained through late-life maturation. In the case of those Jewish men who were most active religiously, there was a clearly articulated need to contribute to and preserve a cultural heritage. With those Christians who were most closely involved with organized religious affairs—such as attending

Mass daily for the Catholics or close association with a local church and church community for the Protestants—there was often a clearly marked spirituality, a concern with the afterlife and a desire to personally gain spiritual comfort.

Successful recovery from ill health may also be retrospectively viewed as a type of "passing through," a side trip off the main road. One effect of being sick often noted by the men is to "draw" a person away from his normal social relations. One man summed up the effects of a serious ulcer condition this way: "The sicker I was the less I was inclined to see anyone. You get sick, you tend to stay inside and not want to see anyone at all." The condition is now successfully treated with a new sort of medication. The illness is now seen as an unpleasant event which was lived through: "Now things are better. I enjoy going out."

Both of these concerns—the theme of "passing through" and an interest in religion—are discussed in more detail below.

Individual Sense of Time

Often, the question concerning orientation to time concerns an individual's overall orientation to the past, present, or future. This is a very difficult question to evaluate because it is hard to imagine that one ever holds a single orientation. Nevertheless, individuals hold characteristic attitudes to time. The following feelings about time were characteristic of the men we interviewed.

1. A sense of connection to the past. The feeling that events of the past cannot be divorced from one's current life was voiced by several men, primarily widowers, who still felt a profound connection to the life shared with the spouse. Here some men even tended to "live in the past," in environments fundamentally unchanged from a time when the wife was living. In this regard certain events, therefore, were not "passed through" but continued on.

Associated with this was the notion that "something perfect in the past can never be recaptured," yet this was combined with a compulsive need to try to maintain it, ultimately leading to disappointment.

2. "I live one day at a time." This is a very common attitude. One man said, "At my age, each day becomes a unit. You can't plan much in advance." For many, the idea was to experience each

day fully and extract pleasure from it. For others, life was so un-bearable that one had to take life slowly so as to minimize jarring. Living one day at a time and having a strong connection to the past are not incompatible (cf. Rubinstein, in press).

3. "I have overcome or passed through events." This theme deals primarily with the bracketing of the past from the present. The here and now is distinctive, better and freer. This segmented view of time is not incompatible with living one day at a time (number 2), particularly in its pleasurable sense. Nor is a sense of connection to the past (number 1) incompatible with the idea of "passing through" events; both can exist together.

4. "I wonder what the future holds?" A degree of uneasiness about the future was characteristic of the sample. This was so both phys-ically and spiritually. The prospect of declining physical and mental abilities was greatly feared, not only intrinsically but also because of the burden it would make, or worse, the lack of anyone to give a burden to. In a tongue-in-cheek way some men hoped they would die "in my sleep" and without loss of faculties. Yet the fear of dying alone and not being found for weeks was mentioned by several men, in general more by the never-married men. Spiritual uncertainty affected some men, and several indicated a real fear about their fate. Four or 5 men spontaneously indicated their desire not to be kept alive artificially "by a machine."

Uncertainty about the future was compounded in reference to financial matters. While an income might be "adequate" today, "who knows about two or three years from now?"

An inability to make specific, long-term plans is also characteristic of this uncertainty. Men felt they could look forward to little with certainty. With the exception of declining health and death, none of these men was generally future-oriented except within specific activity contexts ("The club will meet next month"). Notable ex-ceptions to this were those men who were oriented by means of their faith to believe that they would experience a happy afterlife.

Uncertainty about the future is compatible with the idea of living one day at a time. It is also compatible with the idea of "passing through," in which the present is happy—a state to be desired—in comparison with the past and in comparison with the uncertain and potentially dangerous future. Uncertainty about the future is compatible with a sense of connection to the past (number 1) in that the future basically does not matter to a present which enduringly contains the past, except in the threatening sense that it makes the past more distant. Here the future is to be denied.

Achieving the Status of Elder

In a popular image of old age in the past, older men became patriarchs, achieving the powerful and influential status of "elder," one considered innately respect-worthy. If this ever was true—a highly doubtful idea—it certainly is not now. Eldership is not necessarily an ascribed phenomenon.

Rather, eldership is innately ambiguous. We are admonished to "honor our fathers and mothers" and to have "respect for the elderly," but our society is also quick to categorize the elderly in a variety of negative ways.

Theoretically, then, our ideology holds that an older person should be respected and awarded an "elder" status by society. Positionally, an elder may receive the *emeritus* or *laureate* status. A man may become a "grand old man" or a "patriarch."

It would appear that the old view, that the elder status is an ascribed one, is an idea which grew up when there were relatively few older people, and is being replaced by an attitude which stresses achievement of the eldership status.

The fact is that many of the men we interviewed had nowhere gained the status of elder. This was particularly true of the never-married men and to a lesser degree of senior center members.

One purpose of the centers is to turn the individual experience of old age into a community affair, no longer focusing on the "specialness" of eldership but rather its common attributes and the need for age solidarity in the face of a sometimes uncaring society. Chronological age ironically takes on a new importance here in that the oldest person at a center is often specially honored.

For those men who had achieved some of the status of elder, it was always within a specific context. The most important was within a family. Here, the greatest amount of respect and love was received. Eldership may also be awarded within organizational, occupational, and community contexts.

Loss of a Personal Network and Friends

Another important personal transition involves surviving the loss of key associates—family, friends—and the incorporation of loss as a permanent feature. As one man put it, "I've gone to a lot of funerals in recent years."

If it is true that an important role of close friends is to help a person maintain a social identity (due to the sharing of experiences and mutual reinforcement) and if there is any validity to the notion of disengagement, such losses of friends and confidantes are possibly the core of disengagement. Life becomes a search to replace, if possible, what has been lost, and, at the same time, an effort to adjust to changed or reduced social circumstances.

In some cases, however, close friends and associates drop off so fast that one has no hope of ever replacing them. One man whom we discuss fully below, in a very distressing situation, had, along with his wife, lived through the death of two middle-aged sons, a close step-sibling, close in-laws, and two daughters-in-law in the space of about four years. In the fifth year his wife died. This man, in his fifth year of widowhood at the time of the interviews, was still distraught. It is difficult to see how the notion of the possibility of replacement has much currency here.

In an opposite way, however, the experience of replacement can be a powerful one. Four widowers who had reorganized their lives successfully and all of whom had high levels of activity and large and involved social networks had managed an unusual feat of replacement by forming a relationship of confidential intimacy with a woman each had known or known about prior to marriage (3 cases) or prior to the death of his wife. In the 3 former cases, the lives of these men had achieved a kind of full-circle quality. One's marriage, now over, was bracketed through the experience of bringing premarital and postmarital history together.

Personal Changes and Neighborhood Changes

The way in which one experiences the neighborhood in which one lives can also be part of a sense of personal transition. The neighborhood is a fertile field for the playing out of a number of powerful personal themes: continuity vs. change; personal control vs. external control; power vs. powerlessness; comfort vs. danger; familiarity vs. newness; neighborliness vs. alienation. There are many others. Thirty-four of the 47 men were residents of their immediate or larger neighborhood in excess of ten years, and many for much of their lives.

In our conversations, themes of personal transitions, of growth and decline, of family, and of aging were made with reference to changes in the neighborhood milieu. The neighborhood took on meaning in terms of the associations (real and fantasy-derived) a person had about it and the projections one made based on personal issues. In this regard, the importance of neighborhood has been discussed by Rowles (1978). Certainly, the ability of men to relate life changes to the neighborhood was dependent on a variety of personality factors. But this tendency was wide-spread. Again, associations and projections were made especially in the case of widowers who lived with continued unhappiness. Thus, for example, one widower said that he could no longer walk on a particular street or go shopping because that had been one place he had walked with his beloved wife. But it was not only widowhood which led to such usages. One man associated his own declining health with the declining "health" of his neighborhood by describing the reductions of his "zone of safety" in the walks he took over the past ten years. "I used to be able to walk ten blocks in any direction and feel safe. There was a park I could sit in, undisturbed. It seems like every year it's grown less and less. I wouldn't be caught dead over there [ten blocks away] now. . . . It's not only that it's unsafe, but my legs aren't quite as good. . . . Now it seems that it's only safe to walk in the block around here, and I even wonder about that."

The knowledge held by some older men of their neighborhood and the changes which have occurred was phenomenal. One interviewer took rides or walks with some of the men, and they could easily point out distinctive features, places where events had happened, and changes which had occurred.

Such changes are not innately negative, but can also signal the arrival of a "fresh wind" to old, worn-out places, as well as the destruction of "beloved places" to make way for "heartless" progress. The interpretation made by an individual is likely to be on the basis of a number of psychological factors.

Entering the Senior Milieu

The personal transition by men to the "all-senior" environment of a senior center can be difficult because it may occur along with changes in self-perceptions and in social roles (Jacobs 1974). Many of the men who attended senior centers volunteered that they entered center life very gradually, months or even years after first hearing about a center, and only becoming a more complete participant over a period of many months. In the early period of feeling one's way into center life, social contact may be friendly but restrained. While chatting and card playing are ongoing, men consistently noted that they knew little of others at the center and often did not know the names of people with whom they associated (this information came from men who did not usually stint on details of other people).

Once men pass through an initial stage and become more complete participants, the center can become an important context of friendship and interest. All in all, however, men appear to do less well than women at centers, in the sense that they participate less in formal activities and are more uneasy and isolated in the center. The overwhelming majority of center men appear to keep their center and noncenter lives separate. While meetings with other friends did occur outside of the center context, most were unplanned and informal. The center usually came to represent a concentrated area of social contacts.

It is the partial resolution of an important crisis that brings men into a center. Widowers do not enter center life when deeply bereaved, but rather when they begin to "come out" after mastering their grief.

Poor men may hear of a center and, due to their poverty, are attracted to the low-cost meal and the snacks.

Men may tend to drift in and out of center life, but more commonly, once participating—having survived the initial period—they tend to stay. Despite the often large disparity in number between men and women, many positions of authority at centers, such as committee heads, are often filled by men. The center provides a powerful *context* as well as a place for doing things. Often these things amount to nothing more than talking, joking, eating, or playing cards, but it is the special context of these events which is also important.

In addition to senior centers other significant steps in entering the senior milieu are the receiving of Social Security—a major indicator of a change of social status, decrease in income, and dependency— and engagement with the Medicare system, a system which brings for most men tales of bureaucratization and error.

CHAPTER 3

Widowhood

We raised a question earlier about the various life transitions we discussed, namely, whether any one of them seemed to be especially salient or to especially influence the others. We concluded that for many of the men we interviewed, loss of the wife and the subsequent period of widowhood were such influential and salient changes, and were, in part, the major transitions of late life. The death of one's wife was viewed by many men as the major event of late life, the one which conditioned the remaining years. For some men, widowhood and old age are synonymous.

While loss was a profound event in the lives of all the widowers we interviewed, these men varied considerably in the impact of the loss and in their abilities to reorganize their lives after the loss. Below, we judge such life reorganization on the basis of its relative success, depending on several criteria. By successful reorganization we generally mean the achievement of a new life-style centered around a new relationship of intimate companionship with a woman, the successful working through of most of the grief and the diminution of profound loneliness, and/or an ability to be engaged meaningfully in projects and activities. By unsuccessful reorganization we mean the more or less permanent establishment of a life-style characterized by the psychic continuation of the former marriage, an inability to form new, mature relationships, or an inability to find much satisfaction in activities.

Widowhood does not necessarily entail living alone, of course, but for most of the men we saw, the motivating circumstance of living alone is widowhood in late life. While we have yet to address the subject of living alone in detail, it is important to note here that it is an experience which is colored for these men, to a great degree, by the experience of loss, both for the widowers and the never married.

Our perception of the significance of loss and the problems of life reorganization was derived from conversations with men and from their statements about their lives. Yet there is a profound contrast between those widowers who now live successfully and those who live unsuccessfully, almost as if we are dealing with two separate species. Certainly, the process of recovery after loss by a man who is 70 or 75 years old, after forty or fifty years of marriage, is difficult, but many do manage it.

We begin our discussion with some general comments on the elderly widower and then a critical examination of the literature on widowhood, primarily divisible into that with a social and social-psychological basis and that which treats intrapsychic processes. We borrow the notion of reorganization from the work of Bowlby (1980) and Glick, Weiss, and Parkes (1974), who find it to be an analytically useful construct, but we find it necessary to introduce the notions of successful and unsuccessful reorganization in order to describe conditions of life characteristic of the elderly men we interviewed. The successful group of men consisted of those who were functioning well, who appeared happy, and who had managed to detach themselves from continued participation in a former marriage. The unsuccessful group admitted various degrees of unhappiness and appeared to be still married, psychologically, even after the passage of years, and were unable to reconstruct full life. Nevertheless, in both instances, life had been reorganized in the sense that new patterns of living had been established and maintained over time.

While the above are considered the basic criteria of successful or unsuccessful reorganization, in our judgment, a number of other specific features became apparent from our conversations with the widowers and were characteristic of each group.

Thus in our discussion of reorganization we single out a number of important themes which serve as *primary* contrasts between the two groups. These are the ability or inability to create a relationship of intimate companionship, differences in levels of social contact and social involvement, and the quality of relationships with children. These are areas of significant differences between the two groups and each is especially germane to issues of reorganization.

Also we distinguish a *secondary* set of attitudinal themes which further elaborate the differences in styles of life reorganization. These themes represent conscious and unconscious ideas expressed by these men in the interviews, and are ideas which appear over and over in the interviews. Thus the presentation of these secondary themes below represents our best translation of inner ideas expressed by individual men in each group.

THE ELDERLY WIDOWER

There is little doubt that the loss of a loved one can be the most devastating experience a person may have. While this is true at any age, each age has special problems attached to the experience of loss within it. The effects of widowhood in old age often occurring after many years of marriage are profound, can be deleterious, and may lead to considerable stress and to life-style changes. For men in old age, the thoughts which color the experience of widowhood and bereavement may include, among others, a perception that there is not enough time left to make an adequate life change nor to alter deep emotional patterns associated with forty years of marriage; a low self-image; or an inability to overcome functional dependency. In many cases the painful intrapsychic efforts of widowhood are mitigated over time, or at least the episodes of grief become fewer and occur with lessening intensity. Grief may be mastered and intense mourning passed through. This initial, emotion-filled period may last a year or more.

Beyond this is another period in which social adjustment to the new circumstances of widowhood is necessary and must be commenced. Adjustment includes both the altering of relationships with the outside world as well as inner-directed tasks of self-redefinition. In this regard there is always a tension between the inner and outer goals. While full of grief, an individual may cut himself off fully from the normal social stream and involve himself completely in his emotions for a time. Yet most individuals reflect directly, at least to some degree, on their own experiences and do not give up caring about their own social identities and social needs. Bereavement is essentially a process of "being inside" (self-involved) and "coming out" again.

Widowhood in old age can hide multiple deficits. The devastation-through-loss is one component, certainly the major one. But equally crucial is the degree to which loss will be connected to the ongoing experience of old age as a whole. Loss may trigger continuing feelings of disillusionment and low self-worth. Loss may be directly equated with old age, not an uncommon reaction from the men we interviewed. As one man put it, "When my wife died, I became an old man." Some men believed that the death of the wife was the first real evidence they had which indicates that society's worst thoughts about the elderly are correct.

For some men, then, the experience of loss sets up and strongly influences the whole of late life.

Thus widowhood in late life takes place in the context of normal late-life adaptation and change, but the effects of each are difficult to tease out. In a nutshell, the experience of loss may greatly influence adaptation and change, or, conversely, adaptation and change may greatly influence the experience of loss. We will take up this point in more detail below.

As we have noted, the common reaction of older people to widowhood is not to remarry. The rate of remarriage for elderly individuals is quite low. In 1970 3 out of every 1,000 brides were age 65 and older, while 17 out of every 1,000 grooms were age 65 and older (Treas and Van Helst 1976). Also, widowhood is primarily an experience of old age. In 1970 only 23 percent of widows and 19 percent of widowers were under the age of 70 (ibid.). While widowhood is primarily a phenomenon of later life, the literature of widowhood is nonetheless biased in favor of the young.

STUDIES OF WIDOWHOOD

Studies of widowhood have sought to understand this phenomenon from two perspectives: by analyzing the social and social-psychological aspects of widowhood, and by studying the intrapsychic or experiential aspects of widowhood.

In analyzing the social aspects of widowhood, gerontologists, social psychologists, and others have sought to describe and compare widowhood in its relation to morale and well-being and to isolate key variables within the widowhood experience which are significant in contributing to positive or negative self-perception. This research has also sought to compare the experience of bereavement of men with that of women and to understand the relative impact of widowhood on the quality of life and mortality of the survivor.

Mortality and Widowhood

Many studies have appeared that have highlighted and documented the stressfulness of widowhood which may lead to an increased rate of suicide (Bock and Weber 1972) and overall mortality. A recent paper by Helsing, Szklo, and Comstock (1981) has reviewed the literature on stress, mortality, and widowhood. Their own research demonstrated conclusively that male survivors have a higher rate of mortality after widowhood than do women. Experimentally, they identified some 4,000 survivors in a Maryland population who became widows and widowers between 1963 and 1974. Each widow or widower was matched for age, sex, race, and geographic location with a married individual. Widowed men showed a significantly higher mortality rate than that of married men, while there was no significant difference for the mortality rates of married women and widowed women. The rate of mortality for widowers who remarried was lower than the base rate for all widowers, while remarriage had no significant effect on the mortality of women. Finally, the researchers found that living alone was associated with a higher mortality rate for both men and women. These findings were applicable for sample members of all ages (the sample included individuals age 18 and over), although 44 percent of the sample was age 65 or older.

Social Aspects

Research on the social aspects of widowhood and on constructs such as social isolation and integration, the quality of life, and well-being and morale has been undertaken by a variety of social scientists. In much of this research, the experience of widowhood has been taken as a central conceptual focus. Some research has sought to isolate widowhood as differentially experienced by men and women and to compare it between the two sexes with regard to its distinctive features and relative deleterious effects.

Without a doubt the most comprehensive body of literature which has appeared to date on widowhood is the work of Lopata (1973a, 1973b, 1979). Her approach is thoroughly sociological and embarks from a theoretical interest in social roles, social integration, and "support systems" of the widow, an individual in "the last stage in the role of wife" (1973a). This research has clarified much about the social lives of widows and has described many of the common problems and experiences of widowhood.

There is no body of work about widowers which is equivalent to Lopata's in its depth and scope, although the work of Berardo (1968, 1970) is often taken as a starting point to some areas of male widowhood.

Berardo's thesis is that while the aged widower experiences different problems from those experienced by the widow, he encounters more severe difficulties in facing the single status than do widows. Berardo concludes that aged widowers are often socially isolated and experience "high rates of mental disorders, suicides and mortality risk" (1970:11). The empirical basis for his conclusions comes from a study done by him in Washington State in the 1960s. He also cites supporting evidence from studies by Townsend (1957), Tunstall (1965), and others.

Berardo's thesis has received only limited support from other sociologists and social psychologists. Pihlblad and Adams (1972) studied 1,551 community-residing married or widowed elderly age 65 and over in several small towns in Missouri in 1966. They found that widows are more "activity-oriented" than are widowers. They found no changes in activity patterns among women after widowhood, while widowers, on the other hand, demonstrated a "linear" decline in activity with length of widowhood. This conclusion would tend to support Berardo's thesis.

More recently, Hyman, in performing a secondary analysis of several large national data sets for the enduring effects of widowhood on those age 60 to 79, found some information which supports the notion that widowers do not fare as well in many areas. Concerning feeling, tone, and satisfaction with family life, "negative effects are more prevalent among widowers than among widows" (1983:89). According to Hyman, his data on older widowers as well as older divorced and separated men support the Berardo thesis in a number of areas.

However, Arens (1982), in an analysis of NCOA data, found that while widowhood had a generally negative impact on well-being, the data showed no reduction in levels of social participation for men. Direct effects of widowhood are insubstantial after taking into account factors such as health status and levels of social participation. Berardo's thesis concerning the special case of widowers is not upheld.

Gallagher, Breckenridge, Thompson, and Peterson (1983) examined bereaved elderly some two months after the death of a spouse and compared this group with a nonbereaved control group. While differences in distress and depression were found between the bereaved and nonbereaved groups, they found no differences within the bereaved group on the basis of gender which could be attributed to the loss of a spouse.

Carey (1979), in assessing a sample of 139 widows and widowers, age 28 to 70, thirteen to sixteen months after the death of their spouse, found that adjustment was more difficult for widows and that widowers were significantly better adjusted. He cites cultural reasons for this, noting that women tend to build their identities around their husband and that for men remarriage is easier. Individuals age 57 and older were better adjusted in the sample; he also found that higher education level, higher income, and greater reported happiness in the marriage were associated with better adjustment. This too fails to support Berardo's thesis.

Atchley studied 902 men and women age 70 to 79. He concluded that the effects of widowhood were felt severely by working class widows, especially, while other groups felt the impact of widowhood less. Atchley concludes that his data do not support Berardo's thesis. He finds that widowers in general fare better than widows and that "people are generally able to cope with the changes widowhood brings" (1975:176).

A similar conclusion was supported by Heyman and Gianturco (1973), who found that long-term adjustment to bereavement was generally characterized by emotional stability, stable social networks, few life changes, and few bereavement-related health deficits. The 14 widowers interviewed for the paper had an average age close to 75.

Finally, Morgan (1976) studied 232 widowed and 363 married women, age 45 to 74. She concluded that lower morale among the widowed may not be a function of widowhood per se, but may rather be attributable to other factors such as loss of income, low employment status, and the low availability of alternate roles.

This conclusion is similar to those of Harvey and Bahr (1974) and Hutchinson (1975). Harvey and Bahr found that negative and long-term consequences of widowhood derive from socioeconomic deprivation rather than from widowhood itself. Hutchinson, in a study of low-income elderly, found that marital status, as a predictor of self-reported happiness, makes no difference below the poverty line.

This social-psychological work supports a variety of conclusions. The style of reaction to late-life loss of the spouse appears to be somewhat different for men and women. Whether the outcome of loss is "worse" for men or for women remains unclear. Conclusions about the effects of widowhood are also diverse.

Intrapsychic Aspects

In analyzing the intrapsychic or psychological effects of widowhood in adult and late life, researchers have come to the more definite conclusion that widowhood is extraordinarily stressful and that analytically and experientially it can be separated out as a distinctive entity in its own right, regardless of socioeconomic or other variables. Studies by Bowlby (1980), Parkes (1972), and others have clearly shown that the loss of a spouse and the subsequent period of bereavement are often deeply felt and long-lasting in their effects. It has also become increasingly apparent that ties to the deceased spouse (as well as to other deceased individuals) do, in fact, persist over time as part of "normal" bereavement and as part of permanent adjustment. Below, our own material provides some evidence of long-term ties.

A major body of work concerning attachment, bereavement, and loss is that of Bowlby. His approach combines aspects of ethological and psychoanalytic theories. He has analyzed data (1980) on the experience of bereavement by adults after the loss of a spouse in the middle age and in late life, relying on his own clinical work, results from eight studies of bereavement in Western society, and ethnographic materials. The eight studies of bereavement in Western society, on which he draws heavily, discuss samples of mourners who consist to a large extent of women or of individuals under the age of 60. The study of bereavement in late life has, we believe, been inadequately examined.

Bowlby describes four distinctive phases of adult mourning. These are:

1. A period of *numbing*—an inability to believe that the death has occurred—lasting a few hours to a week after the spouse's death.
2. A period of "yearning and searching" for the lost figure, "lasting some months and sometimes for years" (1980:85).
3. A period of "disorganization and despair" in which the loss is recognized as permanent and the task of rearranging life is painfully faced and commenced.
4. A phase of reorganization—getting over the loss and building a new life.

The period of numbing is also characterized by feelings of anger. Parkes (1972) has described aspects of "yearning and searching" and the quite literal form that such longing takes. The phase of "disorganization and despair" represents confusion about one's place in life and the variety of feelings attached to the prospect of "coming out from under" the experience of loss and reaching the conclusion that life must go on. Reorganization represents the achieved style of life attained by each survivor. We will take up the last two stages below.

Bowlby (1980) lists three phenomena which are characteristic of the response by adults to the loss of a spouse. These are the *persistence of the tie* to the deceased by the survivor, *emotional loneliness,* and *ill health.* We will discuss each of these in turn.

It is quite clear that the relationship to the deceased may persist and continue in the mind and in the behavioral repertoire of the survivor for some time. Typical of persistence according to Bowlby are spending time thinking about the deceased, even after a year has passed; experiencing the "presence" of the deceased; dreaming about the deceased; or engaging in mock conversations with him. These and other evidence of a continuing and persistent tie are recognized by Bowlby as *typical* rather than atypical behavior. More recently, Moss and Moss (1984) have elaborated aspects of "the persistent tie with the deceased spouse" among elderly widows and widowers. They recognize that enduring ties with a deceased, longtime spouse continue "after the first few years of separation and mourning have passed." They isolate and amplify six aspects of this continuing relationship: caring, intimacy, family feeling, commitment, identity support, and a sense of home. Elsewhere (1980), they have described how the relationship between a survivor and a new spouse is essentially triadic, as it includes the old spouse as well as the survivor and the new spouse.

For the widowers, loneliness is typically experienced as a specific reaction to the loss of a spouse. Among the widowers in our sample, the greatest degree of loneliness was reported by those who were in their second to fifth year of widowhood. We discuss loneliness in chapter 6.

Finally, Bowlby mentions ill health as a characteristic of bereavement, and he summarizes several studies which indicate that an adult bereaved person experiences an increased likelihood of ill health. Fundamentally related to this topic of ill health is the question of the duration of grief. Studies discussed by Bowlby show considerable variation in typical duration of grief experienced by subjects. There seems to be no way to account for these differences. Bowlby concludes that a "substantial minority of widows never fully recover their former state of health and well-being" (1980:101; this, it should be pointed out, was concluded from samples primarily *under* 65 years of age).

In regard to the duration of the experience of grief, one important preconditioning factor may be that of anticipatory grief, or the grief experienced by a closely related survivor of the deceased prior to the actual death. Anticipatory grief usually occurs in the case of a chronic illness in which a foreknowledge of the impending death is available. Here, however, evidence on the effects of anticipatory grief is not conclusive. For example, Gerber et al. (1975) interviewed 81 surviving widows and widowers six months after the death of their spouses and found that the survivors with chronic (long-term) ill-nesses fared worse in their adjustment than the survivors of spouses with short-term illnesses. Presumably, the increased time available for the experience of anticipatory grief and the foreknowledge of eventual death should have mitigated, to some extent, problems of adjustment, but they did not.

A similar conclusion is supported by the work of Clayton et al. (1973), who studied survivors of spouses with short- and long-term illnesses, and who found that the surviving widows and widowers of individuals who had long-term illnesses felt worse than the short-term group one month after the death, but after one year were no better or worse in their adjustment. Gerber et al. (1975) also found that of all survivors of spouses who died from chronic illnesses, men fared worse. On the other hand, Glick et al. (1974) found that recovery from grief was inhibited and delayed in the case of those widows whose husbands had died suddenly (for example, in an accident) and who had had no forewarning of the death. Survivors of those who were chronically ill fared better in that it took them less time to reach a fair degree of recovery from the loss. Carey (1979) found that widows who had forewarning of the husband's impending death had a significantly higher level of adjustment thir-teen to sixteen months after the death, but forewarning was not a factor for widowers.

As we have mentioned, we find it useful to think about successful and unsuccessful reorganization, which we defined and characterized at the beginning of this chapter. We found it necessary to introduce this distinction after considering the phase of "disorganization and despair." While there is no timetable involved, the experience of these feelings of disorganization and despair is generally superseded, Bowlby notes, by a reorganization in which old patterns of thinking and feeling are discarded and "the corner is turned" in the fight against grief. A shift occurs which is well described, according to Bowlby, by one London widow who noted, "I think I'm beginning to wake up now." Nevertheless, as we described below, the corner was never turned for many of the widowers we interviewed. Elements from the phase of disorganization and despair continued on. Or, more to the point, life was reorganized by these elderly men around the idea that the loss is permanent and living will be diminished until death. Although unsuccessful reorganization can change and a man's condition in life improve, one is facing reality by noting that a life adapted to the permanency of a loss and diminished in richness four or five years after the loss is unlikely to change.

Thus while the phase of "disorganization and despair" exists, it appears to have two outcomes among the elderly widowers we interviewed. Disorganization and despair are overcome, the "corner is turned," as it were. And elements of disorganization and despair continue to be a central focus.

The men who had continued to suffer from the effects of bereavement, even after the passage of many years, could themselves distinguish a time when they had been "worse," and they noted a passage from a time of total disorganization to the current time in which life was somewhat improved, *but it was organized around issues which derived from the loss.* That is to say, life was reorganized but it was reorganized around the loss. While Bowlby's stages are meant to illustrate phases of intrapsychic experience, they can also be viewed with a concern for sociality. The stages represent a process of descent into internality followed by a gradual rise to externality. Immediately following the death of the spouse, deeply felt emotions "come out" fully and consciousness is oriented inward, toward them. In time, pain and loss are experienced only as a part of consciousness, and as episodic. Consciousness is redirected outward. Because of this, stages of bereavement must take into account a social component. Thus the phase of "disorganization and despair" applies not only to the inner, mental world per se, but also to the relationship between the inner world and the outer, social world. Inner states including conflicts, emotions, confusions, and other contributors to disorganization may be projected as outer social disorganization as well. The phase of unsuccessful reorganization was one which took the form of outward orientation, but the content was one of loss. Procedurally, these men "went about their business" as if things were normal, but they were not.

Bowlby's work (1980) on adult bereavement owes a large amount to the prior work of Glick, Weiss, and Parkes (1974), in which "reorganization" received definition and explanation. This earlier work presented a study of the *first year* of bereavement of 49 widows and 19 widowers all *under* the age of 45 at the time their spouse died. Subjects were interviewed four times following the loss: at a few weeks, eight weeks, and thirteen months after the loss, with a follow-up interview held between two and four years after the loss.

Glick and his colleagues found five "patterns of recovery from bereavement" which form the typical patterns of reorganization. These patterns represent three types of life-styles distinguishable on the basis of their orientation to remarriage. Specifically, these patterns are (a) the reestablishment of a marital relationship and a return to a married life-style; (b) the establishment—as a central life component—of a non-marital relationship with a member of the opposite sex; (c) reorganization of life around a close, supportive relationship with a kinsman; (d) the establishment of a life relatively independent of any close ties to other adults; and (e) an inability to establish any satisfactory life organization pattern.

The various phases of bereavement and recovery are illustrated in table 3.1.

TABLE 3.1
Phases of Bereavement and Recovery

"Numbing"	"Yearning and Searching"	"Disorganization and Despair"	"Recovery and Reorganization
			Five Patterns:
		Intrapsychic aspects	Remarriage
		Sociocultural aspects	Nonmarital relationship with a member of the opposite sex
			Close relationship with a kinsman
		Gender-related aspects	Life independent of any close ties
			Inability to establish a "satisfactory" pattern
		Common difficulties:	
		Ill health————————————→	
		Emotional loneliness————————→	
		Persistence of ties————————→	

Source: After Bowlby (1980), Glick, Weiss, and Parkes (1974), and Moss and Moss (1984).

All of the individuals interviewed in the Glick study fall into one or another of these patterns. These five patterns are all-inclusive and take into account the variety of possibilities of life reorganization after a spouse's death. A majority either remarried or led life-styles independent of close association with other adults at the time of the follow-up interview, some two to four years after the spouse's death. Nevertheless, they represent a kind of "fairy tale" in comparison with the lives of the elderly widowers we saw. Clearly implicit in the categories outlined by Glick et al. is the notion that bereavement resolves itself into one pattern which represents a *successful* adaptation or a *successful* recovery from bereavement. In their view, it appears that the only failure is the inability to achieve some sort of pattern. In living chaotically ones lives unsuccessfully.

In the Glick sample (1974:241), for those individuals who have attained a life-style which is relatively independent of close relationships with other adults, the resolution of the bereavement experience into this pattern represents, in the minds of the authors, a fundamentally *successful life-style* because all were viewed as functioning well on their own (1974:242). But our interviews with older men living alone showed that while a pattern of relative independence is common, one's existence within it may be generally happy or it may be uncomfortable and unhappy. There is, therefore, a distinction to be measured between "patterns" as *de facto* form and as content. Given our own sociocultural conventions, there are only a limited number of possibilities for people who have lost their spouse: remarriage or not, associations with others or not. Through these must run the theme of individual success or happiness; for Glick and his colleagues this issue is an implicit quality in most categories.

Many of the widowers we interviewed can certainly be classified as having a life-style which is "independent of close associations with other adults." This, however, may be an unsatisfactory state of affairs for them. It may not be the way they want to live, but it may be difficult for them to change due to a variety of external limits, the strength of the tie to the deceased, and a particular age-related self-conception.

There is a middle-age bias in the Glick categories. Another problem with these patterns is that they fail to give enough weight to the issue of age in the recovery from widowhood. The basic question is, how does a 70- or 75- or 80-year-old man make a life for himself after the death of his wife. The prospects here are clearly more limited than for the under-45 groups.

Thus the younger one is, the longer each new pattern—be it remarriage or the independent life-style—has a chance of remaining established. The older one is, the greater the chance of each pattern changing due to the greater probability of mortality. The younger one is, the greater the chance of approximating or recreating what one had before because any "new" relationship has time to generate enough history of its own to make the earlier relationship distant. (There is little information on the average distribution of time passed between one marriage which has ended in widowhood and a remarriage. In this regard it would be interesting to see how many "patterns" of independent life-style eventually, after several years, end in another sort of pattern.)

There is a tendency for certain patterns to predominate at a given age. For the young or middle-aged sample discussed by Glick et al., the "recovery" patterns of remarriage and independent life-style occur most frequently. In old age we know that the frequency of remarriage decreases while that of a close relationship to a kinsman may increase. At both stages the independent life-style remains an important pattern.

Many of the men we interviewed had moved on from the full disorganization and despair which had characterized their lives immediately after their loss. Their lives had been reorganized in a particular way, such reorganization forming a distinctive pattern, organized around or away from the loss. In cases of unsatisfactory reorganization, the subjective meaning of "old age," as well as the psychological nature of the ties to the deceased, served to lock a person in what is probably a permanent pattern. Further, it seems to us that there is considerable individual variation in passage through these phases, which are at best high-order abstractions. These are the lowest common denominator of actions and feelings derived from individualized systems of meaning. For certain people, there is no doubt that the experience of passing through bereavement follows phases that have more or less clearly recognizable beginnings and ends as well as key events which mark transitions between the phases. Nevertheless, for many there is no such sharpness of transition. Grief subsides some, becomes episodic, reduces in intensity, but always remains. Some important disorganization may become permanent or continuing if some element of "organization" which was performed by the deceased is not adequately replaced. Passage into a "pattern of recovery" may itself be *de facto,* ascribed rather than achieved.

For any individual, the death of a spouse and subsequent recovery must be viewed in terms of the problems and satisfactions encountered at the stage of life in which it occurs. For elderly men, the issue of spouse loss and adaptation to such loss is one which must be viewed within the adaptational problems and challenges indigenous to late life. Loss in late life cannot, therefore, be divorced from other adaptive tasks and freedoms of late life. Clark and Anderson (1967) suggest that five adaptive tasks are necessary for the process of late-life aging to be successful. They suggest that each individual must (a) define her limitations so as to conserve and use wisely her available energies; (b) redefine her physical and social life space so as to preserve her ability to control it; (c) find alternative sources of need satisfaction, focusing on those interests and activities which are feasible; (d) change or reassess her own criteria for self-evaluations so that standards of what is desirable or worthy are keyed to the present set of roles and activities; and (e) reintegrate values and life goals so that experiences in late life have meaning and coherence. These are listed as optimal tasks. Very few people do all of them and most may do only a few. They find that the third one, substitution of new sources of need satisfaction, is the most difficult and most crucial task.

If widowhood, bereavement, grief-induced disorganization, and life reorganization after bereavement occur in late life (as they often do), they will occur within a total adaptational milieu. Separating the tasks and issues of reorganization after bereavement from situations of late-life adaptation and understanding their relationship and mutual influences is difficult but necessary. For so many of the men we will discuss below, widowhood "sets up" the remaining years; it becomes an axiomatic principle in each individual's style or "culture" of living, a central entity of social identity. An individual's assessment of himself in light of his own experience of loss, grief, and bereavement strongly influences his perceptions of his own aging and what he will be able to do now and in the future. In turn, one's perception of aging, the curse, the opportunity, or some combination, will also influence the quality of life reorganization after a spouse's death.

This is a very complex area with many components. For example, Nydegger has noted the great difficulty in untangling role and age transitions. She describes problems that exist in understanding which life course transitions occur on the basis of age alone, which occur on the basis of role alone, or which occur in some combined form when "age . . . exerts an independent influence to *modify* the role transition in some significant way" (1980:128; emphasis in original). Such a combined form, Nydegger notes, is probably the most frequently occurring type of transition.

Widowhood will therefore be occurring in an environment in which change—both specific and generalized—is a common feature. The effects of widowhood may act in concert or in conflict with other, specific or general changes. There is no way to know if the effect of such compound change is beneficial or deleterious. For example, the occurrence of both retirement and widowhood within a close period of time may act to effect long-term devastation or, together, to "clear the slate," so to speak, depending on the personality and situation of the survivor. It is certainly the case that the life-style of relative independence from other adults can come to have a variety of meanings. It is not merely the resolution of a deficit. It is a lived-in state in which life continues to adapt and change.

LIFE AFTER LOSS

Next we will turn to a discussion of life reorganization in widowhood. This stage concerns us here for a variety of reasons. This is the phase of reorganization which was primarily seen by the interviewers as the interviews were ongoing. We do not have much information about specific events in the earlier stages since retrospective accounts of painful events are notoriously inaccurate. Also, we are concerned with the question of how people construct and depend on meaning in their lives and, therefore, in how lives are reorganized after crises. Again, this is the stage when individuals try to build a viable life for themselves after most of the immediate impact of the loss has been diminished.

First, we will discuss the characteristics of successful life reorganization, isolating and describing the various themes which emerged in the interviews. Then we will take up unsuccessful life reorganization in a similar way. Finally, we will contrast the two.

In all, we interviewed 29 widowers, excluding the 1 man widowed in excess of fifty years. The case material will be derived primarily from interviews with 25 of the 29. We have omitted 4 for a variety of reasons, but primarily for a lack of complete data. The average age of the 25 men at the time we interviewed them was about 78 (the range, 67 to 92). Table 3.2 shows those by cohort.

TABLE 3.2
Widowers by Age

Age	Number (=25)
65–69	2
70–74	5
75–79	9
80–84	5
85–89	2
90 and over	2

The average age of these men at the time their wife died was about 72; they were married for an average of thirty-seven years (range, seven years to fifty-four years).

Successful Reorganization

There were 11 men who were judged to have successfully reorganized their lives after the death of a longtime spouse.

A successful reorganization of life after the death of a longtime spouse may be viewed as having two stages, although the second stage is not a necessary development after the first. In the first stage of reorganization, these men had mastered their grief. The painful events surrounding the wife's death no longer preoccupied them. The feeling of loss and devastation which had at one time been pervasive no longer seemed to thoroughly influence or infect most of their lives. They experienced loneliness sometimes, rarely, or never, but not often. They managed to keep busy and to fill in time so they were not anxious or bored when alone. They could be engaged meaningfully and ongoingly in projects. In general, they functioned well, although they were still in a process of recovery. They had interests and contacts and had made a life for themselves, however tentative. They were active and were sensitive to events outside of themselves.

The second level of successful reorganization consisted of a more complete life than that implied by merely the mastery of grief and "getting by." In this more complete form of successful reorganization there has been a replacement of parts of life which are deemed by an individual to be crucial for him. Further, for these men life is active and rewarding. Some men continue patterns of a high level of activity which has been typical of them prior to the wife's death. Several men—as far as we can tell—seem to have increased their overall activity above what it had been during the last years of marriage. Nevertheless, even if increased activity or a high level of activity was not characteristic of these men, their current lives, as they were talked about, were displayed as something with an internal coherence and patterned meaning and something from which satisfaction was derived. Some men achieved a new life-style centered around a new relationship of intimate companionship.

Several topics which relate to successful reorganization should be mentioned here. First, the meaning of living alone is one indicator of successful reorganization. We discuss living alone and the meaning of living alone in chapter 7. For those widowers who had had successful reorganization, living alone was often viewed as important in that it enabled an individual to actively get away from others after a busy day; the home was viewed as an oasis in a desert of demands, an environment which could be (blessedly) regulated and controlled. For those men who had successfully reorganized their lives, but who had reached the first level or reorganization, the home was an embodiment of important ties to the deceased wife, and, to a certain extent, represented continuity with the marriage-that-was. Yet in comparison with those widowers who were unable to successfully reorganize their lives, the sense of continuity and embodiment was diminished. For those men who had not successfully reorganized their lives, living alone was viewed as a continuation of living with the wife in the sense that once the wife was gone, things continued unchanged, the widower attempting to fill in the tasks once performed by the wife as best he could, or by leaving them undone, marking her continuing role through her nonreplacement.

All of these men feel the loss, but some have more trouble accepting it. One may distinguish, then, as we do below, between living alone as discontinuity and living alone as continuity, or, put another way, active living alone and passive living alone. It should be noted that for men who have successfully reorganized their lives, grief and despair have, for the most part, been worked through, the reality of the death of the wife faced, and life "gone on with." In this way living alone represents discontinuity in two ways. It represents discontinuity with the marriage-that-was. And it represents discontinuity with daily activities; men "go out" and "come home" at the end of a day, home and out of home representing two distinctive domains.

In successful reorganization, a man has found replacements for some of the roles played and some of the activities performed by the deceased spouse. For those elderly men we interviewed, the role of "intimate companion" seemed to be especially salient. An intimate companion is a woman of the same age range who acts as a confidante, with whom a man has a special, subjectively placed bond, and with whom he does things. The relationship may not be sexual and may not be marriage-oriented but may exist as a relationship separated out by its specialness. Such a relationship allows involved individuals to have a relationship of friendship or a marriagelike tie and yet maintain an independent life-style. In such relationships the wifely role of "intimate companion" is replaced, but other roles such as "mother," "sexual partner," "homemaker," "income earner," and "housekeeper" may not be. While it is not true that having an intimate companion negates the need for these other roles to be filled, it would appear that for those men with intimate companions, these other roles do not seem to be quite as important.

A higher level of activity and social contact seems to be characteristic of the second level of successful reorganization after the death of a spouse. In our total sample, those individuals who had the highest levels of activity were widowers, although those men who had successfully reorganized their lives in fact covered a wide range of activity levels. Those men who had successfully reorganized their lives also had a variety of patterns in regard to the continuity of activity through the life course. This, of course, was difficult to ascertain retrospectively.

Interestingly, for those men who had successfully reorganized their lives, the period of time which had elapsed since the wife's death varied considerably. Of these men we discuss below, 3 had been widowed for three years or less, 5 had been widowed between three full years and seven full years, 3 had been widowed twenty-one years or more. It would appear that the passage of time does not uniformly reflect successful reorganization.

Conceptually, a number of themes seem to appear or may be teased out of the statements made by these men in their interviews that illustrate commonly held attitudes or thoughts which typify or embody successful reorganization. We go into these in detail below, but here an example will suffice.

For these men, "present time" is viewed as part of "future time," and both are associated with a positive self-image and a feeling of confidence that new and/or rewarding things are yet possible in life, before it is over. For men who have not successfully reorganized their lives, "present time" is tied closely to "past time," and "future time" is viewed suspiciously as an element which will bring about further unwanted separation from the past.

Even in successful reorganization, time only heals some wounds. Many of these men have warm and telling memories of their deceased wives, and these deceased individuals are, to some extent, included in everyday life through photos, objects, and memories.

In successful reorganization, relations with children seem to be more cordial and the goals of the relationship more clearly defined and mutually supportive than in occasions of unsuccessful reorganization. Below we discuss relationships with children within successful and unsuccessful reorganization.

We begin by looking at intimate companionship, levels of social contact, and social activity. We take up the question of relations with children, and finally focus on thematic elements which appear frequently with these men. Also, we take up the meaning of living alone in chapter 7 and the question of ongoing memories of the deceased spouse in the section of loneliness, chapter 6.

CHARACTERISTICS OF SUCCESSFUL REORGANIZATION

Intimate Companionship

One important aspect in the successful reorganization of life after the death of the spouse was the ability of some men to establish a relationship of intimate companionship or a confidante relationship with a woman. Of the 11 men who seemed to have successfully reorganized their lives, 9 have had involved relations with women since the death of the spouse. These relations have existed in a variety of forms; they are not always—or often—sexual.

The renewal—in late life—of an old acquaintanceship. Three men had renewed relationships with women whom they had known or known of in their younger days. These relationships seem to be especially meaningful and satisfactory although the history of each is somewhat different.

Mark Miller is an 88-year-old retired businessman who was active in business and civic affairs prior to his retirement and since that time has been active in religious and community circles. At the present time his closest nonkin relationship is with a woman about ten years younger than himself, whom he knew originally from an earlier part of the century and whom he remet about fifteen years ago, six years after his wife's death. He discusses his relationship with her in the following way.

"When I get lonely, there is a lady I call on the phone, a very good friend of mine. . . . Let me tell you something. When I first met this lady, I was 'going out' with a sister of hers, but it didn't amount to anything. . . . That sister and I drifted apart. . . . My current friend, she was the youngest child in that family; the one I was going with, she was older. I learned sometime later that the one I was going with and had broke off with was engaged to another man. In fact, I was invited to the wedding. We were still amicable.

"Well, things went on, and I met my wife, and got married, and so on. . . .

"Now comes the curious part. Forty-five years after I saw this lady—my friend—I was living here. I was looking up a name in the Philadelphia phone book . . . and totally by accident I came across the family name. Their last name was a little bit unusual, and I thought, 'My goodness.' I recognized the name so I called her up and said, 'Are you Arlene so-and-so?' So she said, 'Yes.' I said, 'Are you one of the so-an-so children?' She said, 'Yes.' So I introduced myself and I found out she was living not too far from here. So I drove over, and I've been going over to visit her ever since. We are good friends.

"The funny thing is that she's about eighty now and I'm close to ninety. But when I knew her before, I was in my twenties and she in her teens. That was a tremendous difference then, but the difference between eighty and ninety isn't so much.

"I often go down to see her. She lives near downtown, so if I happen to be that way, I'll stop in. More importantly, whenever I get lonely, I'll call her up on the phone. . . . I tell her things I wouldn't broadcast to everybody. Opinions, or things that are happening.

"I've known her since she was a youngster.

"It's funny how things like this happen. So much of our lives is controlled by chance . . . being at the right place at the right time. My parents would have called this 'predestined' because they were great believers in that occult stuff."

Hubert Smith, now age 83, has a similar kind of situation. He grew up in a small, mostly black town in the South and came north in the 1920s hoping for work. One of his childhood classmates, Elsie, was a "girlfriend" at that time. After Mr. Smith moved north, he and his girlfriend drifted apart. Each eventually married another and raised families. Now, both of their spouses are dead. Elsie lives in Washington, D.C. Mr. Smith's wife died in the 1950s and since that time, although he has had a string of girlfriends, he has never remarried. During the time Mr. Smith was married, he continued writing to Elsie: "We never let six or seven months go by without a letter."

Mr. Smith now feels that he is close to Elsie. "I call her up every holiday. We talk frequently. I visit her down there once a year. . . . We talked about getting married after my wife died, but there was a lot of reasons we didn't. We both still had children then, I was working up here, and she was down there. But we're still close . . . we keep in touch."

Mr. Smith identifies Elsie as his closest friend. It is her picture (not that of his wife) which hangs on the dresser mirror near his bed.

A similar event happened to Steve Thompson, age 77, a retired businessman. His wife died five years ago in 1976, after more than forty years of marriage. For the last few years, he has been "going with" a woman whom he had known about earlier in life through an association with her husband. Steve Thompson, his former wife, and his current girlfriend all hail from the same small neighborhood in Philadelphia and knew of each other in "the old days."

"You should know about my lady friend. . . . She's a widow. Her husband and I were in the same elementary school and same business. In fact, Betty [his girlfriend], I knew of her back there, then, too. She was very good-looking and everyone knew who she was.

"I met her again after my wife died, at a get-together. We struck up quite a friendship. She is my best friend now, the person I'm closest to. . . . Our relationship is not sexual. . . . However, we spend a good deal of time together. We have dinner together every night. . . . Our friends recognize us a 'a couple.' We travel everywhere together; we see each other every day."

The renewal and continuation of old relationships is a happy event for these men and is certainly one event which has enabled them to "get over" the loss of the wife after many years of marriage (thirty to forty years in each case). In each of these instances, the relationship has operated over a period of time greater than that of the long-term marriage. Certainly, these cross-sex "old friend" relationships are ones whose initial development has been thwarted by marriage, and these have bloomed, in a time of need, after the marriage is over.

Functionally, these relationships satisfy needs of identity as well as more utilitarian ones. Mr. Thompson's friendship is a practical, day-to-day affair. Although he and his friend maintain separate residences, they otherwise function together as a couple, dining out, entertaining, shopping, pooling resources. There has been some talk of marriage, Mr. Thompson preferring it, and his friend not. Mr. Miller renewed an acquaintance after almost fifty years. For him his friendship is a considerable advantage when he is feeling low and presents a place for him to go when he is downtown. He also mentions that this relationship is one which is important to him when he feels "neglected" by his children, when they are busy with their own lives and do not have much of a chance to get in touch with him. In the case of Mr. Smith, his friendship is an embodiment of strong ties to his own past and the farm community in which his family lived and where he grew up and was educated. Each man talked directly about these functions.

At a less utilitarian level, these relationships have one function of giving life a "full circle" quality. There is some element of one's youth which is being "returned to," because in these cases there was much of life, family, neighborhood, and community that was shared years ago by these men and their friends and which forms the basis of the current relationship. Indeed, these relationships seem to say that things survive as well as change. In each case, although this is difficult to assess, the marriage relationship, which has taken up a good portion of life, can be viewed as one episode in a whole life, rather than the subject matter of most of life itself (as may be the case with men who have not successfully reorganized their lives after the death of the spouse). Early and late life are tied together through the presence of a significant other who has been present, part of, and privy to both.

Another theme, although one which was not spoken directly, nor acknowledged, but was apparent from the way in which these men spoke of their friends, is that each man has maintained an interest in what has happened to the "girls" he knew before, that this interest was latent throughout married life, and it was something which was easily activated. None of these men currently has sexual relations with his woman friend. But among them was clearly the realization that things could have—very easily—turned out differently, and that these individuals might have been married today.

A somewhat similar pattern was followed by Bill Franklin, age 80, a retired electrician. He has been a widower since 1978, after forty years of marriage. In 1974, while still married, he started an affair with a younger woman who was known socially to both Mr. Franklin and his wife.

"I don't believe that my wife knew about it. We had known each other several years, socially and in a business relationship. Alberta [the girlfriend] was divorced, after a stormy marriage. On occasion, the three of us—Alberta, my wife and me—went places together. My wife and Alberta were close friends.

"I never had any affair in my life prior to this. I guess my relationship with my wife wasn't good sexually . . . we had separate bedrooms. But I loved my wife. She was a remarkable woman. . . .

"My relationship with Alberta has continued until today. It started discreet and it is still discreet . . . none of my friends knows about it. It's important for both of us to keep it quiet—it's more important to her, I guess. She has a certain position. . . .

"She is my closest friend. We're in constant touch by phone. Before I go out or after I come back, she'll call or I'll call so she knows where I am. She spends the night here at least once a week, although sexually I've slowed some—I'm not as good as I once was."

This relationship started in late life. While it does not have the full-circle aspect of those mentioned above, it is one which existed outside of the context of marriage and continued when the marriage was over. One wonders, of course, whether Mr. Franklin's wife really knew about it but chose not to say anything. From what Mr. Franklin said, his wife was kindhearted, patient, and religiously motivated. She seemed to be the kind of person who would know and not say.

Mr. Franklin's relationship with Alberta is one of great significance to him. It has some of the advantages of marriage with few of the disadvantages. It allows both individuals a great deal of personal freedom, but gives Mr. Franklin a feeling of being supported. It is the major source of warmth and friendship in his life.

Relationships with newly met women. Of those men who have substantially reorganized their lives, 3 have managed to start intimate relationships with women whom they met since the death of the wife, while 1 man is actively "looking." Interestingly, none of these men is currently "going with" anyone.

Frank Walters, age 73, is a retired City of Philadelphia employee. His wife died in 1975 after about forty years of marriage.

"We had a house in Arbortown. After my wife died, I was living there. . . . Grieving takes a while. I didn't come around until about a year after my wife's death. . . . I moved into an apartment when I retired. . . . Later on, I started going to the center [the local area senior center].

"I got to know a woman named Margaret there. She was a widow. She was very kind to me and a nice person. She was Irish like me. I thought a lot of her. We even talked about marriage. The thing was, she died suddenly, over a weekend. I tried to find out more from her children, but they weren't very nice to me. They put me off."

While Mr. Walters managed to "get over" the death of his wife and form an attachment to another woman, he has had to get over this loss as well. It is obvious that he experienced considerable sadness concerning the sudden loss of Margaret, about eight months prior to the time he was interviewed. At that time, he was still wearing a ring she had given him. Nevertheless, Mr. Walters did not dwell on this loss, managing to stay active and to "get out" as much as possible. For him, this meant both center and church activities.

Henri Minsk, now in his early 80s, met his second wife at a social gathering. He was married to her for about ten years when she died, about three years ago. He has gone through a second period of grieving: "I was married almost forty years the first time and ten years the second time.

"I was very sad, very depressed after my [second] wife died. . . . I was lonely. But little by little you get yourself together. Time is the best healer—but you also need an ability to adjust yourself. . . . It takes a strong will to control yourself and to reconcile yourself to things. But life has to go on. It's better that you don't think as much as you get older. . . . You don't have another eighty years."

For Mr. Minsk, his first wife "fit" with his first career of parenting and business; his second wife fit with the life-style of his "second" career—volunteer work. He continues his volunteer work, but he feels emptiness at times.

Horace Adam, about 80 years of age, has been a widower for six years after more than fifty years of marriage. His participation at a senior center has enabled him to meet several women. He feels a debt of gratitude to the center for having improved the quality of his life since his wife passed away.

"Since I've been going to that center, there is one lady with whom I've gone about, but we've long since broken off. I haven't seen her in some time now, although if I wanted to I could. . . . She is someone who has had several men guests. Now I have several lady friends, but these aren't [of a sexual nature] like the other one was. Of these, there was one in particular I was going with, but we've broken off now. We often went out togehter, to local restaurants or to other places. However, we've been drifting apart. In the past year—last year—we discussed marriage, living together, arrangements, but it won't work out. We still see each other occasionally—or even more often—but that's all."

One of Mr. Adam's acquaintances suggested to the interviewer that Horace is looking for a wife. "He doesn't get around quite as well as he used to and he's afraid he'll have trouble. He's looking for someone to help him out."

"Looking for a woman" is also a theme in the life of Tony Johnson, who is about 80 years old, in very good health, and has been a widower for seven years, after almost fifty years of marriage. Mr. Johnson appears to have "gotten over" his own grief at his wife's death, although he is occasionally still bothered by anxiety attacks which began after his wife died.

"I don't want to remarry . . . fifty years was certainly enough . . . I don't want any more. I'd never get married again.

"One problem is that although I go out with women—they're younger than me—in their late sixties—all they think about is marriage. They're Catholics, 'good girls,' and they won't 'play around' outside of marriage. I wouldn't mind living with one of 'em, but they'd think it was a sin.

"On my mind is that I want to get something going with someone. It's harder when you're older because it takes you more time to get aroused, to get an erection. Somebody I knew knew someone who knew someone who had connections with a 'house.' Until a few years ago, I'd go there, but unfortunately the girls don't know 'the special needs' of old people . . . they work 'piece work' (ha-ha) . . . for them the faster the better. For me, I won't come up so fast anymore. . . . My first times were with 'girls' too . . . back in 1915 or 1916.

"But now I'm looking. I date once or twice a month. I know women from this neighborhood and the suburbs too. Maybe we'll go to the shore. I'll proposition 'em, ask 'em to stay overnight [and have sex] in a hotel. . . . I don't 'con' these women—I tell them right out that there's no marriage involved. They'll turn me down. But I admire women who won't . . . who want want marriage first, although it makes it hard for me. I haven't had sexual relations for about two years, now."

Later on, at a last meeting, he added: "There's another woman I know, I'm gonna ask her about Atlantic City, ask her outright." ("You mean about sex?") "Yeah . . . I'm hopeful. I don't think she'll turn me down."

Men with no intimate companions. Several men who have successfully reorganized their lives have not developed intimate relationships with any women.

Ed McBride, age 80, married for fifty years, has been widowed for less than three years. "I've done my crying over my wife. We had a good life together. I'm satisfied that I did my best by her. . . .

"I spend most of my time here at home. I manage to pass the time all right. Occasionally, I'll go downtown. I've never felt lonesome—there's always something to do.

"I don't think of remarriage. Things are fine the way they are. I'm doing O.K. as I am."

Mr. McBride says that he has no close friends, no intimates. "I don't confide in anyone, not even my family. . . . I don't even think I confided in my wife that much."

To an observer, it is nevertheless clear that there is a loneliness in Mr. McBride's life. He has recently announced an interest in attending a senior center or in doing volunteer work to fill in his free time. From the way he speaks, it is also apparent that he has conflict within him still lingering over the death of his wife. His wife's death was an ordeal. She was ill for several years, incontinent and progressively senile. Mr. McBride served as her primary care giver. He experienced relief at her death. Nevertheless one hears, still, his fondness and longing when he speaks of her. While these conflicts have not been resolved, Mr. McBride is, himself, resolved to go on and is just now (at the time of the interview) making the transition to being socially active again.

We consider Mr. McBride to have successfully reorganized his life because he is in the process of making a transition to a full and somewhat more satisfying life-style and because he has broken the active ties with his wife. While it is true that no tie is ever really broken, from the point of view of his life reorganization, the tie no longer prevents him from going on.

Lou Giordano, "a young seventy-six," says, "My wife's been dead twenty years now [after thirty years of marriage]. So I've been alone quite a long time . . . it isn't bad . . . I'm all right. At first, I used to miss her bad, but I'd say to myself, 'Lou, it's no use in feeling this way.' Even now, if I begin to think about her and I miss her, I just go out . . . and I talk to anyone about my wife."

In his apartment, he keeps a special bookcase on which stand photos of his wife and his mother as well as religious items such as a crucifix and a Bible. He prays "to them" and "for them." He believes that he will be joined with them, again, in the Hereafter.

He feels the sadness of missing his wife "sometimes," even after twenty years. He has not been able to transfer his desire for companionship onto another, even after the passage of this time, but rather, in a curious way, still views himself as being married to his wife. However, he seems to be functioning well. He has successfully reorganized his life in that he has mastered his grief and learned to accept and live with the loss. Nevertheless, it appears that his manner of acceptance has been to continue living in the way in which he had been living before, eliminating those things done by his wife, and never replacing them. In this case, less clear-cut than those above, it is hard to say what constitutes successful reorganization, except that his general tone is happy.

Levels of Social Contact and Social Activity Experienced

In general, those men who have successfully reorganized their lives and who have adjusted to the death of the spouse show a high level of social activities and a high incidence of social contacts. Clearly, the sheer number of social contacts is no direct indicator of the degree of successful readjustment, but, rather, it is one element in a total picture. Thus 8 of the 11 men now have what may be described as a "high" level of social activity and social contacts (see chapter 5). By this we mean that, broadly defined, they are participants in at least two social circles or groups in which they are active and invest at least three hours three times a week (social groupings or stages for roles such as clubs, paid work, volunteer work, church, senior groups, and informal—but recognized—activity-oriented circles of friends); that participation in these circles or groups seems to have some subjective significance; that they usually have some family matrix with sustained and warm contacts; that they have at least one or two individuals whom they recognize as close friends and acquaintances; that they have a large number (at least five) of peripheral, yet subjectively significant, acquaintances; and that they have a number of definite roles they play and places they "belong to," or feel a part of.

It is important to note that this level of activity is extraordinarily high and probably not typical of the majority of elderly.

In assessing the level of social contact and activity, we also want to treat the following issue: Did the death of the wife bring about a permanent change in the number or quality of social contacts and activities, or does the relatively high level of social contact represent a long-term pattern?

Continuity in high-activity or social contact level. Most of the 11 men had total patterns of high activity which seem to be extensions of patterns held in earlier life. For example, Mr. Miller, mentioned above, was someone who seems to have had extensive responsibilities in all periods of his life: "I went straight through school and quickly to the top of my profession." He worked for more than forty years in one capacity, retired, and then continued on with two other firms for fourteen additional years. Finally retiring from the work force, he has achieved positions of responsibility in community and religious circles. He is still extraordinarily active. And he is candid about himself: "I like to be in charge." He speaks of one social grouping of which he is the head: "People there are extremely mediocre. . . . I don't know any person I can talk to . . . maybe one or two, but they keep to themselves. I know this sounds a bit braggadocio . . . and I don't mean to be bragging, I assure you."

Similar long-term patterns are described by another man. "My life now is focused around what I call my 'hobbies.' I have been an official of my church for more than forty years. I've been involved with fund-raising and management of overseas charities for twenty-five years. I've been with the Police Athletic League almost since its beginning some fifty years ago, and I am on the board of one community agency for more than ten years." This man stopped working five years ago at the age of 75. Since then, he has filled in his time with these and other activities and may attend several meetings a week in connection with them. Moreover, he receives and makes several phone calls a day concerning his "hobbies." He has considerable paperwork attached to these activities as well.

Other patterns. A total of 7 men (of the 11) followed a similar pattern of continuity. For several of these men, since the death of the wife occurred some time ago and most of the experience of bereavement was in the past, it was difficult to assess how long and to what effect bereavement interrupted the continuity of activities.

At the time of our interviews, 1 man was just at the point of coming out and beginning to socialize again after the death of his spouse some three years ago. In this case, Mr. McBride—mentioned above—now appeared to be interacting with a number of people in excess of those he had seen prior to his wife's illness and certainly while he was nursing her. However, these interactions did not yet appear to have much subjective significance for him. The individuals he met did not seem to be signposts in his life.

Finally, 3 men were quite difficult to place in terms of the continuity of social activity. One was a widower for thirty years, another for more than twenty years, and the third seems to have entirely dismissed his wife from his life (he did not even own a photo of her), and it was difficult to get a sense of what life had been like for him in the past.

Relations With Their Children

Of these 11 men, 8 have children. Of these 8, only 2 mentioned problems with children either in response to specific questions or in general, open-ended conversations. For these 2 men, problems with children were nagging, long-term, and subjectively significant.

One man, who had eight children (two sons, six daughters), was asked to list problems in his life now and replied, "I have one problem. It's my son Dan. Things haven't been right with him now for some time . . . with him and his wife. It was all over something that happened at a wedding of one of his children . . . he says that I was rude to him and his wife and since that time we haven't been close. . . . That was a few years back. He doesn't live very far from me but I don't go there and he doesn't come here. He never calls me up; sometimes I'll call him, but he's always 'too busy' to come to the phone. Dan don't see his sisters, either. . . . You know, I think a lot about this. It's really eating me up, hurting me. I'd like to stop it, but I'm not sure what to do. We haven't spoke in more than a year."

This man seems to have cordial relations with the rest of his children (this despite personal difficulties several seem to have; one has been an alcoholic, another has had considerable problems in her marriage). He talks about his other children in the following way: "Butch . . . my [other] son . . . we talk or see each other every two weeks or so. Four of my daughters I see or talk to at least once a week. They all live close by. One other . . . she lives in Jersey. I see her about twice a year, but I'll talk to her every week. There's one down south, in Texas, I've been visiting her every February for the last few years. I'll stay a week or two. . . . I'm close to the girls and to Butch, but not to Dan."

Two of his daughters in particular take care of his heavier household tasks such as cleaning and laundry (although at times he will take care of these things himself). Several of his daughters and their families helped him move into and fix up his latest residence. One daughter has taken the role (held formerly by his wife) of reminding him when birthdays and special occasions are coming up, so he can remember them. He says, "I show my appreciation to my family often."

The other man with troubles with his children, Andrew Hart, age 74, has a difficult relationship with one of his two children, his son. The son, a man in his 40s, who lives with his family in a town in the Midwest, has a life-style and values which are at odds with those of his father. Mr. Hart's other child, his daughter, lives in the South. The "differences" between Mr. Hart and his son do not consume him, however. Mr. Hart, a man who still works part-time, has a "lady-friend" and is active in his church. The dispute between Mr. Hart and his son is best symbolized by the fact that they have seen each other only twice in the last seven years, despite the fact that both men have sufficient time and money to go traveling. Nevertheless, they talk "regularly" (one to two times a month) on the phone.

Although it is easy to overgeneralize, the remaining 6 men seem to have fairly good relations with their children. By good, we mean that there are no specific or general disputes which prevent interaction; hatred, anger, or contempt do not appear to be major themes in relationships. Domains of interest are demarcated. Fathers know when they should or shouldn't involve themselves in the affairs of their children. There is a sense of family continuity and wholeness. The goals of the relationships between father and children are held in common; the needs each participant in the relationship has are not mismatched with the possibilities offered by the relationship; if they are, they are adjusted.

Mr. Walters, mentioned above, has three children. "My children all live far away. . . . I hear from then once in a while. . . . I get letters every couple of months [he has no telephone]. They got their own lives to live now. I'm happy with the way things are with them." He saw them last two years ago, when they came, as a group, to visit.

Mr. Minsk also has three children. "I'll be ninety in a few years. I can see my choices as an 'old age home,' living with one of my children, or staying here in my home. Since my health is good, I'd rather be here. I like to see people of all ages, like I do here. You have more spirit and vitality. I'm close to all of my children, but my eldest son in particular. My children, they inspired me when I was depressed, after my wife died. You need to have someone to give you encouragement, and my children do that for me. We all experience tragic things and we all have the need to go on. . . . The urge to survive and continue is strong.

"I am close to my children. My son calls every day at a certain time. . . . I talk to him and his wife; they ask me how I'm feeling and what I've done all day. My daughter and my younger son, I hear from them maybe twice a week. They all live in this area. My son has achieved a very high status in his profession, and his professional status means a lot to me. I worked on trucks and on docks. That's all right, I made a living. My son has gone beyond that. . . . Something that made me especially happy was when his son, my grandson, got his Ph.D.

"While being close to my children is important, I still would rather by my own man. It's hard for you, a younger person, to know what pleasure I derive from watching the sun come up or taking a walk down the street . . . all by myself, independently. I often have to make a concerted effort to do things, but I force myself to. . . . There's a lot of water under the bridge but the river's still flowing."

Tony Johnson: "I get along good with my kids and my grandchildren. My idea is to keep everything even. I see each of my children every month or so, maybe to spend a day or a weekend with each one and their family. I'll do that once a month or so.

"I've made a will. Everything is split evenly in three ways. This is how I want things to be. I try to keep it all even, to give equal gifts and to have no favorites.

"Like I said, every month or so, I'll go to one of my children's, stay overnight or for the weekend, so I may be over there, ten, twelve times a year." In an interview held on a Monday afternoon, he said, "I still have some of a hangover today. I was at my son's this weekend. Saturday, I went shopping with my daughter-in-law. I help around the house when I'm visiting, do the dishes, and what not. Saturday night, we went to a party at some of my daughter-in-law's relatives in New Jersey. I was drinking . . . I had a good time there, saw some old friends. Yesterday, we were in, watched some football games, drank a little bit more. Today, my stomach don't feel so good."

What the actual nature of such relationships is, is a difficult question and one which is practically impossible for an outsider to know. Nevertheless, these relationships are presented in a way in which conflicts—to whatever extent they exist, and they certainly do exist—are not presented as a dominant theme; this is in contrast with the case with so many of the men whose lives are not satisfactorily reorganized, as we will see.

Major Themes

In evaluating our interviews with those men who had successfully reorganized their lives since the death of the spouse, we selected a number of themes which were recurrent in the interview material of these men. These are not meant to be used as a basis of specific comparison with the men who have failed to successfully reorganize their lives, but rather to represent and express feelings in the lives of the men we are discussing here. These themes may be stated as a series of generalizations which ring true for most or all of the men and which as generalized propositions seem to capture the sense of individualized experience. Below, we have listed these themes and we discuss specific manifestations of them. Following each listing, the number of men for whom the theme appears to be appropriate is given. The total number of men we are discussing here is 11.

1. "Life is good." (11 men)

This overarching theme covers a variety of statements concerning satisfaction, well-being, morale, etc. Such satisfactions may be absolute ("Things are better than ever") or positive, but conditional ("All things being equal, I'm doing fine").

For example, Tony Johnson, mentioned above, said, "I have no real problems now. Everything is sailing along beautifully. There's only a couple of trouble areas, but nothing great. I'm very satisfied with life. I love going out and having a good time. . . .

"I've run into lonely people, but I'm not one of them. Some old-timers, they don't know what to do with themselves. They keep to themselves a lot. The worst is when they don't talk about it, especially for these old-timers, when they lose their wife. They sit and brood all by themselves and they don't talk. They got to be lonely. You can see it."

Mark Miller: "Sometimes, people will find out my age and say to me, 'God bless you.' I'll say, 'He already has.' And I mean that. Look at me. I'm near ninety, my income is sufficient—more than sufficient for my needs; I'm still healthy for a man my age, certainly. I'm still active. My children are fine people. They have married fine spouses. I've lived to see grandchildren and great-grandchildren. . . . I don't know what comes next, but I've enjoyed myself here."

Steve Thompson: "I'd say that I'm satisfied with life now. There's only one or two things that bother me, but I hope to be able to change them when they become issues. The major thing, it seems to me, is that I'm healthy. I pray that my legs will hold out so I can continue. Nevertheless, I have a happy life now. It is rewarding."

Satisfaction with the way things are was found consistently in the interview material with the 11 men, and was strongly expressed as both responses to specific questions and open material. Successful reorganization could be judged on this criterion alone.

2. "Despite changes and losses in late life, it is a time in which there are new, positive things." (11 men)

This theme is a significant one and was expressed in a variety of ways.

Certainly, all of those men felt some conflict between "self," the basically youngish person inside, and "nature," the cruel and impersonal force that slows down and eventually does people in as they age. All of these men recognize that compromise and adjustment are necessary in the wake of uncontrollable changes. Indeed, they had already made many adjustments in their living.

To generalize, these men had an image of old age as "Father Time" using his scythe to cut down and lay low men. Spouses, friends, relatives, had fallen in a great harvest. Using such an image of the generalized "other" elderly, many of these 11 men, themselves survivors and in good shape, could compare themselves with the elderly depicted in this image and also envisoned as lonelier, poorer, and less satisfied, and take some satisfaction themselves from the results of this comparison. Others die or are poorly off, but these men continue and do well.

Further, good health in late life was taken to be a gift from "nature," conceptualized, to be sure, in a variety of ways individually. The gist of the gift, stated directly by several of these men, is that "others of my age haven't done as well as me, God has given me an extra helping and I pray it continues."

Thus several elements combine here. The impersonal force of "nature" moves inexorably but inexplicably. This force may be understood by some men within a personalized meaning system such as a religion, theory, or philosophy. What is important is that such a perception of "nature" combined with common social attitudes to the old lead to low expectations about what is possible in old age. Given these low expectations, actual experience is, in fact, much better. Thus many of these men have a not-to-be-quibbled-with experience of old age as something good, better than was expected. Expectations are low, actualities are high, and seem higher still given expectations.

For certain men, such an understanding of things leads to a broadening of possibilities without a concomitant of increased expectations.

For many older men, old age is viewed as a "natural" (e.g., biological) event and not necessarily a social one and therefore not subject to normal social factors like class, income, ethnicity, family, etc. "Old age" affects everyone and it cannot be prevented by a high income, although it may be experienced more or less comfortably on the basis of income. These 11 men tend to view other elderly men as less well-off than themselves. They do not necessarily expect to be doing as well as they are. Their happiness, health, etc., is a gift which is somewhat inexplicable. Without expecting much of themselves, without expectations or fear of failure, some may feel free to try things—new activities—which they find out are pleasurable. Or they might take increased pleasure in old mundane things. Concerning new activities, several men could point to specific new things.

Lou Giordano: "I attend the center every day, from about ten to one. I have never been involved in any social clubs before. I just didn't go. . . . I guess I was busy with other things when I was younger. . . . Now I come every day. I would never have thought about doing anything like this in the past. It's an entirely new sort of thing for me, and it's been a great help to me in many ways."

Bill Franklin: "I am always as busy as I want to be. The only thing I did was 'retire,' but that didn't mean much. I just continued doing all the things I had been doing before or expanded on them. . . . I don't think too much about being old."

Another man: "Through the center, I've been able to take a French course. It's new for me. We've been learning different phrases in French and songs. . . . I feel there's a lot of opportunities out there now."

Another aspect of this "freeing up" is the ability to take a new pleasure from old things. Thus events such as playing cards, "joking with people," and the like become newly pleasurable.

3. *"All things considered, I'm in good health and this is a big factor in my current good fortune." (11 men)*

All of these men isolate health as a factor which, subjectively, is of great importance in their current active and relatively happy lives. These men also contrast themselves with others of their acquaintance or with the deceased wives for whom poor health was a factor. Most of these men see doctors regularly, but at least 1 boasts of his failure to have seen a doctor for several years. One man told this story: "The doctor suggested that I start walking with a cane, 'cause I have a bit of a pause in my step. I said to him—without stopping to think—'Cane!? Those are for old people!' He looked at me funny."

4. *"Religion is very important in my life." (11 men)*

To a man, formal involvement with religion and involvement away from the formal setting were highly characteristic of these men. Most of them attended a worship service daily. Prayer at home was also universal in the group. The attitude of one man was typical: "I feel very much personally close to God. Prayer is an important part of my day [he prays in the morning, at meals, and before bed]. . . . I never used to be like this. It's something I've come to in the last few years." Another man puts it in this way: "I like to think that I got a little religion, but I know I can use more. . . . I've made mistakes in my life. . . . I like to know wrong from right.

"But I'm no fanatic. . . . There's a radio station with a Bible reading show on every day. I'll try to tune into that every day. I always try to set time aside for it. I'll follow along in my Bible.

"I'd say that the religious life is important to me."

5. *"My income is sufficient for my needs and wants." (11 men)*

Although income varied widely, it was higher, on the average, for these 11 men than for the group as a whole. (The monthly range for the 11 men was $440–$3000; the average for 10 men—excluding the man with the highest income—was $916; the average income for the whole sample was $626.) Interestingly, despite the wide range, income was described as "satisfactory" or "more than enough" by each individual. One man indicated that although he had enough for his current situation, he was only "one step ahead" of inflation.

More typical is the statement of Horace Adam: "I've got more than enough money for my needs. In fact, I'll give money away to people who need it. There's nothing I want that I don't have, and nothing I need to buy."

6. *"I have a definite opinion of my social needs." (11 men)*

Each man could make a definite assessment of his social needs which seemed to ring true. Most (8) viewed themselves as highly social and freely indicated that they "needed," "loved," or "liked" people. This attitude was expressed by Lou Giordano. "I know when I have to be with people. I am very social, very sociable. I know where people are who can talk to me, up on the Avenue, or elsewhere. If I need to, I get out and find someone."

Two men felt that, temperamentally, they were not especially social but they liked people. One man claimed that he was not social and did not especially enjoy people: "I don't need contact with people now as much as when I was younger. My wife used to arrange all of our social activities—the bridge club and whatnot—but I don't feel interested or motivated to arrange that now. . . . I feel I've outgrown a lot of people I knew before. . . . I'm very critical of such friends and I see their faults too easily."

7. *"I feel that I am in control of something important or that I otherwise fit in in a significant way." (11 men)*

This is an important theme because it says a lot about an individual's conception of his own relationship to the world outside himself. This theme covers several areas.

Several men, the most active, are in fact at the head of some particular group or entity and take pleasure in this. The notion of "I am in charge" is clear here, as when Mr. Miller said, "I like to be in charge." For 2 or 3 men, this need to control is directly expressed and directly achieved.

A related form of this theme is "I am important." This is more difficult to abstract from interview data but can be culled in several ways, particularly through statements which indicate that a person has particular needs and is unconflicted and active in satisfying them. This theme seems to combine elements of "I am in control" and "I can still fit in."

Edward McBride, in his early 80s, expressed this theme in the following way. "In my mind, work is what helps to dignify a man. . . . A lot of problems with colored and whites would disappear if everyone had a job. . . .

"I am working now, one day a week, for a place that handles magazines. They do one or two big days every week, when the magazines come off the truck, so they hire extra people to help out. The magazines have to be taken off the truck, untied, addressed, sorted, and bundled. There's some heavy work involved. My base pay is ten dollars an hour and often there's overtime. I'll clear close to a hundred dollars for a day, sometimes. I have enough income on my own to make it, but this helps a good deal. . . .

"I would say that this job is important to me. It makes me feel a lot better about myself. I look forward to going in. I feel good because I can keep up with the younger people there, at least for that one day. I must admit that at the end—and I've been on my feet most of the day—I've had it.

"I feel sorry for people without work. The young blacks without jobs, I feel sad for them. For older people, it really depends on their health, or if they want to work; many of 'em don't. . . .

"I'd say that my work helps me to be independent. Even though it's one day a week, it gives me something."

Mr. McBride does not want to be in charge of some large domain, as Mr. Miller does, but he does want to fit in, maintain himself, be independent, be like others, within certain limits. Within these limits, he can do the work and derives a sense of mastery and dignity from it. He is especially happy to be paid at the same rate as everyone else.

"Fitting in" is related to a sense of control, and the theme may be stated as "In fitting in, I demonstrate control, in that there is something I do well." The standards of measurement here are the expectations and achievements of earlier life ("work"), recast in terms of the real situation in late life ("I don't have the stamina to work full time"), so as to satisfy personal needs ("But work is a meaningful endeavor to me, so I'll do it one day a week and be paid handsomely"). "Fitting in" may be thought of as "a continued ability to control one's own life and be independent." Horace Adam also expresses this sentiment. "I have a lot of options now. Every one of my daughters [and he has several of them] has told me that they would like me to live with them if I want to. But I like it here by myself. . . . It's true that I get lonely at times. . . . but my life here is certainly preferable. Having plenty of options, I guess, makes it easier to be independent."

Another element of the theme of control is "Through service, I demonstrate control." From one point of view, service—volunteer work—can be viewed as the relinquishing of control in the sense that one takes orders and follows the suggestions, commands, and needs of others. But from another point of view, service can give one a sense of control in that a person has an independent life which he can command, or he can still "fit in," or he can master time, by giving structure to his day. This is the case of one man who spends three days a week, regularly, as a hospital volunteer. He says, "I am happy when I am at the hospital. This work, this experience, is rewarding to me. I feel better when I know that I have somewhere to go, something to do. . . . It's like a second career. This work is designed to free up the nurses so they can spend more direct time with patients. We do a lot of stuff like moving patients around, delivering mail and charts. It is important work for the hospital. The work does not at all seem menial to me; rather, I feel highly rewarded for it. Regular hours, a good cause, nice people. . . . I feel that I am contributing."

8. *"I have a close friend who is important to me." (8 men)*

As we have mentioned, several of these men have relations of intimate companionship with a woman. Also, 2 had women friends whom they met in late life and who died. Several men could name a male friend to whom they felt close. Only 1 man could state that there was no nonkinsman to whom he felt close.

9. *"Ties to the past are important." (11 men)*

This theme was expressed in the interviews by almost all of the men, although there was no uniformity in the mode of expression nor in the emotional content. For these men, in no case is the past "all-consuming." The present is important and acknowledged as such, and these men tend to live in the present. The "past" is often related to the present through symbolic channels which emphasize particular themes, objects, or individuals. Certain ties to the past, therefore, take a specific and narrow and emotionally laden form. Consider the story told by one 82-year-old man, who says about himself that "I don't need stuff [objects, mementos] for old memories, because

I am more involved with the present than with the past. I don't have time to dwell on the past.

"We were farm folk. . . . I left our farm in North Carolina after my parents died and I came north. . . . I still think of North Carolina as home.

"I got nothing here [in my apartment] from the past, no mementos, photos, anything. I used to have my mother's eyeglasses, but my daughter took 'em. I don't have anything else from my folks.

"Every year, I visit my sister down south. She doesn't live far from that farm we used to have and the town where I was raised. . . .

"One of the things I do every year is visit my old schoolteacher's grave. We went to school in a one-room schoolhouse. That man was college educated. He went to one of the Negro colleges. . . . I was a real 'poor boy' then. That man . . . he used to whip me when I did something bad, and now I thank him for it, 'cause he cared enough about me to make sure that I did good and went straight. . . .

"A lot of that town is gone now. Our farm was sold for taxes. Where the school was, there's a highway through there now. Even his grave is covered up, all honeysuckle grown all over it. But I know where it is; I don't think anybody else does. I go there and spend a few minutes, every year.

"He's been dead fifty-five years now."

There is a good deal of meaning condensed here, involving ideas about "family," "home," "the past," "land," "growing up," "transmission of values and ideals," with deeply held emotions. This pilgrimage to the hidden grave site is annual, bounded as an episode, and combined with a visit to a sister and to the old family home. This pilgrimage is but one rather direct channel to the past, coming from a man who has few tangible mementos of the past.

Another style of ties to the past is that of the "broad" set of connections. This style is illustrated by the situation of another man whose parents left Russia prior to the turn of the century. For this man, his identity as a Jew is very important to him, something which he feels places him with "a cultural and religious tradition thousands of years old," as he puts it. Although employed in another field, he has always had a scholarly interest in Judaism and with the history of the Jewish people and owns many books dealing with topics pertinent to Jewish culture. Some of the books he owns date back to the middle of the eighteenth century. He keeps these books displayed and handy in a glass-fronted bookcase built by his father, and he does his work on a desk also built by his father. For him, while the past and the future are distinctive, they blend in an important way. Thus while he views his children and grandchildren as part of "the future," he also sees them as part of "the past," within this tradition. His grandchildren keep the connection strong. "I'm the only member of my family who does not speak Hebrew. And the reason for that is that I was brought up on the old-fashioned education which consisted of translations of the Bible and no emphasis laid on conversational Hebrew. . . . My granddaughter can speak Hebrew as fluently as I speak English." He views this grandchild and his others as being more closely tied to Judaism than he is, keeping alive and contributing to important traditions.

Much of what this man does in his day-to-day life revolves around a Jewish cultural heritage. For him, the past, present, and future have a close and thoroughgoing unity.

Both of these examples portray an individual's ties to the past as part of a general personal disposition. In the first case, one particular channel is emphasized, while in the other case, there is a broad spectrum of associations. Related to the general disposition are two other sorts of ties which are of importance to these men. These are memories of the deceased wife and memories of a particular old neighborhood. In fact, in some way these two may be associated; in 9 of the 11 cases, a man and his deceased long-term spouse came from the same geographical area—mostly the same neighborhood. We take up these sorts of ties in more detail in our sections on loneliness and living alone.

10. "I've passed through the storm." (8 men)

Related to the theme of "Ties to the past are important" is the notion held by 8 men that they had passed through some occasion of living hell which had nearly destroyed them, but that was all in the past now. Most typically, this unhappy episode was the death of a man's wife and the following period of bereavement. These men were able to look back on these events now and feel that they had weathered the storm. This feeling could take one of two forms. For most of the 8, the attitude was that "I was bent out of shape, but I'm now myself again." Things got very bad for a while, men were not themselves, but with the passage of time, things returned to normal. The other version of this, experienced by only 2 men, was that it was only their deep sense of continuity and dedication to "going on" that prevented them from being destroyed or being "done in" by the period of unhappiness. They would not permit themselves to be "bent out of shape."

The first style of "passing through" is illustrated in the following case. One man, in his 80s, views his life now as generally satisfying, involved and productive. To get it to be this way, he has passed through some hard times: "After my wife died [in 1975] I started drinking—I started soon after her death but got into it a few months later. . . . It started small but soon grew. I was spending ten dollars or more a day on drink. They know me at every bar from here to the Avenue. I had a routine: start at one, move to the next, and back again when I was at the end. Between times, I'd ride the buses and travel around. I was on the skids. It was no life.

"One time I was sitting outside of a bar. A lady passed me on the street. She stopped to talk with me. She asked me, 'What are you doing this for? Why are you drinking like that?' I didn't really know what to say. I was very lonely, though. She said, 'Why don't you come to the center?' And she told me about it. I can't remember if it was the first time I talked to her or later on, but I started going. When I started going, I stopped drinking. It was very, very hard to stop, but going to the center helped me. I stayed with it. Now, I don't even know how to go to a bar. It's not the same anymore."

Interestingly, another experience, occurring some six years after his bout with alcohol, led to a similar feeling of "passing through." This was the occasion of a series of cataract operations, which had been proceeding successfully, at the time of the interviews, in a step-by-step fashion. The emotional lift of having progressively poorer vision improved is substantial and for this man seems to have acted as yet another element in "passing through."

Similar accounts of "passing through" were given by a number of men. Two men on the other hand stressed that it was a deep commitment to continuity in their lives that prevented the deep falls which other men might have. In both cases, one reason for the continuity was that the men perceived themselves to have experienced "hard times" and "passing through" at an earlier age, so that they were prepared for the tribulations of bereavement. In 1 case, a man spoke of his father's death when he was in his late teens as a formative experience. He viewed his father as a sickly and somewhat mediocre man who did barely enough to get his family by; for him his father was a distant figure. He says he wonders, however, "Why was my father sacrificed to make me a man?" His father's death, he says, galvanized him into filling a role in the lives of the survivors, of taking charge, supporting his mother and two younger brothers, earning a living, paying for the house, going through school. He was ambivalent about this new role. It gave him opportunities to be in charge and lead, two admired abilities, but his new role also left him "depressed." He gives the impression that this experience—his father's death and his subsequent role acquisitions—challenged him in a positive way, but left him full of anxiety and fear. He says that he has learned, however, the way to deal with tragedy "is to get up and continue with life . . . life goes on." This sense of continuity or at least the ability to continue derives strength from two significant areas in his life—his religious faith and practice and his work (at age 76, he still works at least half time). While the death of his wife was a great blow, it does not appear as if it doubled him over, as is the case with several other men. It was an experience of "passing through" hard times, but one in which continuity was stressed.

Two of the 3 men for whom the theme of "having passed through" was not appropriate, or at least not as an experience of late life, were men who had been widowers in excess of twenty years.

CHARACTERISTICS OF UNSUCCESSFUL REORGANIZATION

We found 14 of the 25 men to have a pattern of unsuccessful life reorganization as widowers. Unsuccessful reorganization occurs in several ways. If a period of deeply felt grief is extended and compulsive, a survivor may fail to establish any satisfactory pattern of life. His unhappiness may be extensive and unrelieved. In a case where the experience of deep grief passes, an individual may indeed establish some sort of pattern of life, such as the pattern of independent life-style suggested by Glick, Weiss, and Parkes (1974). Yet this pattern may be an unhappy one; life may be unfulfilling and participation in activities hesitant and tentative. Ties to the deceased spouse may not prevent the survivor from living some sort of productive existence, but such ties may also limit an individual in seeing possibilities for himself and in working toward goals.

Our own focus on elderly men living alone precludes us from commenting on the existence of unsuccessful reorganization in the context of remarriage. It would appear that there are few data on this important question. Those older men living alone who had reorganized their lives most successfully followed patterns in which a nonmarital opposite-sex relationship was a central life component and in which there was a close (but not central) association with one or more kinsmen. Those with least successful—in our definition, least happy—reorganization were men who had established a life independent of any close ties as well as those whose life-styles were somewhat chaotic.

We judged men to have an unsuccessful reorganization after the death of their wives on the following basis. In certain cases, some five years or more after the wife's death, overt grief was still profound. In less dramatic instances, those in which overt grief was not apparent, conversations led us to understand that a preoccupation with the deceased spouse was still an important life theme and that the deceased spouse still exerted considerable influence on the life of the survivor. Some men had a hard time making a go of it, their attempts at new attachments limited and ineffectual. Characteristic of a majority of these men with "unsuccessful" reorganization was an ongoing dispute with a mature child. Of the 14 men we discuss here, 13 had children (2 of the 13 had stepchildren), and of these 13, 8 had ongoing disputes with children and were dissatisfied in their relationships with them. In general, these 14 men were unhappy and presented themselves as depressed and unsatisfied individuals. Several had health problems which they associated with their period of mourning and widowhood or with "old age."

Here we will discuss these individuals from the basis of intimate companionship and continuing attachment to the deceased spouse. We will also touch on the question of the continuation of the level of social contacts and activities, on relationships with children, and finally, on thematic material which appears frequently in the interviews.

Intimate Companionship

As far as the data gathered in our interviews may be considered reliable, only 2 of the 14 men have had affairs or attempted relationships since their wives passed away. In neither case had the relationship been successful according to the needs and desires of the men who had them.

We will deal first with those men who have been widowers six years or more at the time of the interviews. These men have had ample time to reorganize their lives. In terms of patterns, these men fit into the pattern of independent life-style. Two have had affairs, but neither has been able to form more permanent attachments.

Men widowed six years or more. Len Silverstein is age 73, a retired lawyer, who has been widowed six years after thirty-eight years of marriage. He lives alone in a large house in Philadelphia, filled with antiques, memorabilia, and bric-a-brac. The house is no longer neat, as it once was. He feels self-conscious about allowing the interviewer into other areas of the house besides the entryway and the living room. He impresses the interviewer as a bicameral man who on the one hand is analytic and intellectual, still abreast of developments in his profession and with a keen interest in several areas, while on the other hand is deeply emotional, tending to repress his feelings and to be depressive. Since the death of his wife, he has been unable to achieve a whole life for himself, isolating himself and concentrating on accruing parts rather than a whole. His wife still plays an important role in his life; nevertheless, since her death he has been involved with several women.

Interviewer: "Since your wife passed away, is there any one person you've been closest to emotionally?"

Mr. Silverstein: "Yes . . . that was a woman who died almost two years ago [in 1979]. . . . I met her through a relative of my wife, this woman was an acquaintance of my wife's cousin. After my wife died, her cousin invited me to some affair, and that's how I met her.

"She passed away suddenly. She was about ten years younger than I am.

"The relationship was something unexpected. She was married at the time I first met her; then, we had a friendly relationship. She took a friendly interest in me. Her husband was a wealthy man. He was out on business a lot, all the time, and she said, 'Let's have dinner,' or something. Or I would do some work around the house for her, if she wanted something fixed up. But the relationship was built on a friendly basis.

"Her husband suddenly got very sick. I was the one who took him to the hospital. He had a heart attack and died a few days later.

"After that we became sexually intimate. We were very close.

"A problem arose in time because she wanted the same setup with me—the ability to sleep with other men. I didn't like that.

"We broke up. However, we remained good friends.

"Any relationship I get into would have to be one hundred percent. I can't give the exact attributes I would want from another person, but it would have to be one hundred percent. I don't believe in a halfway basis."

Since this time, Mr. Silverstein has started seeing another woman, one whom he met recently. He described her as the "youngest woman I've gone out with." She is 38. Although it is clear that he likes this woman, he does not appear to have a particular goal in mind.

He finds it difficult to extricate himself from his marriage, which has continued in many ways, despite his wife's death. He feels considerable guilt about her death and ambivalently still feels considerable warmth for her and for the home they created and which he continues to inhabit. These feelings give him considerable reticence in dealing with people.

Among his tactics is frightening people away. "When I meet women, one of the first things I tell them—and they are generally younger women, some much younger—immediately, I tell them my age. I make no bones about it [Mr. Silverstein indeed looks younger than his chronological age]. I do that to frighten 'em off . . . if they want to be frightened off immediately. I just tell 'em, that's all. Because first of all, I'm proud of my age. I am saying, 'You haven't made it yet; maybe you'll never make it, but I've already made it and I'm still going!' So I feel that my age somehow gives me a certain advantage—it helps me sort people out: 'I don't care what, you haven't made it yet. I've made it and I'm going to make it a lot more from here!' My age gives me a feeling of superiority. I get rid of people who would be afraid of me."

Nevertheless, for him this is only one posture. The air of superiority and freedom leads to guilt: "I feel quite guilty—bad—about my wife. She was several years younger than me and she died first. I am living financially better off today because she died. If there were two of us to support, it would be difficult, and most likely I would still have to work to support us."

Clearly, his wife is still a factor in his life, even directly: "I feel my wife is still with me in some respects. I am not morbid about it or anything . . . I just have a warm feeling about the house. It was her doing. She put everything together here."

As he reports it, he separates his inner world, still closely connected with his wife and home, from the more social world outside: "I never entertain. . . . That is absolutely out now, although when my wife was living we did a good deal of it. I haven't had a woman in this house since my wife died. The house isn't kept up as it used to be. . . . There's no real reason for this; it just turned out that way. I keep the house separate from any other activities. Nothing from the outside penetrates into this house. Except me. The house and the outside world are two separate entities."

It appears that Mr. Silverstein has considerable ambivalence about what to do. He is active in a number of social circles but many of his activities are of the solitary sort, although they may be done in groups. He has no close relationships with people. Nonetheless, while he is satisfied with his own role in his life, he has questions about the places of others in his life.

Another man, Manny Gulzer, has had similar difficulties in establishing relations of intimate companionship. A friendly, independent, and intense man, he is often depressed about his life. He is subject to periods of ill health and seems very tense at times. He has a heart condition and has had a pacemaker installed. The fear of a heart attack is ever present; he keeps a packed suitcase by the door in case he must enter a hospital in an emergency situation. His weight fluctuates; when his weight is down, he smokes a good deal; when he stops smoking, he eats.

He is 67 and has been widowed for ten years. He lives in a small (one room, kitchenette, and bath) apartment, which is cluttered, unkempt, and dirty. He has three children whom he does not often see. He has had a major altercation with one of his sons. At the time our interviews commenced, he had not seen or talked to his son in more than four months.

Mr. Gulzer has had relations with several women since his wife died. In fact, in one instance, he was set to remarry, in 1975. "We had a date set. As the time approached, I kept learning more about her that dismayed me. She wanted too much from me. She wanted me to buy her a mink coat and a new car! As soon as we married. She was working at the time and I was just retired. Also, I had a lot of expenses just then, in connection with my children. It became more and more apparent that she expected me to buy things for her—I didn't have the income—and that she expected me to support her. That was no good. It turns out that she wasn't too nice. She was self-centered and greedy. So I broke it off, about a month before the day."

Mr. Gulzer got the last laugh. "I've been able to follow her, since we know the same people. I found out that she met a fellow, had the same ideas about him, they got married, and now *she supports him!*"

Currently, Mr. Gulzer hs a "girlfriend," Fran. She is several years younger than Mr. Gulzer. In 1980 she spent several weeks "living with" him in his apartment, but since then she has moved out. Mr. Gulzer views Fran as his closest friend: "When I'm down, she's the one who brings me out of it, cheers me up. She calls me often." But he also views her as being too dependent on him. For example, during the course of the interviews, he went away for one weekend without telling anyone where he was going. When he returned, a neighbor told him that his phone had been "ringing off the hook" all weekend. (Mr. Gulzer lives in an apartment building in which noise travels.) He was quite pleased that someone had been trying to reach him all weekend. Later, he learned from Fran that it was she who had been responsible for many of the calls. He was very pleased by her attention, but he said of the situation, "Let her wait." Indeed, the theme of "I am taken for granted" and "I wonder what they'd do if I disappeared" were often brought up by Mr. Gulzer.

Mr. Gulzer's relationship with Fran is not currently a sexual one, although he says it was in the past. Fran is separated from her husband, who lives in another city. She is residing with her daughter and her father. Possibly, Mr. Gulzer would marry Fran, but he is ambivalent about getting remarried in general: "If I date a woman and there's any pressure for marriage, I drop them." He does not date Fran exclusively.

"I might remarry if the right person comes along. It would be for love. Money is not important.

"I know where to get sex. That isn't a problem for me if I feel that I need to have it. I have 'friends.'" There are about four women I know, some are single, some divorced. One was a close friend of my wife. After the funeral, after we sat *shivah,* she came to me and said, 'Manny, you know what a friend is for.' She meant sex. I've been with her four times in ten years.

"There's another one, a widow who's in her forties. I have had relations with her on occasion. I like her, but not to marry. She is not a 'one-man woman.'

"Thirty-two years of marriage, I never cheated on my wife. I knew what I had a home. I don't play around. Now, I only want it when I need it."

Mr. Gulzer usually talks to Fran daily. While he has periods in which he wishes to get away from everyone, in general he seems to be quite solicitous of her. During a hospital stay, he visited her daily and spoke with her on the phone in the evening. The trip to the hospital required a considerable departure from his daily routine, but he was happy to do it.

There is some chance this relationship might lead to marriage. It is difficult to assess. In many ways Mr. Gulzer has gotten over his attachment to his wife, although he admits that he experiences her presence from time to time, and when he has to deal with problems, especially those concerning his children, he imagines what she would say about it. Nevertheless, he has been unable to form a relationship of intimacy or to fully trust other people. Even his friendship with Fran is periodic. In the final meeting, he told the interviewer that ultimately, he hoped to move from Philadelphia—to the Southwest—to start over. He said, "I have nothing holding me here."

Tom Fredericks, age 77, is a quiet man who has been widowed for about ten years. For him widowhood has been mostly an unhappy time, a slow march away from the life with his wife which he enjoyed.

Mr. Fredericks is a slight but wiry man. He is generally close-lipped, and difficult to talk to, difficult to get to know. He chain-smokes when he is interviewed because, he says, he is "nervous." He lives in the bottom floor of a two-story row house in Philadelphia.

He married late, at age 40, to a widow with three children. His wife died in 1970.

"It took me about three or four years to get over my wife. When she died, I was very lonely. Since that, I can't say that I've had much sadness . . . nothing can compare with that."

During the series of interviews, he claimed both that he was "over" his wife and that was not. When he was asked to describe a "happy incident," he described "when I got married and settled." He con-cluded that he still misses his wife, "although it is not as bad as before."

Mr. Fredericks' life today, almost more than any man we saw, is one of routine. His days are divided up, his activities regular, his friends and circles well charted and established, his holidays routin-ized. His circles of friends have been his for many years. He is still close to his in-laws and to the small group of men he knew as a young man in the 1920s and 1930s. In this way, he has maintained a level of continuity with the past. However, he has found no substitute for his affections and no effective way to vent his emotions.

This has had an effect in the two areas of life over which he has had problems of control. His relationship with his stepchildren is not as secure as he would like it. For example, he does not know what their attitude to him would be if he could no longer take care of himself. Would they take care of him or not? He finds himself slowly drifting apart from his stepchildren, and is not sure to what extent he can count on them, nor does he want to ask them about it because he is afraid of the answer. For him to renounce the tie to their mother, in favor of a tie to another, might put in jeopardy one important area of possible support. His emotional attachment to his wife is a form of emotional entrapment for him.

Second, he has had a number of recurrent health problems in the past few years to which he ascribes moodiness and social isolation: "When you feel bad, you don't feel like seeing anyone." His health problems are part of a greater concern—fears about his own degeneration and mortality. His wife was his only intimate. Even among those whom he has known for years, he cannot talk of intimate things. He has no way to deal with his feelings except through withdrawal and through prayer.

It is more than likely that he will never remarry. He has been unable to get over his wife's loss within the context of the independent life-style he has established for himself.

Men in the fourth and fifth years of widowhood. Three men were in their fourth and fifth years of widowhood at the time they were interviewed. These men stand out as individuals with some of the most difficult problems of adjustment.

Henry Heller is 89 and had been a widower for more than four years at the time of our meeting. He lives in a small row house. The inside is neat and orderly, receives a good deal of sun, and seems very still and quiet. The furnishings are old and well kept.

Mr. Heller was married for fifty-seven years. "Her name was Mary Teresa O'Rourke. She was a sweet, kind woman, a real peach. She was a gentle person. We were married for fifty-seven years. I remember clearly how we met and when we married. . . ."

He has been saddened considerably and harmed irreparably by his wife's death. Besides his continuing great sadness at her loss, he suffers from a variety of physical health problems, including circulatory difficulties, which preclude him from "getting out" as much as he would like. He says, "If anyone tells you that retirement is the Golden Age, don't you believe it. It's not. It's pure hell." Unfortunately, we do not know much about the genesis of his health problems nor how they are related to his period of mourning. In all likelihood, they are. We do not know much about this because soon after the series of interviews started, he entered the hospital for an extended stay and the interviews stopped. At one point, however, he told us that he wished to die. Besides his health problems and his sadness over his wife's death, he now has a very stormy relationship with his son, a man who he says refuses to visit him in the hospital and who, he says, will not come to call except to take things of value to sell.

The issue of health problems in relation to the experience of bereavement is also important in the lives of the 2 men we discuss below. Although each lives an "independent life-style," neither has successfully reorganized his life since the death of his spouse.

Freddy Williams is age 71, a widower for four years after thirty-six years of marriage. He is a man of medium height who moves slowly through his home. Almost all of his time is spent indoors, in his three-story row house in an old neighborhood of Philadelphia. Mr. Williams, one soon learns, is an angry and impatient man, punctuating his conversation with both sarcasm and outbursts of direct insult. He also is a very sad person, his grief for his wife still very apparent and very much on the surface. It is clear that he feels abandoned by her and still tightly bound up with her.

Although he lives in a three-story house, he spends most of his time during the day on the ground floor, in the living room, where the big color TV is, and where his easy chair sits and his stacks of paperbacks. The room is overseen by a large portrait of his wife.

He is not very well, suffering from vision problems, circulatory difficulties, and shortness of breath. His ability to walk is restricted to an area of only a few blocks, and such a trip must be done in spurts. It is not his breathlessness which prevents him from walking, but loss of power in his legs.

He is still actively involved in the loss of his wife. His living room is set up as a combination day room and museum for her. In a corner is the chair which belonged to his wife: "That was my wife's chair. We called it 'The Queen's Throne.' " Next to it is her sewing stand and on top of that, a leather cigarette and matches case, with his wife's last package of cigarettes, on the tabletop since 1977. On one wall is her picture, taken by Mr. Williams in his amateur photography days. "Sometimes, even now, I'll look up at that and start to cry."

Often, Mr. Williams takes little pleasure from his existence. At times, he describes eating as "feeding myself."

His wife is still dear to him. He speaks fondly of their relationship. He feels that, as a couple, they worked things out well, recognized one another's interests, and divided the labor beneficially: "She let me have my areas and she had hers. The things that concerned both of us we decided together. She let me have a lot of independence and I liked that. She made decisions about herself and I made mine."

Such independence in marriage has re-formed itself as dependence after marriage: "My wife . . . people used to call her 'oddball' because she was tall and lanky and thin. She had a good sense of humor. Since she died, that's something I've lost all of. Life stinks sometimes. I have only *one thing* to look forward to. Day after day, I have nothing to do. I have bad breathing and my legs are bad . . . they hurt or they just won't go. I sit here, look out the window. The feelings are real, real deep in you, deep inside. It's bad on rainy days, especially; there's no hope of going out."

His inability to walk far is, subjectively, the major effect of his circulation problems. For this difficulty, he blames his period of intense bereavement: "When she died, I stayed inside the house for a whole year. I didn't want to see or talk to anybody. I did not go out at all; I had no exercise for a whole year." His grief was complete and uncompromising; and in the process, he managed to do himself in: "Can you imagine what it's like for a man who's been athletic all his life to be cut down in this way?"

Mr. Williams has two children. His relationship with his son is problematic; his relationship with his daughter seems warm but is troubled by what he sees as her failure to meet his needs, her inability to see him as much as he wants.

Due to his physical disabilities as well as his disposition, he has not been able to reorganize his life in a successful and productive way, and at times he takes little pleasure from it. He has seen no women since his wife passed away; he has few callers and he socializes very little.

Thomas Bergen is age 77, widowed for five years after fifty-two years of marriage. He too has been laid low by his grief, much in the manner of Mr. Williams, but he is a more delicate man, with less of the anger of Mr. Williams and with a greater acceptance. While his reaction to the death of his wife has been similar to that of Mr. Williams, he seems, nevertheless, a freer person and a more open speaker. He too is a row house dweller. His furnishings are worn, but neat, and his small house uncluttered. His physical and mental health has also suffered considerably since his wife died. At that time, Mr. Bergen had an episode that may be described as a "nervous breakdown," which he described as "nerves," uncontroll-able sadness, and crying which went on for many months after his wife's death and to which he is still subject, several years later, although with increased infrequency. It is not merely the death of his wife which has contributed to his great sadness. Together, in a period of about five years, he and his wife experienced the death of two middle-aged sons, close in-laws, siblings, and two daughters-in-law. In the sixth year, his wife died suddenly: "Before my wife died, she said to me, 'We'll make it through, hell or high water.' When she died, I said, 'I'm gonna do the same . . . I'm gonna make it as long as God leaves me here, through hell or high water.' It sounds funny, don't it?" (Interviewer: "Do you still feel almost as if she's here?") Yes, all the time. I hear her, see her. Once in a while I'll get awake and I think I hear her calling me [weeps]. That sounds crazy, don't it?" (Interviewer: "No, it doesn't.") But see. We were together so long and it happened so sudden. . . ."

After five years the tears and pain have been mostly contained and affect replaced with resignation: "Sometimes, I get thinking back to the kids and my wife and how we used to have a good time, going on picnics and going swimming, going visiting upstate to her people.

"Sometimes when I'm thinking back on something that happened, all of a sudden, I'm like a baby. I start to cry for a while [laughs].

"I'm perfectly satisfied in the way I'm living. You'd be surprised but I am. It's enough for me.

"I'd never go out again or meet other women! There would never, never, never be anybody who could take her place."

Over time, Mr. Bergen has come to accept the loss as a fact of life, but at the same time has acted to reject acceptance by tying his current life to his past. He cannot yet bring himself to sleep in the bed he shared with his wife. He sleeps on the sofa in the living room, an old thing, once brightly colored, now worn and covered with a sheet. From the sofa, he can see the television, and when he sits up, he can see out the front window over the porch onto a wide street. "My clock every day is the noise of the schoolchildren going to school and coming home. I always pray that nothing happens to them and that they arrive home safely." He ventures upstairs only to use the bathroom or to change his clothes. "When I go up in the morning to get dressed, I'll look back over at her picture in the back room [where they slept] and then like a damn fool, I'll say [laughs],

'Good morning, doll.' Or, if it's a bath, 'Hiya, doll, I'm just going to take a bath.' [Weeps.] You know, them nutty things. But it's very important to me."

His life is not chaotic, nor is it "independent" in the sense described above. His life is not a full one; rather, it is a continuation of the life he led formerly, but with one party gone. He does not wish to accept the social status "widower" and seeks to continue the marital tie indefinitely. His poor health, especially vision and circulation problems, prevents him from "getting out" to a greater extent than he does. Nevertheless, he does go out, once every few weeks, and even more often, to a neighborhood bar. Much of his shopping is done for him by neighbors. A surviving child visits him rarely, less than once every three months.

Mr. Bergen has not been able to disassociate himself from the past so as to form a new relationship of intimate companionship. He now has few close relationships, primarily those with a nearby neighbor and with one grandson whom he helped raise. For Mr. Bergen, his grandson embodies many of the ties he had with his deceased wife, since it was Mr. Bergen and his wife who, for long periods of time during the grandson's life, were responsible for raising and taking care of him.

Men in the first, second, and third years of widowhood. Seven men are in their first, second, and third years of widowhood. None of these men has, of yet, managed a new relationship of intimate companionship with a woman, although many of them are outgoing and sociable. Their lives are, in general, independent of major attachment to other adults, and they are in the process of working through ties to their deceased wives. These are men who feel themselves to be between things. For these men, the past is a defined realm and the present is really part of the past, although the crushing blow of loss has in fact separated the two. For these men, the future is unclear, and to a startling extent, the to-be-lived future does not concern them. Some of them realize that being a "man in-between" may be a permanent affair.

How the past colors the present is illustrated by the activities of George Lancaster, 75 years old, who was widowed for less than one year after about ten years of marriage. A good deal of his social activity now revolves around membership in his church. He stressed several times in the interviews that it was his wife who got him involved, originally, in church attendance and activities. Also, he feels that it has been church members who have provided him with the greatest amount of comfort and support since the death of his wife. He has no children. He claims that it is his strong religious faith which has helped him adjust to living alone and to his wife's death: "When it's time to go, He will come for me; when it's time to go Home, I'll go to Him. I'll meet my wife again, but up there we'll be like strangers . . . it's a new life, a new world . . . we will see each other, but we'll not be like husband and wife. There will be a new start for everyone.

"I have tapes of my wife's voice, recordings made of her in church, talking and reading the Scriptures. I spend a lot of time listening to those tapes. Listening to them takes some of the burden off. I'll just play those church tapes. In the afternoon, I'll sit out front on the 'glider' and listen to the tapes." He has been taping church services for five years, and has several years' worth of listening ahead of him. He is confidently between things. His past is part of his present, and for him his future is clearly marked. His intimate companion is still his wife.

John O'Brien, 77 years old, had been widowed for about two and a half years at the time of the interviews, after twenty-five years of marriage (he was married one time previously for a short while). He has several health problems. He is blind in one eye. He spends most of his time almost entirely in the downstairs living room because the stairs are difficult for him to climb and, moreover, because "there are too many memories up there." He has left the house "exactly the way it was when my wife died . . . with all the knick-knacks she loved to collect." He is living in a world largely shaped by the memories of his wife. This is not merely an artifact of his poor health or of his inability to get out more; it is a state of experience in itself. He says that he is often lonely and that he finds it difficult to live without his wife. For him, much of the meaning of his current life is derived from the past. He is still deeply involved with missing his wife and has found no one to replace her with. He is between a hauntingly active past and some uncertain future.

Five other men have similar degrees of close, continuing association with their wives and have been unable to find, indeed have not sought, a new source of intimate companionship to replace that which has been lost.

Two of the men have situational constraints: 1 is blind and another has a reduced capacity to walk. They, and the 2 who are healthy, nevertheless, are still absorbed by the life they had with the spouse.

One 1 man of this group has made any motions to change his life. This man, Max Flowers, is still strongly attached to the memory of his wife, who died about one year prior to the interview (they were married for forty years). On the one hand, he has made some real attempt to alter his life. On the other hand, he also recognized his own ability to do much about his attachment and to replace it. He says, "I am not interested enough in other women to go looking." While recognizing his own present inability to remove himself from his attachment to his wife, he has made, nonetheless, a concerted effort to define what he needs and what is possible for him at this time in his life, and to seek it out: "When I turned seventy [about six months before his wife died] I threw out all the rules, restrictions, and regulations. Time—as it was, laws—they don't exist for me anymore. No rules, as long as I don't hurt anyone else. Now, I do what I want when I want." He adds, "I have to be like that because my life is incomplete without my wife."

He suffered a profound depression after his wife died, a kind of wasting away. A move away from the home they had shared together to new circumstances helped some, as did involvement in some social activities. He has slowly been pulling out of his depression. Temperamentally, he remains circumspect, a "loner," and says that he is peripheral to groups and sympathetic to people to whom others will not talk, the shy and the socially awkward.

He says, "One of my favorite people now is my ninety-two-year-old aunt. I call her 'aunt' but actually she's a great-aunt of my wife. She's been in the hospital, but she's at home now; she's okay. She's on a very restricted diet, her doctors have really limited her. Once, every two weeks or so, I get in the car, go over there, take her out to lunch. We go to a particular restaurant [names it], where they know us—and she has a corned beef sandwich. According to what she should be eating, this is *totally outrageous!* She enjoys it tremendously. Why not? *After all, she is a ninety-two-year-old lady!* Why not enjoy it? Her mind is sharp and we have a good discussion. . . . Family things or general topics . . . I enjoy it very much."

Mr. Flowers recognizes his attachment to his wife and his attached state of mind as powerful, present, and limiting and perceives his own inability to change them at the current time. Recognizing these things, he proceeds from there. While Mr. Flowers' life still has great empty spaces in it, the interviewer was left with the feeling that Mr. Flowers' life will improve. He told the interviewer: "I'm just like a dog with a bone. Presented with something—some problem—I'll work at it."

Social Activities and Social Circles

The current levels of activities (number of contacts, number of social circles, degree of intimacy) exhibited by the 14 men fall into no general pattern. Interestingly, the overall level of activity for this group of men seems to be only slightly less than that for the entire group.

Common sense would dictate that health is an important factor which serves to limit the sheer quantity of social activity and sustained interactions. Four of the men in this group of 14 had health problems which limited their ability to get out of the house as much as they would like. But even among these individuals, there was considerable variation in the level of social activity.

Consider 2 of the men mentioned above, Mr. Williams and Mr. Bergen. These men are very similar in several respects. Mr. Bergen is 77, widowed five years after fifty-two years of marriage (to one woman). He has one child, who lives in a suburban county. He has several health problems which inhibit his activities. His vision is impaired due to cataracts, which are being surgically treated. Because of circulation problems, he has a limited ability to walk. He has suffered considerably in the aftermath of his wife's death and has experienced serious and long-lasting emotional problems. His health does not prevent him from undertaking daily maintenance tasks such as cooking, washing, and cleaning. His shopping must be taken care of by others, however. He owns his own home in which he has resided for many years. He maintains himself solely on his Social Security check.

Fred Williams is 71, widowed four years after thirty-six years of marriage. He has one adult child in the area. His health problems are almost identical to those of Mr. Bergen. His vision has been impaired by cataracts which are being successfully treated. Circulation problems and emphysema limit his ability to get around almost in precisely the same way that Mr. Bergen's activities are limited. He takes care of the same daily maintenance tasks as Mr. Bergen, but like him, cannot do much of his own shopping. He owns his home in which he has lived for many years. His sole income is from Social Security, about the same amount as Mr. Bergen. His reaction to the loss of his spouse was also severe; some of this has been described above. Both men come from similar blue-collar backgrounds. Of all the men interviewed, these 2 seemed the most similar situationally.

However, their sets of social interactions and the quality of these interactions are quite different. Mr. Williams is extraordinarily isolated. From the front of his house there are at least twenty other houses visible. There are several "short-order" places and at least two "mom and pop" stores. According to Mr. Williams (and verified to whatever extent by our observations), he has little contact with neighbors or the people around him, with the exception of one man whom he sees irregularly to exchange small talk. None of his neighbors, including this man, ever enters his house, nor, Mr. Williams reports, does he enter neighbors' houses. Nothing we saw during our visits contradicted these statements. He receives no aid of any sort from neighbors. It would appear that the primary reason for this is that Mr. Williams docs not wish to receive the aid. He admitted that at one point offers of help with chores such as shopping were made by at least one neighbor. Rather, Mr. Williams prefers to have his shopping done by his daughter. As the schedule works out now, she shops for him once every two weeks—for the larger shopping. Mr. Williams keeps a list of things he needs by the phone, and when he speaks to his daughter, he will tell her the items he needs. His daughter also is the person who takes him to his doctor's appointments. She is his main emotional support. Mr. Williams will not activate ties to his neighbors, although there is little doubt that he could do this if he tried. Apparently, he wishes to maintain his contact with his daughter through her performance of chores for him; he does not wish to expand his networks.

Mr. Bergen stands in contrast to Mr. Williams. Although there are fewer on-street contacts immeditely available to him (his neighborhood is not entirely residential, but is partly commercial, although there are probably as many contacts available neighborhood-wise), Mr. Bergen makes use of his neighborhood contacts. Rather than relying on his son or daughter-in-law for meeting his needs, he has worked out supportive relations with some of his neighbors. Nearby lives a family (mother, daughter, son-in-law) who are longtime acquaintances who do shopping for him. The daughter stops in daily to see how he is doing, to take a shopping list or drugstore prescription. They speak to each other in formal tones, she calling him "Mr. Bergen" and he calling her by her first name. When he was having surgery on one eye, she came to his house twice a day for several months to put eye drops in. Her husband takes Mr. Bergen to the barber, or stops off on his way from work to do errands for him. They have tried to invite Mr. Bergen to eat at their house, but he declines, feeling that they have already been too kind to him. Another neighborhood friend also stops by to see Mr. Bergen, sometimes as often as three or four times a week, and does shopping for alcoholic beverages for him. Mr. Bergen enjoys having a drink "now and then." Despite physical disabilities, he enjoys an occasional (once every ten days) "evening out" at the nearby "tappie" (taproom or bar) where he can play darts, "have a few highballs and a frank," and talk over old times with neighborhood acquaintances. These moments away from tragedy are very important for him. Although his contacts are limited in number and the duration is not usually great, these relations are cordial and are of great subjective significance to Mr. Bergen. He gets outside of himself for a few minutes. He is especially reliant on the neighbor daughter mentioned above and refers to her as "my angel of mercy."

On the surface, then, the resources and situations of these two men are strikingly similar, but their reactions are substantially different. Mr. Bergen does have an active network which he uses for his benefit; Mr. Williams rejects developing one, and has chosen, instead, to tie himself closely to his children.

Implicit in both of these life-styles are complex sets of feelings about children. Mr. Williams hopes to see more of his children; he is very open in stating his disappointment about the limited contact.

His daughter works, and has responsibility for caring for two small children and for her infirm grandmother, Mr. Williams' mother-in-law. His trips to his daughter's house are always a looked-forward-to diversion for Mr. Williams, but they are problematic for him because he does not get along (and never has) with his mother-in-law. It appears that he wishes to maintain contact with his daughter, and one way he does this is by relying heavily on her for all of his out-of-home needs.

Mr. Bergen too has difficulties in working out a relationship with his only son. His son, who lives in a suburban county, sees his father about four times a year. Since his wife passed away, Mr. Bergen has not had a close relationship with his son. His daughter-in-law has only been to his house once in the last six years, right after his wife's funeral. Mr. Bergen states that his son is very busy with his job, but he also says that he is disappointed with this situation. His son offers little in the way of concrete support to Mr. Bergen at the present time, although it is clear that Mr. Bergen has been of considerable help to his son in the past. Mr. Bergen, left to his own devices, has managed to work out a support system to adequate depth and comprehensiveness.

In general, then, these 14 men show no single level of overall activity. Six of these men attend senior centers regularly or live in senior-only housing. The remainder reside independently in the community. None of them are extraordinarily active and involved, and none are unusually inactive. Almost all of these men enjoy some activities, although sometimes for them it is "just going through the motions." These are men in between, in a liminal state after grief and before recovery, after marriage and before something else.

Continuity of activity. It is most difficult to make any judgments about any continuity of activity level between times past and current time. Unless engaged in a longitudinal study, there is no actual way of empirically measuring such interaction. On a more subjective level, it is possible for both interviewer and informants to make such comparative estimates, but this is a very risky business and is subject to severe limitations. First of all, the more time that has passed since the death of the spouse, the more difficult to get any idea of what life was like before and how it differs from current life. Not only is activity difficult to quantify as it is actually experienced, but it is also difficult to quantify retrospectively. Moreover, there may not necessarily be any single identifiable level of activity before or after the spouse's death; a level of activity may fluctuate greatly. Therefore, we are left making estimates about the *tone* of a life—does the general tenor or pace of activity seem to be the same now as it was five years prior to the death of the spouse? It clearly could not have been in the case of the men who suffer from health problems now and have their out-of-doors activities curtailed to some degree. Further, it is very difficult to compare the tone of a life which revolved around a career with the tone of a life in retirement; here specific elements may be more easily comparable.

All these thoughts aside, we might say that, impressionistically at least, these men as a group appear to be considerably less active socially than they were five years ago.

Relations With Their Children

In interviewing these men who had had a difficult time in reorganizing their lives, we were struck by the fact that so many of them had difficult or strained relations with some of their adult children. One characteristic of these strained relations was that the goals of each participant in the father-child dyad seemed to be mismatched.

Relations of enmity. Thirteen of the 14 men in this group have children; 2 of the 13 have stepchildren. Of the 13 with children, 8 men have a variety of disputes, conflicts, difficulties, "differences of opinion," and mismatched relationship goals with some of their children which are mentioned by them in interviews freely as troublesome things or as current "problems." These disputes may range from the extremely serious, so serious in fact that there has been no interaction for some time, to the less profoundly serious disputes which are continual, background, and nagging, but do not lead to a permanent or long-term break. Such a situation stands out, clearly, from that situation of the men who have reorganized their lives successfully.

The following examples give some ideas of the types and ranges of conflicts.

Charles Bravie, age 76, was widowed about two years prior to the interview, after fifty years of marriage. He says, "My children are both ingrates. My son, I won't have anything to do with him now.

My daughter, I've given her and her good-for-nothing husband at least fifty-thousand dollars over the years. After my wife died, they came here and 'cleaned out.' I didn't stop 'em. They took a six-hundred-dollar color TV my wife used to watch upstairs when she was sick. . . . That husband, I've set him up in business. My son, I helped him get into a union. I was sick and in the hospital a few months back. They came, only once, to see me. Once I got out, they wanted to 'borrow' some money. They only call when they want something. Next time I go in the hospital, I'm not even going to tell them. They don't care. They're just waiting for me to die. I hope I never see them again."

Mr. Williams says, "I am dependent on my daughter for a lot of things—for food shopping, for transportation, especially. She is busy, though. She works, she has children, her husband is gone, and she takes care of her grandmother who lives with her. I would like to see her a lot more often than I do, but it can't be arranged. . . . I would consider it a big improvement in my life if I could see my daughter more."

He continues, "My son, I don't know what's with him. I think he's foolish. He's going to be moving to southern Delaware for a job. That move will end up costing me more money, because whenever he calls long-distance, he always reverses the charges. . . . I don't know why he does that. But I don't like it."

A third man describes a more profound dispute. "My son lives in Chicago where he is an artist and an art dealer. He does nothing at all productive with his life. It's all the latest trend this, the latest trend that. I like art, but I object to the way he's living. It's something that's inside of me and just rankles. He has a good education which he doesn't use; it wasn't even an art education. But he decided to become an artist. Even that's okay, but he's not very good at it. He works at it in a desultory way—unproductive and without commitment. . . .

"I saw him a few weeks ago for the first time in almost four years. He happened to be in New York for some art thing and decided to come down to Philly to see an art show! Not to see me. We spent about an hour together and then he went off to see the exhibit. . . . It's not even that that I object to. If we spent any time together, things being what they are, it would lead to battles. What I object to is that he has no steady source of income. He lives in a loft somewhere with friends. He has just been divorced from his wife recently. All I want is him to get a job or do something where he has money he can depend on. He could do anything—write poetry, paint, or whatever, but it looks like he's hanging around with an artistic group and money is no concern to them.

"I've given him money from time to time. I've given him some to get his art dealership started. . . .

"He took it very bad when my wife died. The trouble between us really started then.

"I speak to him on the phone. He calls me to signal that he wants to call, and then I call him back so it goes on my bill. I talk to him about once a month or so. But we always fight. It always boils down to the same end, what is he going to do. . . . I have been thinking of writing him a letter that unless he settles down and gets a real job, I'll cut him out of my will. I would never actually cut him out, but I would let him believe it. It might wake him up enough so that he would mend his ways. I would ask him to carefully consider what he's doing now and what he can expect from me, his income would be so much. . . ."

John Foster, age 77, has three stepchildren who were in high school or younger when he married their mother. In his conversation, the fear often arises that the "step" bond is weak and does not necessarily include support in old age. "I don't know to what extent I can count on anything when I am old and sick. I will plan to look out for myself entirely." He has started to inquire frantically about old-age and nursing homes, about the Social Security and Old Age Care system in his native country (where he still has relations). Only two of his stepchildren live in the area (in two suburban counties). "It's been a long time since either of them has been to my home. . . . The younger one hasn't been here in at least a year [he lives about a half hour drive away]. The older one hasn't been here for six months. I see the older one at her place about once every four to six weeks and I talk to her on the phone maybe every week. The younger one, I talk to him maybe once a month."

From what he says, it is apparent that he feels these relationships are not solid and that they are not on a basis of equivalence. He must give more to keep their attention and affection. He fears losing ties to his children as he grows older. He says that he is also afraid of discussing these fears with them because he doesn't want to "push" them.

Five other men also had similar sorts of difficulties with their children, and in two instances the trouble was much more severe than in those cases reported above.

It is difficult to know what these incidents mean in terms of successful reorganization. For all men, the amount of turmoil and strife and insecurity is increased, but one might argue that such an increase may be a further inducement to remarry or to try to establish a calm social life in other spheres. For all men, the disputes are symbolic of a larger inability to get life ordered and to live happily. But on an individual level, intrapsychically, the individual meaning must be varied. We can suggest several general ways in which strife with children may be structured and may act to prevent successful life reorganization.

1. Anger or hostility to the wife is displaced onto children (her shortcomings become their shortcomings). The survivor acts with feelings of guilt toward the wife (leading to an inability to break fully out of the marriage). His ties to the deceased are strengthened by a retrospective idealization of her (without anger—now displaced onto a child, the wife becomes in retrospect more ideal), and the task of leaving her or finding an adequate replacement becomes more difficult.

2. Children become directly parentified. Faced with increasing deficits due to age, feelings of "not being properly taken care of" surface and are projected onto children. Feelings of having been abandoned by the wife (either emotionally or in terms of instrumental tasks) produce fears of abandonment by children, leading to increased sensitivity to the lack of interest or support on the part of children and an increasing sensitivity to one's own need. A small, bitter cycle develops in which needs are difficult to satisfy.

A father's relationship with some or one of his children may have been mediated by the mother. Left unmediated or unbrokered, difficulties may arise.

Relations of amity. Five of the men who have unsuccessfully reorganized their lives had relations with children which seemed happy, amicable, not generally hostile. The goals and needs of the parents and children were more or less clearly defined and were not mismatched.

This is illustrated in the following case, that of Mr. Flowers, mentioned above. None of his three children lived close to him, and the closest-residing child lived in another city on the East Coast. Mr. Flowers saw his children each about once a year, visiting the one on the East Coast in the summer, while the other two would visit him when they came east on business. It appears that relations might have been somewhat strained in the past, but now seemed to have resolved themselves into generally cordial patterns in which feelings of closeness could be expressed and expectations and rules were fairly clearly defined. Interestingly, this stands in distinction to the situation in Mr. Flowers' own natal family, in which there was considerable strife. One might make several sorts of generalizations about the relationships of Mr. Flowers and his children. First, Mr. Flowers derives a great deal of pleasure from his grandchildren. Second, the level of interest Mr. Flowers and his children have in one another seems to be one of an interest in week-to-week affairs, rather than in day-to-day affairs. Third, Mr. Flowers and his daughter, to whom he is closest emotionally, share a great interest in one particular activity (politics).

In two other cases, the children were concerned with the day-to-day affairs of their father and, in particular, monitored the day-to-day health condition and morale of their father. In both cases, it is clear that the relations between father and children are warm and affectionate.

Major Themes

In understanding the lives of those men who did not successfully reorganize their lives, we have selected a number of themes which appeared recurrently and prominently in the interview material of these 14 men. These are not meant to be opposites to those themes which emerged in the material of the men who had successfully reorganized their lives (although in at least one case this is true). Rather, these were chosen to represent the spoken concerns of these men and the flavor of the ways in which they portrayed their own lives.

1. "Things are inauthentic or unreal." (12 men)

In a recent paper, Clifford Geertz (1975) described the notion of an "experience-near" concept, one which a person might "naturally and effortlessly use" to indicate, describe, or define what he "sees, feels, thinks or imagines." Such a concept is one that a person would in turn understand when used by others.

This theme is our attempt to generalize about the close experiences of 12 of these 14 men. Certainly, some of these men would not use these specific words to describe their lives. Or perhaps the feeling subsumed by these words would be associated with a particular segment of life or a particular type of experience. But for most of these men, the feeling of inauthenticity seemed to infect or disinvigorate much of their lives. Life felt washed out, at times, as if winter went on and on and spring never came. Meanings in life had developed over time and were likely to be derived from married life, from family, and from life activity. Now many important cues, meanings, and signs were no longer fueled by real events.

This theme, that "things" are inauthentic and unreal, may strike one as having similarities to certain key behaviors and emotions which occur in the stages of bereavement described earlier. The unreality of life may be akin to "numbing," or inauthenticity to "disorganization." Certainly this is true to some extent. But what we wish to stress here is that we are talking about feelings in the stage of "reorganization." Life has gone on, resolved itself, but the lingering effects of "social devastation" (Townsend 1968) remain. For many of these older men, life will probably not improve much or regain its color. This is a sort of socialized individual bereavement. To use yet another metaphor, many ingredients are in the pot but the stove won't light.

The notion of inauthenticity or unreality was expressed in a variety of ways. One man, in discussing his present life, said, "I feel out of place . . . I really feel out of place. I don't feel as if I belonged in any group. I know my age—my chronological age—but I don't relate to people of my own age, I really don't."

According to this man, he tries to convince himself that life, as it exists in common everyday experience, is real and should be accepted. But he views his own nature as one which continually raises questions about things. Yet he tries not to because questions

bring on too much discomfort: "To tell you the truth, I don't try
to analyze myself. If I did I might make myself very unhappy. I
just let things go, and as long as I'm not hurting anybody, I'll just
get along and not be too analytical. . . . I deliberately avoid being
that way . . . I don't want to rock the boat. I'm holding on to
whatever I have and not questioning. . . ."

There is a sense of desperation here. What is it that this man is
trying to hold on to? Not only the present, although that is to a
certain extent inadequate in his opinion, but also the past, when his
life was shared with his wife, the time when "the happy years of
my life were lived."

Another man put it this way. "Life is strange now. I feel empty
and lonesome . . . I can't believe that I'm more than seventy! There's
so much more I want to know and do. . . .

"I am somewhat of a loner, I guess. . . . I consider my apartment
my 'last refuge.' I really mean it. No one comes in there. In fact,
the one who most often comes is my daughter [who lives out of
town, about 250 miles away] . . . I really have no visitors. My life
now is incomplete. . . ."

Another man, a widower for about two years, said, "My life has
changed one hundred percent since my wife died. . . . It's just not
the same. I'm seventy-seven and I know it will never change again.
. . . I hate to eat alone, but I do it all the time. . . . I don't have
a set time for meals, although we did in the past. I eat when I'm
hungry and sleep when I'm tired. . . . Nothing is the same."

Thus the theme of "passing through" discussed above is directly
pertinent to this theme of "inauthenticity" and, in fact, "inauthenticity" may be thought of, in some ways, as the obverse of "passing
through," because "inauthenticity" has a component of "being stuck."

In some cases the feeling that "things are inauthentic" comes about
merely because the experience of bereavement is extended in duration
and in feeling. Inauthenticity can exist therefore when the jarring
experience of loss is never reconciled to a new reality. The reality
of the loss is just never accepted.

In other cases—in fact more commonly among these men—much
of the grief has been worked through. Men have "passed through"
their personal anguish, although this may have been a lengthy process.
In such cases inauthenticity comes about not as a direct result of

bereavement. Rather, during this lengthy period of passing through, a number of life changes have occurred. Health is impaired, social networks wither, interest wanes. A diminution of activity occurs— either consciously or unconsciously—so that an individual, passing through his period of bereavement and attempting a return to his "normal self" again, encounters an image of himself as an individual in "old age," and produces an internalized negative self-evaluation, derived from and replete with deficits and diminishing resources and abilities. These have been acquired as the result of the bereavement or in other ways.

Viewed another way, it is almost as if aging adaptation, which under the best circumstances is something that should have been done as needed but prepared for ahead of time and with a degree of rationality, is suddenly forced into a short period of time; adaptation is made to a life of minimal or limited expectations, a life whose axioms derive from the truncated world of the bereaved person. In such cases the experience of bereavement becomes a major arena for late-life aging adaptation and one important means of "socialization to old age." Late life and bereavement become conceptually intertwined.

In such cases the course of bereavement may still follow set stages. Part of the experience of getting over or passing through bad times includes a "turning point," often an episode or event which one can recognize at the time of its occurrence or in retrospect as the beginning of positive change from the dismal state, the beginning of "coming out" or "getting over" the bad experiences. For example, several informants who had successfully reorganized their lives after the death of longtime spouses could name such points (although fewer of the men who had not successfully reorganized their lives could name such an event or episode).

The recognition of such a "turning point" may serve as an uplift. But the effect of such an uplift may be canceled or diminished (depending on the situation) when a negative image of old age, subjectively internalized, is encountered. In fact, it would appear that, depending on how the negative image of current life/old age is perceived, the uplift may never come. Rather, the experience of bereavement and the sense of loss are extended and may exist in a milieu of chronic suffering. Potential uplifts which might come as a result of working through grief and sorting out life (which parts of life can or must be kept or disposed of) are discounted because life *now* is closely circumscribed, diminished, and with few expectations.

Certainly there are a number of ways in which an individual may subjectively tie the period of bereavement to life following bereavement. The encroachment of old age in the negative sense of "I am old and useless" may come as a genuine surprise to individuals. A survivor may be completely involved with mourning, "pass through," and discover that a number of losses have occurred. Retrospectively, social losses may be associated subjectively with spouse loss: the loss of a spouse is transferred to the loss of vitality, interest. Second, on the other hand, bereavement and the negative evaluation of old age may be consciously and directly associated. Loss of a spouse may initiate a frenzy of self-destructive behavior. The feeling of inauthenticity may come about when the expected uplifts associated with "passing through" hard times are not realized.

Several men spoke of their lives in a way in which the association of bereavement and old age is clear. One dramatic case is that of Michael Potniuk, age 76, widowed two years after forty-six years of marriage. Throughout the course of the interviews, he emphasized the great extent to which he felt that his life had been profoundly altered by his wife's death. Upon her death he became fully distraught: "I didn't give a damn for nothing. . . . I sat on the porch and I smoked and smoked and smoked. I started talking crazy and stuff like that . . . my brothers and sisters couldn't help, nobody could. I cut myself off from everybody and everything. . . . We were too close. . . . I think about her all the time; we had forty-six years together. She had been really counting on our fiftieth." His bereaved disengagement led to health problems. Prior circulation problems had necessitated medication. Not caring about the world, he stopped medication; complications set in and his leg had to be amputated at the knee. "I just didn't care anymore. I let myself go . . . I was crazy . . . I didn't care for myself and no one could help me . . . and then I went into the hospital. . . ." Two years have passed. He no longer feels himself to be the man he once was. "Although my wife and I used to take turns cooking for one another . . . there is no one to cook for now, and so there isn't much of a reason to cook too much—no friends come around, so I cook for myself, but not too much. Four of us shop together, two widowers and one about to become one. Somebody'll help me with carrying the bags. My daughter helps me with the laundry now."

He has gone through a self-destructive period in which he has irremediably harmed himself and depleted his energies. His desire to survive and go on has persisted, however, and he has emerged from this period having passed through the worst. On the other side, however, is a life diminished in its possibilities and dimensions. Associated with this is a view of himself as "old": "I wouldn't get married again. I'm afraid that a little excitement would give me a heart attack. I'm better off the way I am . . . I'm not a youngster anymore.

"My health is now better than it's been in a while, but I am older. . . . I can't say there was a time when I began to feel older; maybe it was after my wife died. . . ."

For this man, bereavement and his own slow demise are connected; indeed he has marked his wife's loss on his own body with his own loss. His leg is buried in a casket next to his wife.

Moreover, for Mr. Potniuk, bereavement and the subjective experience of old age are also tied together. For him, his wife's death is the sign-post signaling a final chapter. For a year or more he was in "deep" mourning. Now, having passed through this experience to a certain extent, he is able to reflect on it somewhat, to make some statements about it and to assess his current situation and needs. But his expectations for things are now low.

Several gerontologists have pointed out that a realistic assessment of one's capabilities in old age and a retailoring of one's needs for these capabilities are important components of successful aging adaptation. The assessment that Mr. Potniuk has made of his own situation certainly has a foundation in reality: he *is* infirm and his abilities to get around *have* diminished. Yet it is very difficult to say what his needs are; and he has reduced both his expectations and needs because he feels himself, in many ways, to be socially "nothing," as in the notion "Without my wife I am nothing." Two years after her death he says, "I miss my wife most of the time."

On the upswing from bereavement, he encounters himself as "old" (not wise but infirm). Nor does it appear that he wants to be anything but that right now: having "just enough" to get along is enough for him. His home becomes the most important arena for his life because it was the place he shared with his wife. The home represents the minimum he needs to get by and the maximum he wants and needs. He resists efforts on the part of his children to change, redecorate, or reorder the house. For Mr. Potniuk, the normal course of events has been thrown off; certain elements—feelings about his wife—are supercharged, while the remainder seems diminished, wan and pale.

2. "I'm not sure what I want socially." (10 men)
Ten of 14 men made statements which indicated that they were not clear in their social wants or that they experienced ambivalence about them. This may be viewed as related to a feeling of inauthenticity. In this way a desire to return to a former level of interaction was not generally evident, but there remained some sort of expectations about how social interaction should currently be.

Several examples will clarify this theme. Uncertainty is apparent in the case of another man, who was not sure about the sorts of relationships he currently wanted with people. On the one hand, he looked for a relationship of complete ("one hundred percent") commitment. On the other hand, he says, "I act independently. I never ask anybody for advice. . . . I never ask for advice about personal things, on a personal level." He speaks of a woman he wishes to see on a regular basis, but says that his interest is "just casual." While he has mastered his grief and passed through a painful time, there is much of his life he has been unable to sort out. For example, he views his home as "a bastion of security" which retains his wife's influence and presence. He cannot bring himself to clean up or order the house, however; to do so, he notes, would indicate a fuller desire to participate socially again. "I wouldn't have anyone in here now, the house being the way it is [messy, disordered]. . . . I would have a big job in cleaning up before I could entertain or have a visitor."

Another man, John Benjamin, put it this way: "I have several good friends but sometimes they are busy. . . . Time stabilizes things. Sometimes you get into a rut . . . and you do what you can. I try to go out of my way to help people, but often I'm forgotten. Now, I just won't bother although I'd like to. . . . I believe that we should be kind to others, but often people aren't kind to me. . . . Basically, I'm a fatalist."

Attitudes such as these are typical for 10 of the 14 men. They reflect a sense of inauthenticity in life; some reflection on one's own situation and some satisfaction with certain aspects of it and an inability to come to a decision about others.

On the other hand, 4 of the 14 men had definite ideas on what they wanted socially. These included Mr. Potniuk, who seemed to be fairly satisfied with his current relationships with people around him. Two other men could name specific areas in which there were relational deficits (poor relations with children) and were unambiguous in the desire for improved relations.

3. "My wife is responsible for much of the good in my current life." (11 men)

This theme came up on the interview material of 11 of the 14 men who had not satisfactorily reorganized their lives. Interestingly, this attitude surfaced overtly in the material of only 1 man who had successfully reorganized his life.

Certainly, one factor in the wide expression of this theme is "sanctification," the concept used by Lopata to describe a retrospective feeling held by a surviving spouse that the deceased could do no wrong. Lopata proposes that sanctification is one method a survivor has of getting over grief. The sanctified individual is externalized, seems larger and better than life, and seems to be "outside" the individual. In this way, the deceased is gotten rid of.

It seems too that there is another attitude here, one which is related to the theme of inauthenticity. During the course of the interviews, one man made the statement that "since my wife died, I feel as if I am camping out," and others made statements of a similar nature, while others indicated that such thoughts were an appropriate summary of their feelings. This image of "camping out" is an arresting one because it evokes a sense of man against wild nature, man as an intruder in wild nature, and at the same time speaks of the deceased wife as a "civilizing" influence, one agent responsible for the settling of her husband.

Several episodes make clear the conviction that 11 of the 14 men had that their wife is responsible for much of what is good in their current life.

One man alternated between descriptions of his current life as glowing and as compromised with problems. On his own, spontaneously, he began discussing his relationship with his wife and the effects that his wife had on his current life. He said, "My wife has a lot to do with the way I am now [his present positive state]. She made me feel that retirement was the most wonderful thing for me and she had me look forward to my retirement. And not to feel guilty about anything. As far as finances go, she made me feel that I'd get along and, whatever I had, she would get along with it and there would be no problems. So that was, I think, the greatest factor in my being at peace with myself about retirement. My wife left me well prepared for my current life. . . . She was the one who took the bull by the horns and said, 'Everything is going to be all right.' She was positive in that respect. . . . I owe a lot of my present sense of security to her."

Another man, Mr. Bergen, has been devastated since the death of his wife. He has felt abandoned by both his wife and his son. He says of his wife that "she took care of everything, bills, the family . . . cooking, cleaning, and sewing." Her death left him poorly off and he has had to learn to perform most of these tasks for himself. Yet he also portrays his wife as a person who has left him with the reason and the strength to go on. His thoughts of her, he says, still hold the greatest amount of meaning for him in his life. He says, "Now I am on my own for the first time in my life," as if he is a young man. Yet he also makes clear that he feels his wife to be ever with him.

In a third instance, this thought was more concretely and simply put by another man: "It's true the boom is falling, life is coming to its close. . . . These have been terrible years since my wife died . . . but a lot of what I have, I owe to her."

4. "My independence is important to me." (10 men)

Ten of the 14 men maintained that their independence was an important and precious factor in their lives. They felt that their independence, the ability "to do what you want when you want," as one man put it, gave them the best opportunity to get over their current difficulties. In the lives of these 10 men, too much independence was not looked upon as a burden.

But in 3 cases, men felt they had too much independence; they felt dumped out by family members who were not responsible for them or responsive to their needs.

5. "I don't have many friends." (9 men)

Nine men portrayed themselves as individuals who currently had few friends. This situation may have come about because these men felt that "they never had any friends" or because they had lost friends through retirement and death.

One man, a retired salesman, put it this way: "I am a loner. I can't say that I really have any friends. There's a few people I enjoy 'chewing the fat' with, but that's nothing special and it's not too often.

"When I was a salesman, I had to be a different person, outgoing and talk about whatever was interesting to the customer. But that wasn't the real me. I'm more standoffish, more private," Another man described himself in this way: "I am a loner, really. I don't necessarily prefer it, but I happen to be alone. . . . I have no close men friends, and few women friends. On the other hand, I don't like to be alone. . . . Frankly, the latest I've been in my apartment in the morning is when you come to interview me. I'm always out early and stay out all day. I like to be with people, but I don't have many real friends."

6. "I lack control because old age or illness prevents me from doing things." (13 men)

Many of these men viewed old age as a time of deficits and powerlessness, in stark contrast to those who had successfully reorganized their lives. Here the crucial factors seem to be the subjective perception of illness and old age and the inability to compromise with change. In some cases illness was clearly a factor in limiting activities, but as we have seen, bereavement, illness, and a self-conception of "old age" could combine to act as a powerful limiting force.

COMPARING THE GROUPS

Contrasting the Themes

We have discussed two sorts of themes here. First, there are issues—companionship, activities, children—which are pertinent to both groups and which indeed seem to be opposites as they receive expression in both groups. For example, part of successful life reorganization seems to be a relationship of intimate companionship, which itself is both a symbol and cause of successful reorganization. The first group of issues are meant to be considered as major contrasts. That is, a high level of activity is characteristic of one group while a lower level of activity is characteristic of the other, etc.

The second group of themes ("Life is good," etc.) are given primarily to express the values and feelings inherent in each group. Thus the notion that "life is good" is characteristic of those men who have successfully reorganized their lives. The opposite notion, "Life is bad," is not necessarily a characteristic of those men who have not successfully reorganized their lives, although it may, in fact, be a view of certain individuals in that group. Rather, each set of themes was chosen to express values as they themselves are stated in each group rather than to serve as a contrast or foil to those themes of an opposite group. In the case of "Life is bad," it is true that many of these men are unhappy and believe life to be unfair, but, as we pointed out, they can still feel relatively satisfied with things.

In this sense, then, the contrast for "Life is good" is not "Life is bad," but rather "Things are inauthentic or unreal." There are several themes which might be considered the opposites of those expressed by men who had successfully reorganized their lives. For example, number 2 of the successful reorganization group, "Despite changes and losses in late life, it is a time in which there are new, positive things," has an opposite, but the sense of the opposite is also subsumed by the notion that "things are unreal."

Personality Differences

Undoubtedly, the differences in the attitudes, emotions, and outlooks of the two groups ultimately boil down to basic differences in personality. No crudely put dichotomy such as optimist-pessimist or active-passive is enough to characterize the basic distinctions between the two groups. However, characteristic of the group of men who have successfully reorganized their lives are an ability to overcome dependence, an ability by individuals to focus on things outside of themselves, an ability to channel energies in a certain way, a fluid substitutability as in the belief that something can be as good as something else. Characteristic of those men who have not successfully reorganized their lives are an inability to overcome dependence, a preoccupation with one's self and situation, a minimal amount of outwardly directed energy, a good deal of which is tied up in maintaining the patterns of daily life, an inability to substitute, and a large component of anger.

CHAPTER 4

Never-Married Older Men

The marital relationship is often looked on as the core of adult life. It not only can secure each partner an adult social status but it also can provide a basic focus for a secure later life. As we have seen, loss of such a status is devastating and presents each survivor with a series of problems to be overcome.

Nevertheless, about 5 percent of those people who are today age 65 and older have never married, and most of these unmarried individuals are experiencing and will continue to experience old age without the supports and burdens of marriage. (The actual question of children in old age is in fact another issue entirely, since about 20% of the U.S. elderly population have no living children, while only 5% have never married.)

Although but a small percentage of the total elderly, the never-married elderly number in excess of one million. The never-married are not only subject to the stereotypes which portray the elderly at large but are also subject to a special class of stereotypes of their own. The more familiar of these are "spinster," "old maid," and "old bum," as well as "lonely loser" and "swinger" (Ward 1979).

Little has appeared in the social gerontological literature on the never-married elderly, but what has appeared has been interesting and provocative. Ward (1979) analyzed data gathered by the National Opinion Research Center Social Surveys concerning 162 individuals age 50 and over who never married from a total sample of 3,557 age 50 and older and from a total all-age sample of 9,120 (total never married age 65 and over, 68; total age 65 and older, 1,461). The survey included questions on a "wide range" of topics. In the analysis, never-married individuals over the age of 50 were found to be significantly less happy than married individuals and only slightly happier than the widowed or divorced. For all ages, the never married had slightly more contact with neighbors and "other friends" on a daily or weekly basis than did married people. The never married found family life significantly less satisfying than did the married.

From another perspective, Gubrium (1974) sought to test Townsend's (1968) notion of "desolation." Gubrium divided a sample group of 210 adults, age 60 to 94, whom he interviewed, into desolates (those widowed and divorced people who were recently in the process of being desolated) and nondesolates (the long-term widowed, never married, and currently married who maintain continuity in social engagement). The hypothesis tested was that "relative" isolation— that is to say, desolation or the isolation caused by loss and separation through widowhood or divorce—is more closely related to negative evaluations of everyday life than is absolute isolation. The desolated (the widowed and divorced) were in fact found to be more negative in their evaluation of everyday life than were the nondesolate (the never married and the currently married). Individuals who had been widowed for a long period of time were found to be close to the nondesolates in their evaluation of everyday life.

In a second paper, Gubrium (1975) proposes that single elders "constitute a distinct type of social personality in old age." He assumes axiomatically that people everywhere are "highly social" and have a need for "self-validation" over the life span. Gubrium views marriage as an important form of self-validation, affecting a "wide range of interpersonal expectations and routines." Widowhood in old age means the disruption of everyday routines and creates difficulties in continued self-validation. Never-married individuals are excepted from this common problem of continued self-validation since they have solved the lifelong problem of self-validation in ways other than through marriage. For these never married, then, being single in old age is like a "premium," since the effects of desolation are avoided.

Further, Gubrium finds that studies of the never married (which are few in number and include his own earlier study [1974]) support the following conclusions about the never married in old age:

1. They tend to be lifelong isolates.
2. They are not especially lonely in old age.
3. Their evaluation of everyday life is similar to that of married elders in the sense that both are more positive than are divorced or widowed aged persons.
4. Compared with other marital statuses, being single is a premium in old age in that it avoids the desolation of bereavement following the death of the spouse.

Gubrium also presents an analysis of data on "self-definition" by never-married elderly to further bolster his notion that these individuals are part of a distinctive social type. He reports on responses by 22 never-married elderly (from his original sample of 210 elderly from his previous study). The categories of "self-definition" he discusses are "age-self-conception," "feelings of loneliness," "perception of the life cycle," and "conception of one's future." The data derives from the subject's responses to a twelve-item instrument which sought responses to questions organized around two "cognitive" dimensions, "orientation" (situational vs. personal) and "time perspective" (present vs. longitudinal), and resulting in four possible combined orientations. Thus a situational-longitudinal question is "Would you agree or disagree that life is getting worse, not better?" An example of a personal-longitudinal question is "Thinking back to when you were forty-five years old, would you say that you are lonelier, about the same, or less lonely now?"

From the subjects' responses when asked to describe how they think of themselves "as far as age goes" (their *age-self-conception*), Gubrium concluded that never-married elderly "tend to avoid locating themselves at any one period of life." He found that life is not structured into ages for never-married elderly, but seems to go on as it always has. Gubrium reports that any thought about *loneliness* was anathema to most of the never-married elderly. In fact, he notes that several persons became exasperated with questions about loneliness, and some couldn't imagine why such a question was being asked. Gubrium notes, "Such nonsubstantive replies suggest that the perspective of those who make them may differ qualitatively from others." Several, however, could name some person—often a sibling—whom they "missed." In terms of the life cycle, life was viewed as a *continuation* rather than in terms of stages or declines. In respect to *future orientation,* the future tended to be seen as a continuation of the present. "Death is viewed as just one more event in a chain of ordinary, ongoing experiences."

We have gone to some length to sketch out Gubrium's ideas here because they serve easily as a springboard for our own findings. His conclusions are clearly stated and provocative. Our own data tend to be at odds with some of Gubrium's findings. We will discuss several of these conclusions below.

1. "The never married tend to be lifelong isolates."

We specifically take issue with the terms "lifelong" and "isolate." It is never clear what an isolate is for Gubrium. For him, social selves experience desolation or "relative isolation." After a loss, such as the death of a spouse, people become "isolated." Others (the never married), by virtue of their singlehood, are more "absolutely" isolated, have no spouse to lose, and therefore no reason to become desolated in old age.

This approach seems to oversimplify greatly actual events by making them conform to a particular kind of theoretical construct, that individuals are "social selves." It neglects other aspects of the human personality system and subjective meanings as they evolve over time.

This brings us to the second disputed term, "lifelong." The 11 never-married men we interviewed were *not* lifelong isolates. They spent a good deal of life involved with their family of origin, until the death of key family members, and then were primarily on their own. Table 4.1 illustrates this.

Only one of the men, K., follows the image of the "lifelong" isolate. His early years were spent in "wandering around" from city to city. By no stretch of the imagination may the remainder be called lifelong isolates. It is true that they are not married and that their life-style is not a married life-style. Psychologically, it is apparent

TABLE 4.1
Lifelong Residential Patterns of Never-Married Men

Name	*Pattern*
A.	Lived with both parents until age 38 (when they died). Lived as a lodger in boarding houses.
B.	Lived with his parents until about age 20, when his father died, and then with his mother till age 43, when she died.
C.	Lived with both parents until about age 25, and then with his father until about age 56, when he died.
D.	Lived with his mother until middle age and then with a sister and brother into his 60s.
E.	Lived with his family through childhood and with a sister until middle age.
F.	Lived with his parents until about age 30, when his father died, and continued to live with his mother until age 61, when she died. Lived with an uncle until age 63, when he died.
G.	Lived with both parents until age 56, and then with his father until age 58.
H.	Lived with his parents until age 51. They both died in the same year.
I.	Lived with his parents until age 37. They both died in the same year.
J.	Father died when J. was 13. Most siblings died in childhood. Lived with his mother until age 38. Mother died on J.'s 38th birthday.
K.	Parents died when K. was 4; lived with his aunt as youth. Left home in teens.
L.	Married for three years in his 20s. Wife and he lived with his parents. Wife died. Continued to live with his mother until his 60s.

that these men have had a difficult time "individualizing." But their lives have not been led in isolation. These men are indeed something, but lifelong isolates they are not.

2. "The never married are not especially lonely in old age."

In asking these never-married men about loneliness, we never once encountered hostility to the topic. While the amount of loneliness experienced by these men was less than that experienced by many of the widowers, these men did in fact experience loneliness.

3. *"Compared with other marital statuses, being single is a premium in old age in that it avoids the desolation effects of bereavement following spouse death."*

This statement is true to a certain extent, but it is not, we feel, the entire picture. It is true that being single in old age avoids the desolation effects of bereavement following the death of a spouse; we have seen what a debilitating experience this can be. The elderly in Gubrium's sample portray themselves as relatively emotionless, a fact which in Gubrium's view demonstrates their distinctiveness. He concludes that it is primarily in widowhood that the wounds of separation and loss are felt. This is not the case. There existed for many of the never-married men we interviewed deep wounds and feelings of loss and abandonment upon the death of parents and siblings. The death of the mother triggered a severe reaction among several of these men. This is not the "desolation" experienced by widowers, to be sure, but it is an experience akin to desolation, and it is one which may have equally far-ranging consequences. These men experienced deep attachments to parents conditioned by years of close association and coresidence. For most of these men, such attachments were terminated, in fact, with a death of a parent, most commonly the mother, in the survivor's middle age. The emotional attachment may linger as an important life element for years. In several cases, the death of a parent precipitated a deeply felt crisis of identity. Such a crisis is certainly the same sort of crisis of self-validation that Gubrium notes for widowed people.

Specifically, then, "Does the death of a parent provoke a condition similar to desolation?" The answer is yes and no, in the following ways.

The answer is yes, in that the death of a parent may be devastating in the extreme. Consider the following cases.

Michael Balt, age 66, resides in a row house in a Philadelphia neighborhood. Temperamentally he is a kind man with a soft heart for stray animals and wayward people. He has tried, but not too successfully, to hide his feelings under a gruff exterior. He says about himself, "I am a sucker. I'm softhearted. I feel more sorry for animals than for humans. Humans can talk and talk their way out of things. . . . The way humans treat animals is bad. . . . They use rabbits' eyes to test how products for humans irritate eyes. That makes me sick." His kitchen is decorated with pictures of naked women and women in bathing suits clipped from "girlie" magazines as well as pictures of cats. There are more cats than women.

When he was overseas during the war, his father died. He was in transit at the time and never received official word of his father's death until he actually arrived home because the army was not equipped to send the message when he was in transit. He was shocked by the news when he heard it for the first time when he came home. The manner in which the news came is still a sore point with him. He continued to live with his mother and then, later, with both his mother and uncle until his mother died, and then with his uncle who lived two years more. Mr. Balt was 51 when his mother died.

He has considered marriage from time to time, but nothing has ever materialized. He was "going with" a woman for almost ten years, until the woman died, tragically, in an accident in the late 1970s. While her death hit him hard, his mother's death had a more profound effect on him. He said, "When my mother died, the world went bad. . . . When she died, I had a very hard time." He added, "I've only been out in the evening three times since my mother died.

"You are always a child to your parents. . . . My mother died here in this house. . . . After she died, I slept all over the house. I couldn't sleep good. I heard her talking and I heard her voice in the house. I heard her for a couple of months. Then I dreamed of her a great deal. . . . Nowadays I've been dreaming about my mother's sister. . . ." He traces his current experiences of depression and anxiety to his mother's death, the time when "things changed."

Abner Hatuit, age 80, lives in a two-room walk-up overlooking a busy shopping avenue. He was married briefly, for three years, in the 1920s. His marriage is looked back on with considerable pain. His wife went into the hospital for "routine" surgery and died there from complications. Mr. Hatuit was never on good terms with his son, who was raised by an aunt. His son went out west and Mr. Hatuit heard from him for the last time in the 1950s. Mr. Hatuit says, "I retain some hope that he's still alive, but in my heart I know he's gone."

While Mr. Hatuit was married, he and his wife lived with his parents. After his wife died, he continued to live with his parents until his father died, and thereafter he lived with his mother in the family house and then in a succession of apartments. His mother passed away when Mr. Hatuit was 63; she was in her 80s. She "took sick and died in the hospital." He says of his losses, "When my wife died, that was very bad. When my mother died, that was worse. . . . It was mighty hard."

Jerry Marvine, age 72, lives in a two-room apartment which is dirty and sparsely furnished. He is a loquacious individual and talks freely. He says of his mother, "It just so happens that where she died was the house I bought for her. . . . I'll tell you the reason I bought the house for her. The house we [Mr. Marvine and his mother] were living in was a rented house and it was sold. So we had to move. My sister offered a place to both of us in her house, but my mother said, 'I don't want to live with no married daughter.' So I got my mother a small apartment, she lived alone, and I lived with my sister. . . .

"I had a funny feeling about me. How do you call it? A guilty feeling or what? I wanted to do the right thing in the matter and inasmuch as I was not married and I knew she was not happy and I was not too happy living with my sister either . . . so I went out and bought a house down the street from my sister. It needed a lot of repairs, which I done. I fixed it up beautiful. Well, when I told my mother I bought a house and it was ready, she was overjoyed. Well, the day she moved from that apartment, the two rooms, into the new house was comparable to a new bride moving into a new house. . . . That made her happy, that she was the captain of the ship."

He adds, "I supported her. Maybe that's the reason I never married."

He talks about his mother's death. "After my mother died, I got sick. . . . I couldn't eat much for weeks and I developed sores on my mouth and gums. I was in the hospital and the doctors asked to take pictures of my mouth because the sores were so unusual."

He described his mother as the most important person in his life, still. Her advice on living is still very important to him.

He says, "They say 'a mother is a boy's best friend,' " in a manner to suggest that this aphorism is widely known.

Each of these men, and several others, reckoned the death of the last surviving parent—especially the mother—as a crucial event of life. This loss was at least as devastating as and engendered a concern for reorganization similar to the loss of a wife by the widowers.

To return to our question, these three examples concretely illustrate some of the ways in which this desolation does in fact occur. The loss of the mother is deeply felt and life is viewed as permanently altered. In fact in several of these cases ensuing health problems remind one of the health problems noted by widowers after the death of their spouses.

There are, however, several notable differences between the desolation experienced by the never married and that experienced by widowers. These differences serve to illustrate the "no" component of the answer.

The major differences are two. First, the crucial loss occurs *earlier* in the never-married survivor's life than in the widower's. And, therefore, there are differences in possibilities for life which may be seen to exist after the loss. Second, what has gone into the now-ended relationship is considerably different from the husband/wife relationship.

In most cases the death of the last surviving coresident parent came at an earlier time in the life of the surviving never-married child than did the death of an older man's wife, in average circumstances. Thus for the never-married man, there are most commonly more years to "come back" from the loss than there are for the elderly widower. In several cases the death of the elderly mother of a never-married son brought about some interest in marriage on the part of the son. For example, of the 9 never-married older men living alone who lived with their parents into adulthood (and counting the 1 man who was married for a short time), 4 have had girlfriends after their last surviving parent passed away. Three of these 4 men had had girlfriends while at least one of their parents was still living, but in only one of these cases did the relationship move toward the possibility of marriage. Likewise only one such relationship since the death of the last surviving parent has moved toward marriage. Unlike the desolation felt by many widowers—that it is too late in life for much change—the death of the last surviving coresidential parent, occurring as it usually did at an earlier part of the survivor's life, did not necessarily leave the feeling that there is no time left.

Nevertheless, in a manner similar to so many widowers, the tie to the deceased parent may be experienced as too intense and too important to be actually overcome. Because of the particular personality configuration of the surviving son, life after the death of the parent could be viewed conflictually as a time of new opportunities as well as a life over which the influence of the deceased mother/parent still extended. Thus this period could be one of considerable anxiety, ambiguity, and conflict. For example, Jerry Marvine spoke of his girlfriend, Rhonda, in a way that clearly illustrates his indecision about her.

"My girlfriend—you saw her picture—outside of my mother she was the best friend I ever had in my life. She used to come over here—clean my place and cook for me. She would always look out after me. She gave me many a hint about getting married, but I never did anything about it.

"She died in 1975. . . . She had decided to stay down south with her brother for a while. She was down there only a short time. I think she left 'cause she knew she could never get me to marry her. One day I got a call from her brother and sister. She had died suddenly. It was a shock.

"I knew I should have married her. I don't know why I didn't. It was a big mistake, the biggest mistake I made in my life. She gave me lots of hints but I was too thick-skinned. . . . I don't know why I didn't."

In the case of Mr. Balt's girlfriend, who died in an auto accident, the relationship also lingered on, inconsistently. Mr. Balt was easily able to describe a number of faults which his friend had, that "she was incredibly lazy" for one and that "my mother didn't like her and warned me against her" for another. Yet it is also clear that he felt warmly about her because she represented possibilities for him which he in some way desired but forced himself to deny.

In the case of parental loss, there is more time to "come back" from it. The vista of more time opens up possibilities but at the same time may be unclearly thought out or fail to come to fruition.

Returning to our original point, discussion of Gubrium's contention that being single is a premium in old age because it avoids desolation, we would have to conclude that the cases we discussed above do not fully uphold this assertion. At least 7 of the 11 never-married older men have experienced bereaved feelings of loss and a degree of desolation about the loss of their parents or a parent and have continued this sense of desolation into late life.

In this respect, consider the case of Walter January, a never-married man of about 72. He lives in a rented apartment overlooking a busy thoroughfare. He is not well, suffering from a variety of health problems which limit him, in some ways, from "getting out" as much as he would like. He is not outgoing, and it took the interviewer several sessions to receive replies longer than mono-syllables and simple sentences. He spent most of his days reading or resting or looking out at passing traffic from his front window. His responses to questions were thoroughly unemotional until we got onto the topic of his beloved dog, who had died. The mention of his dog brought tears to his eyes and the admission that "it is still too soon, I still can't talk about it."

What emerged from talking with this man is a story of a life broken apart. His family stayed together until the Depression, at which time all of his family members (father, mother, younger brother) were in and out of jobs. At that time his parents separated. He went to live with his father, and his brother with his mother. This separation affected him deeply and was a split which was "hard to get over." He continued to live with his father from 1930 to 1960, when his father died. His father was an alcoholic and died "from cirrhosis of the liver and other things." Mr. January "did a good deal of drinking myself" when he lived with his father. His mother continued to live until the early 1970s with his brother and his brother's family. He did not see his mother often, but they continued to remain "close."

Mr. January looks back on the 1920s as the happiest time in his life. He had a job working in a toy factory. "I worked there and I guess I enjoyed that job more than anything. It was a good job and there were good people there. The boss used to take me out to his house in the country—and we did some hunting . . . this was before there was all the building out there in the suburbs." Mr. January lost his job at this firm in 1930 (the year his parents separated). "When the Depression hit, no one could afford to buy toys."

Mr. January says that he "often" thinks about the past and about his parents and feels that their deaths are still very close to him and that "you never really get over it." He asked the interviewer, jokingly, if the interviewer could find him a rich widow. He checks in regularly with a nephew, but has no one to talk to if he feels anxious or lonely because "I'm not that close to anybody." Currently, he has most of his conversations with an 84-year-old woman with whom he exchanges books and magazines. His contact with her is marginal, however.

While it is very hard to come to know this man, it appears that the wounds suffered in his parents' breakup and in their deaths are still very current in his life. His sense of desolation is combined with health difficulties, but it is his general depression rather than his physical symptoms per se which prevent him from getting out more. In the last interview, he said, "Getting through the day is not hard. . . . But I feel there's not much I can do about things. . . . It's true that I'm ill, but it's because I'm apathetic rather than anything else. . . . I don't have much ambition to do things. . . . In the last few years, I've done a little bit of crying."

Such parental loss may occur at an earlier moment in the life span, and therefore, theoretically, there may be more time to overcome it. Yet the period after the death of the parent may be charged with similar ambivalences and conflicts that characterized life when the parent was still living.

Finally, although the desolation caused by loss and characteristics of grief and attachment may be similar for widowers and sons, the fact remains that, socially and personally, the relationships which have caused the bereavement are fundamentally different.

Next, let us turn to a discussion of Gubrium's four categories of "self-definition." We do agree with Gubrium that the never married actually *report* less *loneliness* than some widowers. However, not once did we experience the reaction reported by Gubrium, that his subjects treated questions about loneliness with incredulity and animosity. In viewing the other three categories of self-definition, we find little agreement with his conclusions about *age-self-conception, continuity,* and *future orientation.* Our data concerning these time-related categories are presented below.

The notion that the never-married elderly tend to avoid locating themselves at any one period of life (age-self-conception) is not upheld by our data. The ways in which these men organize time periods, in a general sense, are listed in table 4.2.

TABLE 4.2

Person	General Time Scheme
A.	Time clearly divided into "European days and American days." More recent time divided into "when I traveled" and "now, when I'm no longer able to travel."
B.	Clearly identifies the last 6 years as a period of diminishing abilities.
C.	Identifies the "end period" of life when all of his family had died. "I'm the only one left."
D.	Adopts a "waiting for the end" attitude. Has taken care of funeral and burial arrangements and is proud of this. Won't get a set of teeth he needs because, he says, "how much longer will I be here?"
E.	Views himself as last of the family. Time divided into period when "family was alive" and "now, family all gone."
F.	Periods clearly divided into before and after mother died. More recently, a period in which he realizes that he's "slowing down."
G.	Periods clearly marked. We discuss G. more fully below.
H.	Seems to live life day-to-day, without orientation to significant events or eras. The major event in his life is his military service, which continued on and off for almost 20 years. He considers his life now an extension of his military service.
I.	Life periods fairly clear. The time before his parents died (both died in the same year); continued residence in the family house; ownership of own home.
J.	Also seems to live day-to-day without reference to major events.
K.	Not enough data to evaluate.
L.	Personal time divided into periods before and after a stroke. Historical time, before and after his mother's death.

One interesting thing is that work and retirement play very little part in this.

We feel that it is necessary to give a more extensive discussion of Mr. G., a man of 80 years, who lives in a small apartment in one Philadelphia neighborhood. His apartment is filled with photos, some bric-a-brac, and art reproductions which he has picked out himself. Some items belonged to his father and he is especially fond of these.

He is a remarkable man in many ways, remarkably reflective, candid, and friendly. He has never married; he regrets this and hopes to remedy it.

He came to notice and understand his regret several years ago. He speaks of his self-understanding in this way. "A few years ago I was going through a pile of books and I came on one that was about 'understanding yourself.' I wouldn't have paid any attention to it, but there was a line on the cover saying, 'This is dangerous stuff,' 'Look at this book only if you are not frightened to find out about yourself'—something like that. Well, that was a challenge, that was what attracted me to it. So I read through it—it was all about ways of thinking about yourself and asking yourself questions and it led me to do a lot of thinking. . . . All in all, I feel a lot better for having thought about my life in this way. I feel that I am honest—a lot more honest than I would have been otherwise."

In his soul-searching, he has discovered a great deal about himself. "I should have married. If I had it to do over again, I would have done differently. I was kidding myself. . . . I made a lot of excuses for myself and for never marrying. I regret it."

He adds, "I had lots of excuses about it and in retrospect none were true. I felt that I was looking after my mother and father, but they could have taken care of themselves. I asked myself the question, why was I not in love? and I concluded that I kept control too much. I never let go. . . . I never let myself fall in love and I thought I'd be young forever and it wouldn't matter. It was easy for me to find excuses. My brother married late, so I always thought I would. Or I was often out of town for business so things were unsettled. Or other people would say, 'He's doing important work in taking care of his parents.' But it was all excuses.

"The fact is, I was lonely and I didn't know it. In my twenties we were poor and we all contributed to the family income. My father couldn't work; he was nearly blind. In my thirties I felt I'd get married, but I used the Depression as an excuse.

"When I was younger I had a strong sex drive. I had girlfriends in different cities I visited for business. I'm still in contact with some of the families I got to know in my travels.

"Then I had that period of self-realization. I must say that I'm much happier for it. . . . I feel better and easier because I don't lie to myself. . . . I know now that I was kidding myself all those years. I've become gradually more honest and open; I'm better all the time, clearer in my head."

Happily, this man has been able to establish a permanent relationship with a woman who lives in his neighborhood. This woman, a widow, is a few years younger than Mr. G. This relationship is not a sexual one, but as Mr. G. puts it, "We hug and touch a good deal." They spend their days together, as a couple, going out shopping, to movies or restaurants, or staying in. They have a regular procedure of spending time together and taking meals together. For Mr. G., his relationship is a source of much joy and it gives him a feeling that all was not lost, that he has recaptured some of the past about which he had feelings of regret. There is one element of sorrow for him here, though, he would like to get married, but his lady friend would not. While at some level this does not really matter to Mr. G., he still hopes that he can persuade her to change her mind. He listed as his "major problem" that he wants to get married.

Here a separation of time periods into decades, eras, "befores," and "afters" is clear, as is an admission of loneliness. There is a good deal of reflexivity and understanding.

Thus our data do not support the idea that the never-married elderly avoid locating themselves at a particular life period (their age-self-conception), but rather are strongly aware of different life periods. Moreover, life is clearly viewed in terms of stages, although perhaps less sharply than for the widowers. Similarly, the future orientation, especially the prospect of death, served to further charge conflicts for several men. Death was not viewed merely as a "continuation."

A final note on these topics is necessary. The sex of the 22 individuals discussed by Gubrium (1975) is not given. It may very well be that differences between our informants and Gubrium's are gender-related.

CHARACTERISTICS OF NEVER-MARRIED OLDER MEN

In talking with these never-married older men, it became apparent that they could be classified into three general personal *styles*. These may be labeled the sophisticates, the socialized isolates, and the outsiders.

The Sophisticates

Two men could be so labeled. They were cosmopolitan in their worldview, outgoing, interested in people and events, and part of active social circles. Both had a high level of social contact and social interaction. Both were skilled in middle-class social graces and went out of their way to make sure the interviewer was comfortable and at home. Both had analytical personalities and took pleasure in discussing world events and politics as well as their own personalities. Both men had girlfriends; both were relatively well educated. Both had relatives who were professionals. We place Mr. G. in this category.

These men lived in apartments which were clean and orderly. One man was skilled at cooking while the other could not cook.

Although both men had numerous problems and doubts, both presented a general image of optimism and had some orientation to the future.

The Socialized Isolates

Four men could be classed as socialized isolates, indicating a personal style which, on a day-to-day basis, is relatively isolated. Yet at the same time they recognize and seek to satisfy their own social needs, when they come up.

These men had very little family interaction. Three of the 4 men had no surviving family members at all, while 1 man had a few relatives, all distant, both genealogically and practically. Three of the 4 had spent a good portion of their lives in close contact with their family, so their current state of life was in sharp contrast to their past. These men did not regularly participate in formal groups. One man regularly attended a senior center but appeared to be a rather passive participant in it, from his description of his life there.

The income level of these men was low (all under $500 a month). The educational level was mixed.

Nevertheless, each of these men recognized his own need and desire for personal contacts. Each could be outgoing and sought out others when he felt a need for it. Each took some interest in others and events around him. Two men had developed close relationships with women, which were conceptualized as quasi-kinship relations ("like a sister"; "like a daughter"). In both cases these women were instrumental in helping and looking out for the men. One man had had a care-receiving relationship in the past, while the remaining man had had a girlfriend. Further, in 3 cases, each man was part of a regular but informal group of men who met at street corners or taprooms. Each man thus had several emotionally peripheral but regular contacts.

These men may be considered isolates because they had few affectively close contacts, rarely participated actively in formal groups, and tended to spend a good deal of time at home alone. They are "socialized" because they can and do recognize and respond to needs to be with others.

The 2 men who were close to women who helped them lived in cleaner and more well-kept residences than the other 2 men, since their lady friends also helped considerably with cleaning. The other 2 men lived in homes which were very dirty and disorderly and in which very little cleaning ever took place. All had skills in cooking, but it was primarily of the fry pan variety.

Each of these men had worked out a manner of living which was generally comfortable if the pressure of events was not too great. Each was capable of making relationships with some degree of affection and of permanence. Nevertheless, for each there was a conflict between a desire to be alone and not to be attached to others and a desire for contact.

The Outsiders

This term is used to describe the social life of these men who appear to be on the periphery. They are not loners in the absolute sense. In fact, 4 of the 5 men in this category currently are attending or have attended senior centers. However, once at a center, their involvement is marginal and peripheral. This indeed seems to be the case in many endeavors. Their relationships with people seem to be cursory and primarily instrumental rather than affective. None of these 5 men could name anyone as a friend or close friend, although a few do have acquaintances. With one exception, none had family ties. Formerly, all of the men had been close to family members, and their family had formed the basis of their social life well into adulthood. The one man who had contact with family members noted that his ties to them could be closer.

Two men lived in apartments or rooms that were underdecorated—with either only a few pieces of furniture or few or no decorations. Because they were not well furnished, these rooms were neat and tidy; there was little to get out of order. However, 2 men lived in homes which were literally the opposite, homes which were crammed with too much furniture, piles of books, magazines, circulars, newspapers, old clothes, carpet remnants, and the like. Besides the disorder, neither place was clean. (One man was not interviewed at his home.)

Interestingly, each of these men felt especially "at home" in the neighborhood in which he resided. Each man was a longtime resident of his neighborhood. Each had what seemed to be a detailed knowledge of the instrumental resources of the neighborhood and of people and institutions which could serve as contacts for resources, such as rooms to let, meals, and liquor.

The men in the latter two categories of never-married males show, we believe, a good deal of unhappiness, stress, conflict, and ambiguity. Some of these men, especially the socialized isolates, experience loneliness from time to time. In general, the sophisticates and the loners do not.

CHAPTER 5

Activities: Being and Doing

Next we turn to a discussion of the activities of the men in the sample. We wish to deal here with several important questions. First, what generalizations may be made about the activities of all the men in the sample? How do they tend to spend their time? What do they do in common? What activities do they like to do? Also, how do different activities fit into the overall life-style or "system of personal meaning" for these men? What about personal values? And third, what different levels of activity may be discerned among the sample and what do they seem to be related to?

Below, after a short background section, we discuss some of these issues. We begin by discussing the general activity patterns of the men in the sample, what their days seemed to have in common. We then treat activities from the point of view of the individual's life-style by examining in detail the lives of 3 men and some of the specific situations which influence and structure the selection of activities. Third, we attempt to classify the men in the sample on the basis of the level of activity and social contact and in so doing, come to a number of conclusions about the relation of several key variables (marital status, health, and income) and activities.

BACKGROUND

The study of activities is a complex one which exists not only as a part of social gerontology, in which there is a growing concern that the elderly live rich and full lives, but also as an area of study in its own right.

At the most general level, "activities" refers to all "externally observable behavior" (Lawton, 1985). This is primarily a behavioral term derived from the notion that thought and action are separate realms, a dominant idea in Western folk ideology. "Activities" is therefore a term with a great deal of self-evidence to it, clearly denoting the field of action and behavior. The term "activity" often brings to mind such things as sports, hiking, "going out," and the like. The term "activity" has several related notions. Leisure, more or less the opposite of activity, is often viewed as the special province of the elderly. The elderly are said to have "leisure time" (while "leisure" is a life led by the very wealthy). Activities may also be viewed as "obligatory" or "discretionary," depending on their role in normal maintenance.

There are difficulties, to be sure, in using these terms. The obvious one is that "obligatory" and "discretionary" are easily confusable and confused. What is obligatory to one person can be discretionary to another. Moreover, all of these words are deeply laden with preconceptions and assumptions. We do not generally recognize "thinking" and "just sitting and doing nothing" as activities, although they may be so labeled by informants.

The notion of activity has also played an important part in gerontological theory. The basic question in social gerontology has been, what combination of factors leads to the good life (well-being, satisfaction, etc.)? In assessing this configuration of factors, "activities" has always been an important variable. At one time it was believed a reduction of activity was beneficial (Cumming and Henry 1961). Another, more recent school ("the activity theorists") suggests that the continuation of typically middle-aged activities into late life is especially beneficial (Havighurst 1968; Lemon, Bengtson, and Peterson 1972). Other perspectives recognize that activity adaptation is necessary (Clark and Anderson 1967). In all of these ways, "being" and "doing" are closely intertwined.

Activities and Isolation

One distinction which can be made in regard to any activity is whether it is solitary or nonsolitary. This takes on importance in attempting to assess the relative isolation and solitary life-styles of older men living alone. In assessing both the "amount" of social contact and the relative isolation/connectedness of an individual, the first sort must be made around the question of the relative "amount" of "activities" a person undertakes. By "amount" we mean several factors, among them the number of activities, regularity of activity, time involved, strength of subjective involvement. Persons can devote a lot of time and subjective participation to numerous activities, or not, or anywhere in-between, and can be scored and compared on these bases. A second sort can be made around the question, are activities done more with other people or are they done alone? Here, an even finer distinction may be necessary. Are things which are done alone in fact related to a larger, nonsolitary enterprise (for example, studying for a class or writing up minutes alone at home for a service committee), or are they strictly solitary and not tied to a group activity (playing solitaire, watching TV)? These questions are interesting to raise and are significant in understanding the constructs which guide people's lives, but they are not always answerable. Nevertheless, they do draw our attention to a very important fact, that questions of "activity" and "social contact" or "isolation" are fundamentally intertwined.

GENERAL ACTIVITY PATTERNS

First we turn to the general activity patterns of the men, specifically to the question, despite the great diversity of individuals in the group, what are the common patterns or themes which run through their activities? In fact there are several.

The Notion of a Daily Routine

The notions of "constructing" a day and maintaining a daily routine were of importance to all the men we interviewed, whether they were very active or whether they were ill and primarily housebound.

A "day"—a universally, subjectively significant unit—was usually constructed around a daily "highlight," one or two activities or events which were singled out as being particularly important or significant (Rubinstein, in press). Highlights usually consisted of activities which necessitated leaving the home, visiting, going to a center, shopping, taking a walk, hanging out. Highlights were considered to be the day's major business and were typically given as the response to the question, what did you do today (or yesterday)? Besides whatever intrinsic pleasure was derived from an activity in question and the circumstances surrounding it, two other aspects of highlights are significant. First, in most cases highlights commanded attention. There was an "otherness," an objective quality about them which made them seem something outside of a person. Second, in those cases where issues of alienation were present, highlights were looked to as something which could be participated in "normally," and routinely, in the sense of "no matter how alienated I feel, I can still participate in this activity and feel relatively at home and absorbed."

The structure of a typical day in the lives of most of the older men we interviewed appears to be derived from the time-patterning of an individual's former work life. A workday is commonly divided into several major periods, punctuated by breaks and transitions. In a sense, the focus by older men on one or two highlights during a day preserves the workday structure, but, of course, with major changes in the content: new activities take the place of work. The highlight of a typical day for an older man may only consume an afternoon. The typical day outside the house may start later and end earlier than a workday. The transitions between highlights may be lengthy.

For the most active men, the day often started early (six to seven), sometimes with attendance at a religious service before the day's main activity. This might be followed by a morning activity and an afternoon activity. For less active men, that part of a day spent out of home might start somewhat later (nine to ten) and might include but one daily highlight.

Filler Time or Slack Time

Most men recognized the need to be ingenious and to bring will to bear on those periods of time between highlights which had to be filled in. In many cases this was an outgrowth of a philosophy which encouraged men to "keep busy," to "find something to do," as a panacea for social and personal ills.

Several men found filling in time to be a difficult task. Some developed various techniques to "pass the time." One man noted he had turned newspaper reading into a fine art, reading a paper from front to end, savoring each article. TV and radio were recognized as great time fillers. One man ingeniously linked the increasing number and longevity of elderly to the existence of television, which, he believed, involved and entertained them continually.

Most men, however, did not find it such a struggle to fill in empty time between highlights. A majority of men felt they did not have to think much about what to do with slack time, that tasks came effortlessly. At-home jobs and walks were commonly mentioned. Still, even among these men, television and radio figured prominently in passing time. A majority of men kept radios on as background when alone in the house, they said. Stations most frequently listened to were an all-news station, sports events, and call-in talk shows. Television was more watched than kept on as background. Most men watched specific shows in the evening.

While the consciousness of the need to fill in time was universal in this group, it did not seem to be a painful experience for most men in that it was relatively easily achieved and fairly satisfying. Some men experienced a satisfaction due to a perception of limits: "What else is there to do?" Others derived a more basic satisfaction by enjoying filler time.

Time Orientation Distinct from Activities

We find it very difficult to match up our perceptions of an individual's overall orientation in time (to the past, present, or future) and his level of activity, except in one case: those men who suffered most from loss in widowhood seemed primarily oriented to the past and generally had a lower level of activity.

It is counterintuitive to think anything other than the idea that a high level of activity is correlated with an orientation to the present and the future. However, this is not necessarily the case. It is, rather, the subjective meaning of the past, present, and future which is directly tied to the meaning of activities. People can both be active and concerned with the past.

Distinctive Qualities of Nighttime and Daytime

The activity of a "day" generally ends between three and five in the afternoon when people return home. Fewer activities are performed in the early evening; the men spent most of their evenings at home, alone. What socializing does occur at night generally consists of visiting and being visited by relatives. Organized activities in the evening are rare. Often the major social business of the evening is making phone calls.

In talking to men about their evening, one is struck by the distinctive quality they may have. Men tend to be alone, certainly more alone than they are in the day. Men tend to watch television or read. Nights are seen as more private and intimate, on the one hand, but also as something to be passed through. Men rarely go out at night because they do not necessarily want to, but there is also an element of fear in many areas: one does not go out at night without a specific destination and without door-to-door means of travel.

Most of the men we saw had porches or communal building lobbies, and these were utilized to socialize in the early evening. After "going inside" at the end of an evening, a final degree of privacy was reached.

Home Entertaining

Individuals who come into the homes of these men are generally close relatives and, secondarily, neighbors—although there is considerable variation here. Further, close friends of the opposite sex may come to call. However, it appears that close same-sex friends or acquaintances may more rarely come to call.

The older men almost never cook for others (we recorded two or three isolated incidents of this). If a man eats together with friends, it is done at a restaurant or elsewhere outside the home.

There were many activities which had a nebulous status. That is, they neither had the objective status of a highlight, something planned for and looked forward to, nor did they have the status of "filler." Time spent working on small projects in the house, periods of doing housework, and regularly performed activities at an improper time (for example, watching TV in the afternoon) were examples of this.

"Favorite" Activities

We list several of them here.

1. "Getting out." This was often mentioned to be a favorite activity and is important in the context of the daily routine. "Getting out" not only includes the physical, such as walking, but also social aspects such as seeing others. Typical of "getting out" is a nondirected but nontheless purposeful wandering. This activity is called "getting out" because it exists with a lack of specificity, in contrast to specific, named activities such as "going shopping" or "going to the center." "Getting out" may be appended to a named activity. A man may leave for a store early, allowing time to walk, window-shop, stop for coffee, run into others, do his shopping, and return home. For many this is a satisfying form of filling time, of getting exercise, of being nondemandingly engaged, of meeting with others, but not too intimately. "Getting out" is preoccupying to the extent that it can draw one away from inner reflections and "moods," as some men put it.

Walking is a very important part of "getting out," viewed as an intrinsically important activity, and is connected with feelings of self-worth and with self-evaluation of health status. Walking and "getting out" are viewed by men as major techniques of reducing loneliness, boredom, stress, depression, and "moods."

2. Socializing. Attending senior centers was given as a favorite activity of most of those men who attended them. Men liked the centers for the low-cost meal, as well as their role as a place to socialize. Most men had a particular acquaintance at their center whom they could single out as a close associate, although not necessarily a "friend."

While socializing of various sorts was named as a favorite activity, in general men tended to measure it in quantities, such that it could be "too much" or "too little." Men thus reported that they saw "too little" of children or "too much" of an obnoxious acquaintance.

Current contacts which called up the greatest emotional and obligational senses were associations with children and women friends.

Many men we interviewed had no children and no close friends. For them, less intimate, more peripheral contacts were important.

3. *At-home activities.* Two sorts of at-home activities were mentioned as favorites. These were "passive" activities such as listening to radio, TV, or reading; and active, male-oriented home tasks such as "tinkering" and repair and maintenance work. There was, of course, considerable individual variation here.

Desirable Activities If Opportunity Offered

Most men said they were generally happy with the activities they currently participated in, but many could point to some activity they would engage in if they had the opportunity. These are listed below.

1. *Work.* Many men felt strongly that they would like to continue working on a part-time basis, if the work was available. A variety of reasons were given: increased income, meaningful use of abundant spare time, feelings of increased self-worth. While some men had no thoughts concerning a lack of jobs, some directly connected the lack of work to age discrimination and to a commonly held notion that older people should do volunteer work rather than paid employment.

2. *Travel.* Many men voiced the desire to travel. Some recognized this as one major unfulfilled area in their lives, and saw no chance for travel in their lifetimes due to low income and health problems.

3. *Relationships.* Almost all men wanted some sort of a change in their quality and quantity of relationships. Most of the men with close relationships (friend or family) could name one area in which improvement was desired. Most men with no close relations looked to the possibility of the improved quality of relations.

4. *Circulating.* All homebound or partially homebound men named the need to "get out" more as their major desired activity.

ACTIVITIES: THE INSIDE VIEW

The above discussion consists of generalizations about the men in the sample, as a sample. We learn little in the way about the men as individuals.

Next, we look at activities from the individual's or insider's point of view—from the context of an individual's whole life. Activities must be placed in the context of a system of personal meaning for them to be fully understood. All men construct "days" for themselves, choosing from a medley of possibilities on the basis of need and opportunities. Nevertheless, "days" are usually constructed around the influence of a basic issue or issues which are of concern to a person in his or her life. An activity is the end product of a chain of personal contextualization. Two individuals may do the same thing; some of the reasons they do it may be similar, but some may be quite different.

We follow by describing the activity worlds of 3 men we interviewed. The daily activities of each of the men are placed in the context of particular specific issues (feelings, ideas, or themes) which are current and active in their lives.

Mr. Peters: Window on the World

Ed Peters is a short, stout man, 80 years old, and lives by himself in an older Philadelphia neighborhood. His house sits on a street that abuts directly on a small hill which holds an on- and off-ramp for one of the major highways in the area.

His house has two floors but he does all of his living on the ground floor, which is divided, as one walks back from the front door, into a living room, a sleeping and dining room, a kitchen, and finally what was formerly an attached but is now a winterized bathroom. His favorite part of the house is the enclosed front porch. The porch is glassed in, but the glass porch windows can be raised up in the warm weather and be closed in the cold. The porch has no heat but Mr. Peters uses a portable heater which, he says, is warm enough for him in the winter.

Mr. Peters says that he is slowing down. He has "bad legs" which make walking difficult. His memory is "slipping." It is apparent to the interviewer that Mr. Peters is probably in the earliest stages of senility. He does not look after his appearance. He says that he tends to forget things, although he is also aware that he forgets.

Mr. Peters spends most of his daytime hours sitting on his porch. The street that he lives on is lightly traveled. It is primarily the residents of the street who can be seen walking by and the cars of residents and their guests which park there. The pace of the street is quiet, in contrast to the traffic on the highway ramp above. The raised highway is separated from the street by a cyclone fence and a hill consisting of a wide patch of grass with small trees. A metal roadside barrier hides the traffic from the view of people on the street, so that only the tops of cars and trucks are visible as they pass by.

The porch is the center of Mr. Peters' world. He describes it out of the blue as an "ideal place." "I'm out here rain or shine, summer or winter," he says. On the porch he keeps "his" chair, a red, plastic-covered, padded armchair, within easy reach of a number of tables and upended crates which hold, retain, and support the tools and raw materials for the various "do-it-yourself" projects he is continually undertaking.

Mr. Peters is in many ways a "rough" man. He dresses in work clothes and work shoes. His clothing is not too clean. He chews tabacco, using a plastic bucket as a spittoon. The bucket sits on the floor next to his armchair; sometimes when he spits, he misses the bucket, instead hitting the chair arm.

His life has also been rough. He was born in a rural area in a coal-mining community. His father worked in mines. His mother died when he was 12 from the "complications" of giving birth. He remembers her as "a good cook." She was the kind of woman "who would walk instead of riding the trolley, to save money." His father died at about age 50, when Mr. Peters was about 30. He describes his father as a "laborer" who was "normal" in every way. Mr. Peters had two brothers: "There were other children, but I can't remember their names . . . some died and the family split up." One brother in particular he "saw occasionally" over the years. His brother died when Mr. Peters was 79, and he went to the funeral in the South. Mr. Peters does not know if his brother's wife is still alive.

Mr. Peters went through the fifth grade at school. He worked as soon as he was able, mostly in heavy manual work, building bridges and highways, and laying and repairing rail track. He eventually moved to the electric company, working on building and repairing power lines and power installations. He retired at age 65 after "forty good years of service."

He was married for about twenty years, and was then divorced. His wife died in the 1950s. He had six children who reached maturity, although two have died. His namesake, the firstborn, Ed Junior, died several days after landing in France after a beachhead was secured. Mr. Peters says of him, "He was only eighteen. Probably never even kissed a girl." The sense of irony and sadness of this death after the battle was over inflects in his voice. His son's photo hangs in Mr. Peters' living room. A mate of his son's visited the landing site in France in later years and brought back a photo of the area for Mr. Peters. Also, one of his daughters died last year, and he has not seen her husband since then: "I blame him for her death." Another daughter lives close by Mr. Peters, in the same neighborhood. She is the person who has primarily looked in after him, but she herself has been sick on and off in recent months. He expects her to die. Mr. Peters has three other children—a daughter who lives out of town, a son who lives in the suburbs, to whom he is close. A final son, Charlie, is "a bum with no job and no house, who roams around the city. . . . Sometimes he comes by here wanting money, but I chase him away."

Mr. Peters is very much involved with himself and his own activities. Closely tied with this is a perception of time which is extraordinarily subjective. "I have the same routine day after day . . . I eat and 'tinker around.'" What Mr. Peters means when he says that he "tinkers around" is, of course, "tinkering." "Tinkering" is his major activity, what he "does" during the day, what he says he likes to do, and what he admits gives him satisfaction. It is his "tinkering" that staves off the boredom which occurs at times. "Well, yes, sometimes I'm bored, but that's never the case when I'm working on a project." His porch is set up as a seemingly rough but actually finely articulated workshop. In front of his easy chair against a porch window is a low table with a vise for holding projects and an array of tools. As Mr. Peters sits facing out the front of his porch and to the hill and the bit of highway beyond, he can work on projects on the table in front of him. Arranged around Mr. Peters' right is a series of small tables or upended wooden crates, each holding a wealth of parts and small tools. To his immediate right is another small table with more tools and a radio. To his left are the door to the main body of the house and the door out of the enclosed porch onto the small yard and the gate at the sidewalk. The porch is about fifteen feet wide. Prominent in it are several clocks, some of which tell the right time, several of which are off, but running, and several of which do not run at all.

This is the porch world in which Mr. Peters spends much of his time. In many ways it is a rough or "unkempt" place, filled with tools, crates, tables, chairs, clocks, and a plastic spittoon. It is dirty. The linoleum floor is grimy and covered with dust. But this world is intimately personalized. It has the feeling of being self-contained, natural, comfortable, used, lived-in, and it is finely tailored for his purposes. Things are in reach, at hand, accessible, on a personal scale.

Mr. Peters spends much of his daily time "tinkering," as he puts it. His projects include fixing or reworking small devices such as clocks or radios.

But the major focus of his daily energies is the construction of dioramas, encased scenes which he painstakingly builds. Each diorama consists of a glass- or plastic-fronted box, usually about one or two feet high. Inside is a hand-painted scene covering the inside back of the box, and in front of this backdrop, the central element of the diorama, a figure in motion. In order to achieve the sense of motion, the moving part of the figure, be it a boat, a man's arm, or car wheels, is attached on a moving arm to a small, hidden, outlet-operated motor, usually mounted behind the backdrop, which turns at about 10 rpm. For one of his cases, Mr. Peters carved (from balsa wood) and painted a small masted ship, placing it against a backdrop of waves, sea, and sky. The rear of the ship is mounted on an invisible axle, and the front on an arm attached to a small motor. As the motor turns, the ship appears to rise up on the waves.

In another work, a blacksmith again and again raises his arm and hits a small horseshoe on an anvil. At the time of the interview,

Mr. Peters was working on a piece he promised to give to the proprietor of a taproom in another neighborhood in the city.

As it is described by Mr. Peters, his "tinkering" is an all-consuming activity. The world offers little to bother him in his endeavors. He reads no newspapers. He has visitors "very rarely." The most frequent visitor of late has been his son. His daughter, a few blocks away, visited more frequently in the past, but has not been to see him since she was sick. Days can pass without his speaking to anyone. He very seldom goes to visit his daughter and then only together with another child. He knows only a few of his neighbors and only to nod hello to. "I never go in anybody's house. Nearby is a taproom. I've never been in there." One reason for his failure to mix more with the neighbors is that Mr. Peters feels himself to be a newcomer to the neighborhood. "I've only lived here for three years. If I was here longer, I would know more about people, mix more with 'em."

Despite physical proximity to some of his children and grandchildren, he leads a solitary life. His only regular trips away from home and neighborhood are twice-a-month outings to his son's in the suburbs.

There is some aspect of Mr. Peters' whole world which is summarized in his porch-world life-style. It is a self-enclosed world (in an enclosed porch). The street outside is relatively empty but constantly diverting. Inside the porch, everything is arranged for immediate, comfortable use. The porch is almost like a second skin, an intimate, regulated world added onto the body. Mr. Peters' use of neighborhood resources is similar in a way to the style of porch life. It is as if the things he needs are laid out in front of him, a few streets away on a main shopping avenue. From the neighborhood he takes what he needs at the appropriate moment. At times, especially since his daughter has been ill, he may use the laundromat. He may use the barber shop. More important, he takes two meals a day at a local restaurant. Chitchat with the waitress often provides the only talk of the day. He is a "regular" at one place, eating twice a day there, six or seven days a week. He emerges from his house, walks the few blocks to the eatery, sups, and returns home. With the exception of trips to his son's and small shopping trips with his son once every ten days, these are his only ventures out.

Mr. Peters' sense of time is distinctive. He really has no need for the sense of time as it exists in the everyday-business schedule world, and this time framework does not really exist for him. On the surface he is involved with his tinkering. As he puts it, "I cast my mind on my work." He describes the long periods of his day as involved with this enterprise. The average day for him during the course of the interview consisted of three "work periods" (from seven to ten in the morning, eleven to five, and seven to twelve, although a daily nap or work in the garden—in season—were also part of the day). While he sits and works at the workbench, he keeps his radio tuned to the all-news station. Ironically, in light of the presence of a dozen clocks, the all-news station offers numerous "time checks." The cadence of news, time, weather, and ads provides background: a human voice, constant stimulation at a relatively subdued rate, a constant but controlled touch with some outside reality. He also uses the radio to "take in" sports events (especially baseball, of which he is fond). Days are often oriented to the big event—an evening baseball game, for example.

Besides the availability of frequent "time checks" on the radio, Mr. Peters has in his line of vision numerous clocks, some battery-operated, some electric. There are seven on his porch, with the main one right above his line of vision. Several others operate, although the time is off; there are several on which Mr. Peters himself operates, as part of his tinkering. One clock is off by several hours, but Mr. Peters does not want to change it because he wants "to see how long the battery is going to last." Despite the numerous outward indicators of "real-world" time, Mr. Peters has little use for such. He says, "I don't worry about or think about the time. Why worry about it? You have your dark and your light, you pretty much know when things are. Anyway, my belly is my clock. It tells me when to eat."

He says that he often "loses track of time." This is because he is involved in his activities, while at the same time, he often "thinks about the past." His mind can be on his work, but much of his activity is of the background sort, not requiring extensive or extended concentration. His hands move, his mind is busy, but it is also free to wander. He sometimes drifts off to sleep. He says that he often misjudges the day and the date, that days seem to run together and

that they don't have much standard meaning. It is not quite accurate
to say that he is oriented to the present, but rather, he is oriented
to the moment. His thoughts about his past do not represent an
orientation to the past—since concern with the past is not something
that predominates his discussion. Rather, the past may be part of
his experience of the present moment. He thinks little about the
future, he says: "I go from one day to another, and that's it."

He says, "I am happy now. I can do things . . . my fingers are
good . . . I spend money on my projects, but I enjoy that. I just
spent fifty dollars on lumber for the one I'm doing now." He misses
going fishing, but his failure to get out of the house doesn't bother
him. He is also worried about his daughter's illness. One day he
said candidly, "I know she's going to die."

Loneliness bothers him occasionally: "Sometimes, I am lonely in
regards to seeing people, but I'm well satisfied here." His personality
is such that the environment and activity can compensate for whatever he misses interpersonally. Similar compensations exist in other
domains: "boredom" and "depression," both experienced occasionally or "on and off," succumb to his continuing interest and involvement in his projects.

On the basis of five interviews describing almost ten days in detail,
the following emerges as a typical day. Mr. Peters arises at daylight
or shortly thereafter—at five or six. He spends time in the bathroom,
dressing or doing some wash. He bathes and shaves twice a week.
About seven or so he comes out to the porch "to work." By nine-
thirty or ten his stomach tells him that it is time for breakfast. He
walks the few streets to his "usual restaurant." He has his "usual"
breakfast of "grizzled" beef, home fries, and coffee. He is back home
by eleven. The afternoon period is either entirely consumed by work
on the porch or it is "mixed." Very often, he has a nap at about
two. Sometimes he will sit in his backyard, weather permitting, or
work in his garden. One day a week a local service program brings
him a hot lunch, but the service is being curtailed. Otherwise, he
does not eat until about five or five-thirty, when he returns to his
"usual place" for dinner. Dinner is more varied. He returns home.
From April to September his evening fare is invariably baseball ("At
seven, I get ready for baseball; I've been doing it for years"). He
listens to as many games as he can, in excess of 150 a year. He

listens to other sports in other seasons, although not with the same devotion as to baseball. When the game is over, he gets into bed. While baseball is on, he continues to work.

His day is given structure by the periods of work, by his eating habits, by his listening to games. One might say that he has no fixed schedule; this is true in a sense, but it is clear that his schedule *is* fixed and organized around certain key activities and stimuli.

He rarely receives phone calls, letters, and visits. He says, "I ain't got much to think about concerning the future. In five years, I'll be down and done."

He hopes his end is quick and painless: "I know I'm old and my time is soon. But all in all, I'm happy here."

Mr. Cohen: Out and Around

Frank Cohen is a short and broad man who looks younger than his 69 years. In his home, his dress is casual, but outside it is neat and stylish, with a hat, or matching belt and shoes.

Our interviews took place in his apartment, a one-room efficiency in an apartment building in a Philadelphia-area neighborhood. There is one main room containing as appendages a "kitchenette" along one side wall and to the left of the entryway, a closet and bathroom. In one way, Mr. Cohen is the complete opposite of Mr. Peters. Mr. Cohen spends, he says, as little time as possible in his home. But in many ways, his apartment is the same sort of "second skin" projection that Mr. Peters' place is for him. What clothing is to skin—a covering as well as elements in a personal meaning system— this apartment is to Mr. Cohen.

Mr. Cohen is a lonely and somewhat embittered man. Two daughters live in other cities, and although he talks to them with some regularity, he never sees them. He is a widower but never sees his surviving in-laws ("I wouldn't want to see them anyway"). He sees his brother about twice a month, and nieces and nephews less frequently. He says he has no close friends. The interviewer, he says, is one of the few people *ever* to visit him at his apartment, where he has been living for about six years.

He says that his need to get out is often motivated by his detestation of staying in. He often feels cooped up in his apartment, and when he doesn't he has the fear of feeling that way. He says that he tries to spend as much time as possible away from home.

The home he tries so hard to get away from is a small apartment in a rather nondescript, recently built apartment complex. It is in a relatively quiet neighborhood in the city and seems to be free of much of the truck noise which is common in cities. The apartment is reached by walking down a long carpeted hallway.

At entering, one finds a short hallway which opens abruptly onto the one-room square of the apartment. At reaching the point at which the hallway becomes the room, one can survey Mr. Cohen's small world. To the left, one side of which makes up the hallway wall, is a small, closed-off "complex" of bathroom and closet. These are at the front end of the apartment, forming the front wall running parallel to the corridor. Along the left wall of the apartment itself is the kitchen area. Against that wall run a refrigerator, sink, stove, and closet; above the appliances are cabinets. The far wall has several windows which face a courtyard. Mr. Cohen invariably keeps the shades drawn. Beneath the windows, running from left to right as one gazes, are an office desk, a lamp, a side table, a bed (a queen size which juts out into the center of the small room), and a dresser. Along the right wall (adjoining the next apartment) are a chair, a table with lamp, a TV, and a second table. Along the inner wall, the bathroom wall, is another chair. Finally, in the center of the room, but close to the "kitchen" area, is a small card table with a fold-up chair, the dining table.

These are the bare outlines, the skeleton. In point of fact, the place is visually much richer because it is filled, in an ordered disarray, with *stuff*—junk, objects, things, items. The desk, for example, is piled high with papers—newspapers, junk mail, financial records. In front of the desk are about ten pairs of shoes. The headboard of the bed contains shelves which are stuffed with various things: books, novelty items. The dresser is topped with clothes. Items spill out of the closet. The chair is covered with piles of clothes, the tables with books, a suitcase, loose change, combs, playing cards, magazines. The chair near the bathroom is also piled high with clothes ("I wait till there's a special at the cleaners"), and the kitchen table is covered with jars (jams, sauces), food residue, a sugar bowl, a loaf of bread, and crumbs.

Mr. Cohen keeps the room dark—he says the blinds are never opened.

It is easier to describe the room in a general way—that it is messy and cluttered—than to enumerate specifically each of the parts of the clutter. And there are many. But what is most intriguing about the place is that while it is disorderly and cluttered, it is not exactly dirty. That is to say, while there is dirt, the dirt is clearly compartmentalized. For example, cooking utensils and pots are in the kitchen area; there are no dishes in the bed area or the dresser. Decks of cards have their place, on a table. Financial records are on the desk, shoes on the floor. Clothes for the cleaners are in one pile. Thus the "chaos" is organized in its own way. Dirt media are not mixed. Food dirt, for example, is more or less confined to the kitchen area. In fact, in its own way, the one-room apartment represents all the functions of the common family house: kitchen, dining room, bedroom, garage or storeroom, etc.

It appears that this place has several important functions for Mr. Cohen.

First, it represents a kind of staging area for him. Most of what he considers to be his daily activities are performed outside of his home. But his home is his base camp. "People know if they want to get me [on the phone] I'll be here only at certain times." The analogy of a "camp" is appropriate since his style of living in it is similar to camping out. His "camp" is very private, people rarely visit him there. It is shut off: shades are drawn, even during the day. The door is closed. Often the TV is turned up loud so that the sounds from outside and from other apartments are drowned out.

Besides being a staging area for his trips out, the apartment represents a very specialized environment, one which expresses a wide variety of ideas on self, order, and values. "Private" and "public" are kept separate; order is maintained through a notion of standards which conform, ultimately, to public ideas of what order is, but which also challenge these.

Mr. Cohen says, quite clearly, that he hates to be at home, that he feels cooped up, and that every day, regardless of the weather, he spends time outside of the house: "Even in the rain or the snow, I go out." But he does manage to spend a good deal of time at home every day. He is a late riser, preferring to get up at eight or nine or even later. He then often spends about one or two hours at home attending to his appearance, cooking, cleaning, listening to radio or TV, or straightening up. He returns in the evening, often at eight or nine o'clock if he is on his own, or later if he has been at another's house. He remains at home awake from eight or nine to late—one or two, watching TV, making or taking an occasional phone call. Although he says that he hates to be at home, he feels better about being at home in the late evening. From his description, he seems to be more at peace with things, to "glide" over time, without bumps, in evenings at home.

His current pattern of elements selected to fill in a day follows a number of variable routines. He has several regular places he goes daily: restaurants (one or two special places), a social club, two or three homes of relatives or acquaintances, and what might be called resources—places such as stores at some of which he "knows someone" and can get a special deal.

A typical day of activities for Mr. Cohen might be as follows. Leaving his house at nine-thirty or ten, he takes public transportation to a shopping area where he has breakfrast at one regular restaurant and checks a newspaper. While he is known at this place, he does not have any real acquaintances there. He moves on, taking public transport to a restaurant in his old neighborhood. This restaurant harbors a group of "regulars," mostly men but some women. Most of the men are retired neighborhood people, but some are currently employed, stopping in on their way to or from jobs. While there are regulars, the composition of the group shifts over the course of the day.

The owner and staff of the restaurant are important figures in the maintenance of this group. They appreciate the regularity of the customers, so in return for their business and their presence, they permit the quasi-group to stay, allowing them to "nurse" cups of coffee or tea between meals.

Mr. Cohen might arrive at the restaurant prior to lunchtime, have a beverage, nurse that, and then order lunch. There he meets with regulars, some men whom he has known for years, from the neighborhood, from the social club, or from other ways. Later on, he may leave the restaurant and attend to personal chores: shopping or visiting, or he may join a group of men at someone's house for cards. Generally he goes to one of several places for dinner. If he eats lunch with his acquaintances at the restaurant, he will dine with others. After dinner, he may sit until eight or nine, and then return home. Or several nights a week he may attend the social club and there play cards—for small stakes—to late in the evening.

What system of meaning or ideas provides Mr. Cohen with the backdrop for selection of these elements to fill in his day?

Mr. Cohen has two sets of ideas or notions about who he is, or two sets of ideas about things which seem to be in conflict.

On the one hand, he is a man who exists "as part of" a definite social environment. The social world is brought into focus most clearly in the meaningful contrast between home and out of home. His social world rarely penetrates his home environment, which is personal and personalized. Out of home, he is a social man. "People know me," he says, or "People know when to reach me." He is a "member" of the restaurant group—a known quantity and a participant. He is a member of the "social club." He is part of a "regular circuit."

On the other hand, he feels bitter and solitary. His connectedness to various groups and people-filled routines alters at times so that he can say of himself, "I am different from other people," or "I am a loner . . . I have no close friends." He feels himself alienated and becomes a solitary wanderer.

As with most of the men we interviewed, his daily routine has a clear structure: the structure of various episodes is repeated day after day. The elements are selected daily on the basis of how one is feeling on a particular day, and put together into the generally invariant structure, although the components which fit into the structure may in fact vary. The variance seems to depend on which set of ideas about himself is current on a given day.

Even when his impression of himself changes, the grand structure of his daily routine stays the same although the content of the day alters. Alienated, his emphasis in activities is on solitary way stations along the daily path. One weekend he spent "mostly by myself." A birthday was celebrated when Mr. Cohen "took myself out to dinner."

Besides variations in sociality or solitude depending on his mood, there is also a general variation in whether a particular day is classified as intrinsically active or "slow." Even if a day is intrinsically active or slow, Mr. Cohen still has an ability to deal with it as determined by his needs for sociality or solitude. The distinction between active and slow days is emphasized in his evening schedule. Tuesday, Friday, and Saturday, described as active days, are spent at his social club or in a special but recurrent social activity. Monday, Wednesday, and Thursday evenings have "nothing doing." Sunday evening is often spent at a relative's.

Another important theme in Mr. Cohen's life is that of "having knowledge." Although he never had much formal education, he has a large vocabulary and uses words eloquently. He also has a large knowledge of "special deals," particularly where to get things (clothes, cigarettes, food items) at remarkably low cost. His knowledge of "people" and "deals," some of which are not entirely legal, makes him feel good about himself, that he can get along through his ingenuity and superior knowledge. This is especially important in his knowledge of how to get money. Sales of those products on which he gets special deals and his use of his network to get part-time employment are important symbols of this ability. But the foremost symbol is his ability to make use of the Atlantic City casinos.

From Mr. Cohen's point of view, the casinos provide several avenues of possibilities. His attitude to them is much like a hunter in search of game. They are potentially lucrative resources to be exploited; they provide means of getting away from his city and his daily routine; they provide a particular kind of solitude—anonymity in a crowd; they also provide a backdrop for an image of the elderly as "striking back" against exploiters.

One can win money at the casinos; Mr. Cohen has. One can get inexpensive transport out of the city. At the casinos, there are thousands of people, so one can remain anonymous, but be close to others. There is also an aura of sexual possibility, high finance, and glitter which appeals to Mr. Cohen. He also perceives going to the casinos as one way for older people to strike back "against the system."

The image of the elderly as "striking back" actually has a dual sense. Certainly, "striking back" (revenge) is important. But also there is an element concerning those who are considered weak and mild-mannered (e.g., the elderly) winning through craftiness. These ideas appeal to Mr. Cohen and they strike a deep and resonant personal chord with him. He says he feels unappreciated and over-looked, particularly by his family. As a kind of compensation, he delights in telling of winnings at Atlantic City casinos, of being able to take advantage of the "freebies" and "special deals" by knowing the right people, of taking advantage of bus-package tours to Atlantic City in which the cost of the bus is returned by a casino to those over 65. For some time, in fact, various casinos actually gave out a sum of money that was *greater* than the cost of the trip, in hopes that people would come down and be induced into spending (and losing) the money they had been given, as well as some of their own. The ability of older people to resist the temptation to gamble, or to set a limit, gamble, and win was greatly admired by Mr. Cohen. He also admired one couple he knew who managed to *make* in excess of $100 a week by going down to Atlantic City five days a week, when the bus trip was free and each person also received $10 in cash. "Needless to say, as soon as they found out what some people were doing, they stopped being so generous."

Mr. Cohen has won modestly several times at the casinos, but he says that he has generally lost as much as he has won. He uses the casinos to "get away" from the city. Inexpensive bus rides and "deals" on overnight housing make this, in many ways, an ideal escape, an escape from his regular routine. While normally he as-sociates with individuals on a regular basis and less frequently acts as an isolate, his trips to Atlantic City seem to be affairs with roots in his sense of isolation. He goes by himself. He may run into somebody he knows, but most people he meets he knows only peripherally. He says that he can leave his whole world behind.

During one interview, he said the following candidly, about himself: "I have conflicts about feeling neglected and my need for independence. My current life is the best resolution of this."

His feelings of neglect run deep. He feels that his father was responsible for instilling many of them and that his father did not care about him and was unduly harsh. At age 15, having had enough, he ran away from home, hitchhiking south and eventually landing a job with a traveling theatrical company. He ultimately returned home, was drafted, and married. He spent his working career as a salesman in local department stores, and although his tenure at jobs was lengthy, his employment ended dramatically. In one instance, the stored folded. In another, he punched his supervisor during an argument. Finally, at a third place, he retired early under disability provisions of his pension plan.

Drama and tension underlie his relations with his family. After his wife's death, his in-laws, to whom he had been close, "rejected" him. "They turned against me. . . . They brainwashed each other and other people about me." He has not spoken to his in-laws in some time, although he hears of them from time to time. He has two daughters, but says that he is not really close to either one. One lives on the West Coast and he sees her once every two years. Another lives about thirty miles from Mr. Cohen.

Mr. Cohen's activities are constructed with several elements in mind. Every day has a regular structure to it. From his own point of view, the structure seems orderly and useful; from the observer's point of view, it seems somewhat haphazard until one understands his concerns. The structure of the day contains sharp divisions between the home world and the outside world. The world outside contains a regular circuit of places, each designed to fill the need for a particular level of interaction which is felt at a given moment, depending on which view of himself he takes during a day. The movement from place to place—a peripatetic life-style—represents a maximum flexibility. The ability to substitute elements, to be "part of" a regular grouping but one which is informal, to have a matrix of family ties but ties that are interfered with, are all part of a pattern in which, on the one hand, the world appears to be open to manipulation, but on the other, it is estranging. These attitudes are expressed by Mr. Cohen in various ways. During one interview he said, "I'm often down in the dumps. I think to myself, 'Where am I going? What am I doing? Who's feeling sorry for me? Are there people who are worse off than me?' "

Another time he said, "I've been hoping for a long time to get away from Philadelphia. My great hope is to move away and start fresh."

Mr. Lamb: Work and Pride

Nicholas Lamb is an 80-year-old man who lives in a row house in a Philadelphia neighborhood. Born in Ireland, he came to the United States in 1932; "unfortunately, it was at the height of the Depression." He came first and his wife and children followed. Several of his brothers and sisters had already come and several were to follow. After several years of marginal employment, he finally secured work with a large industrial corporation in Philadelphia, where he worked for thirty-three years, until retirement in 1966. He is the father of four children, two of whom live in the area. Several siblings are still living. His wife died in 1978, after almost fifty years of marriage.

Mr. Lamb spends his days in quiet regularity, without as much inner conflict as Mr. Cohen. He says, "I spend most of my time here at home."

While in fact Mr. Lamb spends a good deal of time at home, he has a regular set of "things I do." These include work, one afternoon a week at an office. "There's one guy there who has to look at old contracts once or twice; he leaves 'em in a pile and I come in and file them back. . . . I also look up information for him. It's nice to have extra income." Mr. Lamb also regularly attends services at his church twice a week.

Most significant to Mr. Lamb is the power of activity, the need to keep busy. The need for activity is constant, at work or at home.

"We moved into this house in 1970, about. We moved out of the old neighborhood, which was 'changing.' Since then, I've spent a lot of time fixing it up." He has remodeled the downstairs. His work was interrupted by the illness, the worsening condition, and, finally, the death of his wife. This sequence lasted for about three years, ending in 1978. After her death, he continued to work. "You'd be surprised how many things there are to tinker with or work on at home here."

The place he lives in is a typical row house, like thousands of others in Philadelphia. On the porch, Mr. Lamb keeps a chair and table. At the front of the house is the door and a wide window. The first room one enters is a living room, with a stairway up. A sofa, several tables, and three armchairs make up the furnishings, as well as a wall-mounted mirror, some photos, and a hanging shelf for small porcelain trinkets his wife had. In the dining room are chairs and a table with a white lace and linen cloth, a china closet, a sideboard, and a mirror mounted on the wall. A number of framed scenes hang on the walls. Beyond is the kitchen, with a small, high metal cabinet, radio, and table and chairs, and appliances next to the right wall. Outside is a small, cemented-over backyard. Upstairs are three bedrooms and a bathroom. The house is very orderly and well maintained. There are no piles of "stuff" as with Mr. Cohen and Mr. Peters. The house is kept very clean (Mr. Lamb does his own cleaning, although his daughter will help occasionally). Moreover, it is subject to constant improvement projects—rewiring, fixing, painting. Nevertheless, there was no evidence of work in progress during the period of the interviews.

For Mr. Lamb, "home" and "the outside world" are strong divisions of cognitive space, but the distinction is not the subject of the same set of concerns Mr. Cohen has.

There are several themes which direct the selection of activities or daily elements for Mr. Lamb. One is the notion of "pride" as a personal attribute which is manifest through participation in work and in formal social groups. Second is the need to have social relations with people, but at a level which is not too intimate.

These motivating notions are behind the patterns by which Mr. Lamb selects the various elements which fill his days.

1. On the one hand, he maintains that he can always find enough to do at home and that he is "never" lonely, because there is no reason for him to be. At home here are "always" things to work on. But, on the other hand, he admits that he is beginning to run out of things to do. He says, "There's a lot less to do than before." His current pattern of activities has been partially retained from his life with his wife and before, during, and after her terminal illness. While sustained by habit, they clearly assuage some need. Some patterns have begun "to run out of steam." Nevertheless, the centrality of work, activity, and "doing things" has not changed.

2. Certain tasks become elaborated. For example, paying the phone bill, something which can be completed almost effortlessly through the mail, is upgraded in subjective importance and turned into a complicated "procedure," an event. In order to pay bills, Mr. Lamb makes a special trip downtown, often filling an afternoon, to utility

customer centers in the main office where he can pay his bill. These trips serve several goals. They are important as activities in and of themselves; "being active" is important to Mr. Lamb. They are time fillers, elaborated from a five-minute procedure to an afternoon. They are structure fillers and allow Mr. Lamb to feature another highlight in a day. Further, they express competence, that Mr. Lamb can "still" handle his own affairs. Finally, such trips offer the opportunity to get away and return to places he was familiar with in the past.

3. Mr. Lamb has a need for contact. He describes himself as a loner, with no close friends, with no one he feels comfortable to talk with fully about what's on his mind. Nevertheless, he has a need for contact; contact should not be too intimate to be satisfying.

4. The combination of a need for structure, the need to keep active, and the desire for social contact have led him to join a senior center, one located in his old neighborhood. The journey to and from this center is also elaborated. At the beginning of the interview series, he attended the center twice a week, increasing to three times a week thereafter.

5. Another important factor is his sense of "pride" which he openly states is important to him, and it is clear it is deeply felt. Pride is evidenced in his continuing participation in the work force ("to show myself I can"). It is evident in the way he talks about his continued good health ("The only problem I've had was an ulcer, but that's a lot better now"). Pride is evident in his independence and in his feelings about his lifetime of "hard work" ("Work provides dignity and self-respect"). Further, he is proud of his ability to keep his emotions checked and of his sense of duty and loyalty ("I did everything I could to give my children what they needed"). He is proud of his ability to manage. ("I have no credit cards. I don't buy anything until I can pay for it.")

The process of entering the senior center has actually been a lengthy one. His entry into the center was not the object of a strong desire. "It wasn't that I was lonesome. . . . I didn't have a particular desire to join." He heard about it about a year before he actually started attending. "I ran into a man I knew from work. He told me about it." This was on one of his elaborated "trips" downtown. Mr. Lamb didn't have a particularly strong reaction to the center. He says, "I'm glad I did it." He likes attending for the meal and the companionship and also because it is "something new." But his entry has been tentative. He doesn't know too many people, he says, and fewer names. He plays cards with a group of men, but only knows their first names.

While the center is in another neighborhood, it is not actually far, and occasionally Mr. Lamb will walk home. On his center days, he usually arrives between nine and ten, plays cards, listens to announcements, has lunch, and goes home. Occasionally, he hangs around hoping to play cards, but most individuals leave the center directly after lunch about twelve or twelve-thirty. The center world is left at the door of the center. He never meets with center people outside of the center. His afternoons follow two general patterns, either staying at home or taking trips. "Staying at the house" may include a walk around the neighborhood, to a son's house, or to do shopping or other errands. "Going out" may involve travel on public transportation to other neighborhoods. One afternoon a week, he works. On the days he goes out, the "return home" occurs at about three or four o'clock. Dinner is at about five. With the exception of his children, he rarely has visitors in the evening. He rarely goes out in the evening. He may talk on the phone (about twice a night), and spends most of the time watching TV, reading, or "dozing off."

Mr Lamb reviewed two days which he considered to be "typical." On the first day, he got up about seven. "I just wake up, no clock." He turns on the radio, washes, shaves, and dresses. "I don't take a bath as a rule." He usually attends eight o'clock Mass at one of two churches. "I may nod hello, but I don't know anyone." Done by nine, he has his breakfast ("usually oatmeal, sometimes eggs and toast . . . I've been trying to cut down on my coffee").

One day he went to the center, arriving at about ten, and played cards ("mixed and men only . . . I'll play with anybody who is there. . . . We usually don't talk much. . . . I'm not good at conversation"). From eleven-thirty to twelve-thirty he had his meal and listened to announcements. At about one he took a bus over to a shopping area and did his shopping for the week ("Often, if I need a lot of things, I'll go with my daughter"). Between three and five he took a walk. ("I don't remember where I go; I don't keep track. I think nothing of it.") At five he had dinner (rewarmed meat, leftover from his daughter's Sunday meal). At about six he turned on the TV (the news), and will turn it off at seven, "unless there's a Phillies game. If there's nothing on, I'll look at the paper." He goes to bed between eleven and twelve. He received no personal mail and only one call: "My son called for a chat." Also, "I tried to get my daughter but she wasn't home." This was a "fairly typical" or "average" day. "It's my normal state of life." In response to a question, he says, "I had no especially strong feelings during the day."

On the other day in question, he left home after breakfast to visit his daughter in another neighborhood. "I was there for about two hours. I didn't want to have lunch, but she insisted." On his way home, he made a detour to pay bills downtown. He came home about three. "I was alone here the whole evening." He had no phone calls in or out.

His sense of independence is important to him. "I know how to pass the time. . . . I can go around and do things. . . . I have no problems I can think of. . . . I don't want to live with my family." Independence consists of pride, work, and not bothering others. This latter attitude was present in his entry into the center: he started with the minimum engagement, slowly "feeling" his way in.

When he stays at home and "sits" in the evening with the TV or radio on, but without paying close attention, he says that it's "too late to start anything. I don't think about my sitting. There's nothing else to do, although I can find something if I search. I have things to do, painting and whatnot. . . . There's nothing I keep on a list, and they are all things I could skip if I want to.

"Sitting here is just something to do. It doesn't have any special meaning—just to pass the time. But I like it: there's nothing I'd rather be doing.

"With sitting—and with everything else—I'm free to follow my moods. There's no one else here to tell me what to do. . . .

"There was a poem I learned in school. 'Robinson Crusoe' . . . 'Monarch of all I survey . . . I finish my journey alone . . . Never hear the sweet music of speech . . . I start at the sound of my own.' . . .

"That's me, the monarch of all I survey. I'm my own boss, with no one to tell me what to do. I don't have to answer to anyone in particular. And I like it. After a point, you get used to your habits and patterns and you don't want to change, you don't want to live with people.

"I'm content. That's different from happy. I'm free of a lot of problems and I have enough money. My family took care of themselves and never asked me for nothing. . . .

"I never wanted to take a day off. I am always satisfied to go to work. Work was my major interest . . . I was lucky to have a job.

"I don't like to ask favors."

"I never took from the government."

There appears to be a great deal of "hard" emotion tied to these feelings. Independence, duty, responsibility, form a code for behavior. The softer, sentimental side ties Mr. Lamb to his home, a world of order and neatness. His attachment to Ireland as his home is still strong ("You never really get over that"). He feels proud that he kept his wife "at home" during her terminal illness. "Here, she was among her own. I never would have forgiven myself if she was hospitalized . . . she knew this was her place. She recognized everybody to the last day.

"In her illness, when her mind wasn't right, she wanted to go home, back to her town in Ireland. The need to go home is very strong in all of us."

LEVELS OF ACTIVITY AND PATTERNS OF SOCIAL CONTACT

The men we interviewed fall into several distinctive ranges in regard to their activities and social contacts. The ranges are based on a number of counts of activities and social contacts, and on some idea of whether activities are solitary or nonsolitary, as well as on impressionistic and unstructured material.

The popular image that old men living alone are isolated and inactive receives little support from our data. Twenty-three out of 45 men we considered were assessed as having at least what we label a "medium" level of social interaction. In fact, we were able to interview 2 men, ages 89 and 80, whose range of activities and social contacts was so extraordinary that we had to place them in a special category. Nevertheless, one must recall that much of our sample was drawn from senior centers, an important arena of formal participation and activity.

Because the men we saw undoubtedly represent an especially active group, we were careful, in estimating activity and isolation, to distinguish those men for whom participation in a senior center program was their *only* activity from those for whom participation was but one of many activities. The question is, then, is the senior center the focal activity? The measurement of this must come in terms of the activity of a person's whole life.

Participation in a senior center does not indicate that a person has a wide range of intimate contacts. To the contrary, some of the men we interviewed who were center attenders had few close contacts in or outside of the center. However, those for whom senior center participation represents *the* major daily activity tend to draw a number of their peripheral contacts from the center members. Those who have several social circles and for whom the senior center is but one also may have several spheres of peripheral contacts.

The scale we are using here to measure activity and social contacts is a rough one. While each level of activity and social contact is made up of specific counts (of nonsolitary activities, of the solitariness of social relations in activity circles, of the number of social circles and groups, of close friends and subjectively significant others, of peripheral acquaintances, etc.), the whole is somewhat impressionistic. Further, the activities and social contacts of the men we interviewed may be subject to considerable seasonal variation or daily and weekly fluctuations. However, the whole is useful in sketching out general activity patterns and social habits of those elderly men living alone we interviewed.

Very Low Range

Four men had a very low range of social contacts and nonsolitary activities. These men were part of no active social circles or groups. Three of the 4 men were limited in their ability to get out of the house due to physical disabilities. Two of the 4 had virtually no family, while the other 2 were estranged, to a greater or lesser extent, from their surviving family members. These men had no one they could identify as a close friend. In 3 of 4 cases, contacts with representatives of social service agencies were a significant portion of weekly or monthly contacts. In 2 cases, a whole day could pass without any conversation with another person at all. These men generally participated in no nonsolitary activities, although there were considerable stylistic differences in the solitary activities of these men. Daily activities generally consisted of watching TV, listening to the radio, reading, and "looking out the window."

While it is hard to generalize from a sample of 4, the condition of having very few contacts combined the factors of physical disability, a loss of family ties through death or dispute, and a personality structure which can accept, exist at, or even desire a very low level of social interaction. All of these men showed signs of severe mental stress which had the effect of limiting their desire for nonsolitary activities.

All have incomes of $460 a month or less and 3 have difficulties making ends meet. Two were never married, 1 man was divorced twice after a marriage in which his wife was described as having "turned against" him. All were extremely passive men who felt buffeted about by the world and felt they had little recourse to change things.

Low Range

Twelve men fit into this category. These men are associated with one or no social circles or activity groups. They have few (0–2) close, regular, subjectively significant affective ties to individuals, including kinsmen. They have some (0–5) nonregular but subjectively significant ties as well as some incidental or peripheral contacts (neighbors with whom they exchange greetings, shopkeepers and waiters they know, etc.). They rarely make or receive phone calls (less than four a week), nor do they often write or receive personal letters. Official contacts (landlord, social service representatives, etc.) make up a large percentage of weekly contacts.

For 6 of these men, attendance at a senior center is their major social activity, and many of their peripheral contacts derive from this. However, contacts do not persist outside of the center setting, and outside of this setting the actual number of contacts is low. Involvement with a senior center may amount to no more than three hours a day (maximum) and, because of low income, is oriented around the instrumental activity of receiving a hot meal at noon rather than to the more extensive center programs.

Several of the 6 men who do not attend a center have moderate health problems which may cause them a diminished capacity to get out of their house. Nevertheless, of these men, only 2 are involved with nonsolitary activities of any sort. Most are involved intensively with solitary activities. One of these men, Mr. Peters, is described above.

Several of the men in this group typically spend at least five hours a day watching television, while 2 men spend an equal amount of time listening to the radio or with the radio on as background. One man is a regular church attender. Another has active membership in a group that meets regularly. This man is a recent widower and there is a good chance that he will increase his level of activities as he "comes out" of his grief.

This man and 3 other widowers (of a total of 5 widowers in the group) were rated as having unsuccessfully reorganized their lives, while the remaining widower seems to have attained a satisfactory life-style despite a low level of nonsolitary activity.

One man of this group was divorced, while 6 have never married.

All of these men have few family contacts and little in the way of active support from family members. Only 6 of the 12 men have children, and 3 of these have significant strains in their relations with at least one of their children.

Medium Low Range

Seven men are in this category. This is similar to the low category in substance with the exception that these men have a higher degree of family interaction and have some kind of family support system to fall back on if necessary. Moreover, while 3 of these men have been ill in the recent past, they live in neighborhoods in which there is some active neighborly and family support for them.

Five of the 7 men are widowers, while 1 has been divorced in excess of thirty years. The remaining man was widowed in excess of fifty years. All 5 of the recent widowers have children; 4 of the 5 see their children regularly. Four of the 5 recent widowers were judged to have an unsuccessful reorganization in widowhood, while no judgment was made on 1 man due to lack of data. Most of these men seemed to have generally good relations with family members, and none appeared to have conflicts or long-term, festering disputes with relatives.

Income averaged about $400 a month for this group. Several men mentioned difficulties with living on their income and desired part-time employment opportunities.

Several showed symptoms of stress or anxiety, and 2 had had strokes and suffered slight disorientations. Four of the widowers still suffered from a deep sense of loss.

Four of these men received help with some tasks from children; the others received help, when needed, from neighbors and, in 1 case, from a sister.

Medium Range

Eight men had what may be described as a medium level of activity and contact. This was characterized by an association with one to three social circles or groups (church, senior center, senior housing unit, veterans' club, cointerest or hobby group) which require individual attendance. There is a qualitative difference from men of lower social interaction. The focus shifts from solitary to nonsolitary styles of interaction. Not only does the amount of activity increase, but the attitude toward it changes as well. In this "medium" range, most often attendance at some activity—for example, senior center or apartment activity—is not the primary activity, but rather is complemented by interest and participation in other activities as well. These individuals have some (1–3) close, regular, subjectively significant ties as well as a relatively large pool of marginal or intermediate contacts and at least a few (1–5) nonregular contacts which are subjectively significant. These men may make at least five phone calls a week and will receive personal mail. For 4 of the 8, attendance at a senior center was one of several associations with groups or social circles. None of these men were limited by health in their ability to get out of their home, although they may have had significant health problems.

Five of the 8 men are widowers, of whom 4 have children. Three men are divorced, all with children. Four of these men are attenders of a senior center. Most are attached to some other activity group as well which requires nonsolitary participation.

There was a relatively high incidence of family strife. Besides the divorces, 2 men had significant disputes with children. Most men, however, could rely on their children for help if needed.

Fewer of these men appeared to suffer from observed or admitted symptoms of mental difficulties, although the effects of loss for some men were profound. Of the 5 widowers, 4 were judged to have unsuccessfully reorganized their lives, while only 1 was judged as having successfully done so. The lives of all 3 divorced men still showed signs of ties to their former spouse.

All of these men—with one exception—spent a considerable amount of time during the day out of their home. Most were involved with at least one or two nonsolitary activities; most spent a good deal of time with other people. Yet the effects of widowhood and divorce were still felt.

Income for the men in this group averaged about $620 a month, close to the whole-group average of $627 a month. Interestingly, the income range was very wide, from $325 to $1,000 a month. Fewer men mentioned having actual financial problems (although several men did have them). Some men, however, were very much afraid of the double jeopardy of increasing inflation and governmental cutbacks.

Medium High Range

Six men were placed in this category. It is characterized by an association with two to three social circles or groups and several close, regular, subjectively significant ties (including family). These men also have several nonregular but subjectively significant ties. They have many marginal and intermediate contacts. An association with a circle or group consumes at least three hours a day, four days a week. There is usually regular use of the phone. A high level of contact is made despite any physical deficits.

Four of these men are widowers, while 2 were never married. Two of the widowers were judged to have successfully reorganized their lives since the death of the spouse, 1 was judged unsuccessful, while we did not have enough data about the other to make a judgment.

These men tend to seek out others and spend less time alone than individuals in groups with lower social contacts. Income averages about $577 a month with a range of about $300 to about $900 a month. These men may have periods of time they spend alone, for example, in the evening, but may compensate for this by the large amount and intensity of contact during other times. Only 1 man reports that he has disputes with family members, while 1 has no family to speak of, and the remainder appear to have generally good relations with kin.

High Range

Six men have association with several (at least two) activity circles or groups; association with one of these circles or groups may take all day at least one or two days a week. Each man has four or more close, regular, subjectively significant ties. Each spends part of every day with someone, excluding sleeping time. They tend to be with people more than they are alone. They have several lesser but subjectively significant ties and many marginal contacts. They know a lot of different people. They often have some position of responsibility, be it self-appointed or assigned (a job, volunteer work) in which they are depended on for something. These men usually have close and continuous contact with relatives. They are usually out of the house daily. Only 1 man in this category regularly attended a senior center. Income is generally high. Excluding the 1 man who still worked and whose income was in excess of $30,000 a year, the remainder had an average income of over $1,100 a month (the range was wide, $450 to $1,750 a month, but obviously mostly on the high side). There were no complaints of inadequate income in this group. Since income was generally adequate, paid employment was not looked upon as a goal, and rather, as we have mentioned, volunteer work was common (although, in fact, 1 man was still working). Most of the men appear not to suffer from depression or anxiety.

Five men are widowers and 1 never married. All of the widowers were judged to have successfully reorganized their lives after the death of the wife. Four of the 5 widowers have children. The 1 widower without children had extensive contacts, close relations with existing family, and a girlfriend. The never-married man also had extensive social networks with long histories of ties. Two men reported ongoing disputes with family members.

Very High Range

Two extraordinary men were in this category. Not everyone can be like this. Both men made second careers out of volunteer work after retirement and are associated with several committees, groups, and organizations in active work. Both know extraordinary numbers of people, both are in good health. For 1 man (age 80), his current association with five major charity projects was a continuation of his interest in them from an earlier age. The second man (age 89) started a second career upon retirement from his business which consists of volunteer work in religious, political, and charitable associations.

One man was not classified, since we felt we did not know him well enough.

Levels of Activity: Conclusions

We can draw the following conclusions about activities from the above classifications.

Poor health is related to low activity but not deterministically so. Many of the more active men learn to live with symptoms and minor disabilities. For many of the more active, the level of activity is periodic, depending on health at a given moment.

Low income is generally correlated with lower activity and high income with high activity, but not deterministically so.

Level of education is also correlated, in general, with level of activity and contact, but not deterministically so. The men with the most contact and activity ("high, "very high") had attained the highest educational levels.

Inability to successfully reorganize one's life after the death of one's spouse is, in general, correlated with a lower ("medium," "medium low," "low") level of activity. Those widowers with a higher level of activity had mostly passed through their grief and had established a new life for themselves.

Being alone and performing solitary activities is characteristic of all men, but is less characteristic of those men with a higher level of social contacts and activities.

Attendance at senior centers is not characteristic of men with the highest ("high," "very high") ratings except in an executive or volunteer capacity. Center attendance is flavored by a whole life-style. Men who attend centers may either make attendance one activity out of many or the central formal activity of a day.

Loneliness is correlated with low activity. That is to say, the men at the lower range of activity and contact levels report greater loneliness, but as we have noted, it is the experience of bereavement which causes loneliness and which may also be related to relative inactivity.

CHAPTER 6

Loneliness

In this chapter we explore the topic of loneliness. Our goals here are two in number. First, we describe the loneliness felt by our informants, and second, we relate it to issues in the growing literature on loneliness.

There has been a considerable amount of attention paid by social scientists recently to the topic of loneliness in an effort to counter a long dry spell in research in this area. Loneliness is a feeling or experience which seems to afflict each individual at one time or another. Loneliness is often viewed by many as an acute condition particularly associated with old age. Our own findings refute this rather stereotyped vision of the "old age." Rather, we relate the loneliness experienced by the older men we interviewed to a set of specific circumstances.

The term "loneliness" describes both an *experience* and a *feeling* or *emotion*. In the way it is used it is therefore like many other sorts of emotions. Loneliness can thus be a very specific, bounded experience, for example, as described by the statement "I miss X, I am lonely for X who has gone away but will be returning soon." Or loneliness can be an emotion on a grand scale as described by the statement "I was lonely during my twenties." The former may be considered *specific* loneliness and the latter *general* loneliness. Specific loneliness is often tied to the immediate experience of the *emotion* of loneliness, a deeply felt, intense or throbbing emotion which alters normal perceptions, notions of time and of social procedures. Interestingly, it would appear that specific loneliness, the emotion of loneliness, is very difficult to recall retrospectively (see below).

THE FIRST QUESTION

In an initial or early interview with the older men living alone, most commonly the first one, we asked informants to rate their own loneliness. These responses were grouped into the three general categories used by Townsend (1968) in his pioneering work on isolation and desolation. These ratings represent the sorts of responses that individuals give to the questions "Are you ever lonely?" and "If so, how often?" grouped into three convenience categories.

TABLE 6.1
Self-Rated Loneliness

In response to a direct question, informant states that he is lonely . . .	Number of individuals
"often	6
"sometimes"	19
"rarely or never"	17
	42
(no data, 5)	

The definitions we are using here are as follows. "Often" pertains to loneliness experienced in high or moderate intensity at least twice a week, and/or indicates the fear of experiencing intense loneliness is active and present. "Sometimes"—loneliness felt in various intensities, one or two times a month to twice a week. "Rarely or never"—loneliness experienced less than twice a month or low intensity, or not at all.

One can conclude that while loneliness is a *severe* problem for several of the men, for the vast majority it is *not a severe* problem.

At the end of the sequence of interviews, we were able to make another rating of loneliness, which we call observer-rated loneliness, which represents the summing up of the interviewer's perception of the loneliness experienced by each informant. These are given in table 6.2.

TABLE 6.2
Observer-Rated Loneliness

In retrospect, observer notes that informant appears to be lonely . . .	Number of individuals
"often"	11
"sometimes"	22
"rarely or never"	10
	43
(no data, 4)	

The estimation of loneliness here has been revised upward. Reasons for an observer to label an informant as "lonely" are varied. For example, due to the "unfolding" nature of the relationship between informant and interviewer, it may come about that late in the interview series the informant decides to describe his loneliness, which he has failed to describe to that point. Or, alternatively, an informant may continue to deny an overall sense of loneliness, but he may, through his statements, clearly state that he misses people or admit to periods of "feeling low" from missing people. Or an interviewer may receive a strong subjective impression derived from his perception of an individual's conscious or unconscious presentation of himself that he is lonely. While the category of observer-rated loneliness is clearly a medley of reasons, it does represent one conceptual entity, that of the observer's evaluation of the informant in the context of all that he has learned about him. "Self-awareness of loneliness" can never be a consistent theme in either self-rated or observer-rated loneliness. Those individuals who rate themselves, initially, as lonely must have an awareness of it; while those who do not rate themselves as lonely may in fact not be lonely, or they may be lonely and not admit to it, or they may be lonely and not be aware of it. Similarly, observer-rated loneliness may be a distillation of a process in which the awareness of loneliness appears over time, or it may represent the observer's agreement or disagreement with the informant's self-evaluation. There is thus a discrepancy between self-rated and observer-rated loneliness. This reflects our growing ability through the course of the interviews to come to know our informants.

It should not be thought that the observer's ratings of informants supersede those made by the informants themselves. Both are important and both are correct in the sense that they are purposeful evaluations of a given situation. Statements informants give about themselves should always be valued. Individual statements should be placed in the context of whole patterns. We try to assess the reasons that people give the answers they do, one factor in attempting to get an accurate and meaningful picture of a life.

ANALYSIS

In our analysis of the loneliness experienced by these men, a number of distinctive patterns appear. Before proceeding to a discussion of these patterns, we wish to draw attention to a number of issues which have been raised to date in literature on loneliness.

Theoretical Background

One of the difficulties in understanding loneliness is that it is often conceptually confused with or at least closely associated with a variety of related but distinct topics such as isolation, desolation, loss, depression, sadness, boredom, desperation, estrangement, or alienation, all of which have an unpleasant flavor akin to that of loneliness.

In our own view, loneliness is related closely to loss, or to its opposite, failure to gain, and is tied to stages of development during a life course. Among the men we interviewed, loss played a large—but not total—part in the experience of loneliness.

There are other views. For example, a generalist view is taken by Sullivan, a psychoanalyst, who defines loneliness as "the exceedingly unpleasant and driving experience connected with inadequate discharge of the need for human intimacy" (1953:290, quoted by Weiss 1973:15), a non-situation-specific definition. Similarly, the dictionary defines loneliness as the noun form of "lonely," "without company." However, we view the issues of company per se as actually having little to do with the experience of loneliness. Company per se is really a question of isolation, which, in our view, is a notion suitable to the measurement of the degree of connectedness with others, on the basis of whatever objective measures are used. Isolation can be measured by any number of objective scores or counts, such as the number and duration of contacts with others, the number of meals shared with others, and this in turn can be compared against a norm of some contrast.

Feelings of depression, sadness, boredom, which may be associated with the experience of loneliness, also have no intrinsic association with isolation.

Thus the relationship between isolation and loneliness is clear. As Townsend (1968) and others have noted, isolation may be viewed by the isolate as either pleasurable or unpleasurable. There is, therefore, no necessary connection of isolation to loneliness. The lonely may equally well be found as isolates or as active members of groups (Heltsley and Powers 1975; Riesman, Glazer, and Denney 1961).

However, it is very difficult to dismiss from our minds the notion that isolation and loneliness are somehow connected. This probably has to do with the idea that most loneliness is often experienced in relative isolation (sometimes when one feels lonely, one wants to be alone); that loneliness can be overcome (most people experience and overcome loneliness at some time in their lives, especially at a younger time); and that the more one sees others, the greater the chance that one will find a person or situation to assuage or reduce one's experience of loneliness. One must question, however, if this formula will be *as* successful for an older man who has lost his spouse of many years and experiences loneliness intensely and often as for a younger person.

Another difficulty in dealing with loneliness and its associated emotions and conditions is that they are difficult to measure or discuss objectively. Above, for example, we used a number of extremely simple counts, one based on informants' statements about their loneliness, and one on observers' notions about informants. A more simple set of measures would be difficult to imagine, but any number of technical objections could be introduced to those we used. Not only is loneliness difficult to quantify and compare, isolation, defined operationally as an interactive rather than an intrapsychic phenomenon, is also difficult to measure, and many measures are nothing more than gross counts of interaction (see, for example,

Ferraro and Barresi 1982). Townsend (1968:260), in discussing the social isolation of the elderly, described difficulties in providing an "operational definition" of social isolation and in particular linked the problems of developing objective measures of social isolation to difficulties in quantifying the *intensity, range,* and *kind* of social isolation. He defined these problems in respect to a variety of situational and structural schemes (for example, the problem of measuring the effects of visiting one club five times a week or five clubs one time a week each). It is, of course, very difficult to imagine how one would deal with this "one-five" problem, except either to make a macroclassification which would subsume both or refine categories so as to clearly distinguish the two. Or they can be understood in respect to the particular meaning they have in the life of a social actor.

The difficulties in measuring social isolation and social contact have corresponding difficulties in the measurement of loneliness. In order to discuss these, we may use as a springboard the notions of *intensity, range,* and *kind.*

Loneliness has a quality of *intensity.* A person who experiences loneliness may have more or less internal pain and longing (Hartog 1980), and loneliness may "come on" and recede over time. An individual may feel herself able to play an active part in controlling the intensity of loneliness (as in, "If I get out, I don't feel it as much," frequently expressed by some of the men we saw). Or a person may feel passive and helpless to diminish the intensity of loneliness.

The *range* of loneliness refers to its situational location. Is it experienced all the time, or is it episodic? Is it triggered by certain conditions? Finally, *kind* of loneliness refers to the cause. Most of the widowers we interviewed, for example, traced a large part of the loneliness which they experienced to their loss. Social actors, as well as observers of social actors, make discriminations and construct theories not only as to the source of loneliness but also as to appropriate, available, and possible ways of handling loneliness and getting over the pain.

Let us examine each of these in more detail.

Kind

Several schemes have been proposed in order to clarify and categorize kinds of loneliness. Weiss (1973) recognizes two sorts of loneliness, "the loneliness of emotional isolation" caused by the loss of a significant other, and "the loneliness of social isolation" caused by disengagement from a social network. Both forms are situational; one relating to the loss of a significant individual, the other to the loss or the separation from a group. Weiss contrasts those suffering from loneliness from those suffering from depression, finding that the lonely are driven to find others and to rid themselves of distress while depressives surrender to depression. Weiss (1973:19) has also found that while it is relatively easy to remedy the loneliness of social isolation with access to a new social network, the loneliness of emotional isolation is more difficult to dissolve unless a new relationship is found, one which approximates the intensity of the lost one.

Rubenstein and Shaver (1980, 1982) analyzed a set of 3,500 responses from an all-age group to a questionnaire concerning loneliness. They found that responses concerning both *feelings* associated with loneliness and self-reported *reasons* for loneliness corresponded to some degree to Weiss' distinction between the loneliness of emotional isolation and the loneliness of social isolation. They concluded that the loneliness of emotional isolation represents many sorts of emotional reactions to loneliness such as desperation and also represents self-reported reasons for loneliness such as being unattached. The loneliness of social isolation, they found, corresponds to such emotions as impatient boredom and to such self-reported items as alienation.

Weiss' dichotomy is useful not only for its simplicity but because many other schemes which have been developed to sort out kinds of loneliness can be reduced to it. Weiss' dichotomy stresses an *involuntary* or situational cause for loneliness and the *voluntary* nature of a solution to such problems. Hartog has also discussed the voluntary and involuntary dimensions of loneliness based on a psychodynamic view of human action. Hartog describes various sorts of voluntary "individualistic loneliness, more aptly called solitude or aloneness and sometimes termed alienation" (1980:23). Examples of this sort of lonely person are culture brokers, hybrid professionals, and others who exist at or across boundaries. It would appear, according to Hartog, that nonconformists of all sorts try to deny their innate loneliness by their own voluntary, individualistic withdrawal from society. However, Hartog views such withdrawal and its ensuing (or causative) loneliness as voluntary, while he also ties these to primitive psychological drives which he seems to view as involuntary.

While there is room for greater clarity here, his emphasis on a "voluntary type of individualistic loneliness" is significant. First, voluntary, individualistic withdrawal from society is related to issues of social participation and isolation in old age, specifically, the disengagement phenomenon (Cumming and Henry 1961). This hypothesis concerns the withdrawal of the elderly individual from society and of society from the elderly individual. Moreover, a related notion—voluntary, individualistic marginality—may be characteristic of never-married older men, men who for whatever reason cannot bring themselves to enter into mainstream social life. It is therefore unfortunate that Hartog has little to say on the topic of loneliness and old age.

In his discussion of "isolation, desolation, and loneliness in old age," Townsend analytically distinguishes loneliness from social isolation. In this approach, social isolation is an objective phenomenon, albeit one which is difficult to measure, and loneliness is an unpleasant emotional reaction to the circumstances of social isolation. Townsend (1968:260) distinguishes four types of isolation from society:

1. Peer-contrasted isolation, or isolation from society in comparison with one's contemporaries.
2. Generation-contrasted isolation, or isolation from society in comparison with younger people.
3. Desolation (age-related isolation), or isolation from society in respect to activities and social relations held earlier in life.
4. Preceding cohort isolation, or isolation from society in comparison with the preceding generation of old people.

Most of the Townsend paper is concerned with the first form of isolation. He concludes that living alone and other manifestations of peer-contrasted isolation do not in themselves produce loneliness. In his view, loneliness in old age seems to be accounted for, to a large extent, by widowhood and temporal proximity to it. He concludes that there is no single cause for loneliness, but rather when loneliness is viewed in terms of the life cycle, it is attributable to age-related isolation (desolation, the third type of social isolation). Loneliness caused by social desolation, then, is prompted by losses of loved ones.

How would the notion of social desolation as a cause of loneliness fit with Weiss' dichotomy of emotional and social isolation? For Townsend, loneliness is situational and involuntary (due to desolation), while it is related to events at a given life stage (widowhood in late life). The loneliness of "social desolation" would appear to subsume both parts of Weiss' dichotomy, since desolation refers to the distinction between the present and what has gone on earlier in life, as do both of Weiss' constructs.

Another constituent element distinguishing a type of loneliness is noted by Sadler and Johnson (1980), who describe loneliness as an experience involving an acute feeling which constitutes a distinct form of self-awareness.

This painful self-awareness is created by a "disjunction" (1980:39) in reality as it is perceived by an individual. Such a disjunction may exist on each of the several analytical levels used to discuss human behavior. Thus they recognize that loneliness may exist across four dimensions, each constituting a distinctive kind of loneliness. For them, *cosmic* loneliness corresponds to a sense of estrangement from reality as a whole, from God, or from a person's perceived destiny. (Cosmic loneliness may be somewhat akin to Erikson's late-life despair.) *Cultural* loneliness refers to a sense of estrangement from commonly accepted values and ideals. *Social* loneliness is derived from a sense of exile, rejection, ostracism, or retirement from social institutions or organized relations. *Interpersonal* loneliness represents the experience of separation from a significant other.

Social and interpersonal loneliness would seem to represent the core of Weiss' and Townsend's ideas, and would refer to the emotions attached to loss, change, and separation. Cosmic and cultural loneliness are not represented in the schemes of either Weiss or Townsend, but appear to be similar to Hartog's cultural and idiosyncratic estrangement. (A major difference, however, is that Hartog's psychological approach would ultimately tend to collapse both of these categories.)

Lopata (1973b) enumerated kinds of loneliness described to her by widows "who explain that loneliness is a major problem" for them:

1. Loneliness which represents a desire to continue an interaction with someone who is no longer available.
2. Loneliness derived from no longer feeling as if one is an object of love.
3. Loneliness due to an absence of anyone to care for or to be a recipient of love.
4. Loneliness for a relationship similar in depth to a lost relationship.
5. Loneliness for another person within the dwelling unit.
6. Loneliness or unhappiness due to no one to share work with.
7. Loneliness or homesickness for former life-style or activities.
8. Loneliness as alienation due to a drop in status.
9. Loneliness as a result of loss of someone, such as a husband, which can have repercussions in interactions with others and can become compounded, thus increasing loneliness.
10. Loneliness compounded by an inability to make new friends or the lack of skills needed to build new relations.
11. Loneliness as a composite of any of the above.

In examining these more closely, we notice that they can be grouped into categories which resemble the loneliness of emotional isolation and that of social isolation. Thus points 1, 2, 3, and 4 correspond to emotionally based loneliness, while 5, 6, 7, and 8 correspond to socially based loneliness. Of interest are points 2 and 3, which deal with the loss of being needed.

Points 9 and 10 refer to the relationship between social and emotional loneliness. Loss of a loved one may not only cause the loneliness of emotional isolation, but, ramifying out, may lead to the loneliness of social isolation.

In reviewing the various typologies mentioned above, it is apparent that they can, for the most part, be reduced to the distinction between the loneliness of emotional isolation (the loss of a loved individual) and the loneliness of social isolation (the loss of social network). One exception to this is the place of such elements as "cosmic" or "large scale" loneliness, really a kind of existential estrangement. It is not clear how this would fit into Weiss' scheme or even if it is a commonly experienced type of emotion.

A rather distinctive approach is taken in the work of Peplau and Caldwell (1978) and Perlman and Peplau (1981, 1982). The approach taken there is a "cognitive" one and is contrasted with other approaches such as those described as existential (Moustakas 1961; Von Witzleben 1958), sociological (Riesman et al. 1961), psychodynamic (Fromm-Reichman 1959; Sullivan 1953), and interactionist (Weiss 1973). In the cognitive approach loneliness is collapsed so that distinctions between various "types of loneliness" are blurred and a new focus emerges: "*Loneliness* is the unpleasant experience that occurs when a person's network of social relations is deficient in some important way, either quantitatively or qualitatively" (Perlman and Peplau 1981:31–32). Loneliness is therefore viewed as a "discrepancy between one's desired and achieved levels of social relations" (1981:32). The loneliness of emotional and social isolation are no longer distinguished as the focus shifts the difference between actual interaction vs. desired interaction. Perlman and Peplau note advantages to this approach: it takes into account the actual level of social contact which an individual needs, isolating comprehensively factors contributing to loneliness. Further, it takes into account "cognitive processes" such as causal attribution and perceived control, which mediate deficiency and response.

Perlman and Peplau (1981:37–45) note several antecedents of loneliness, such as changes in a person's actual social relationships or in her or his desired social relationships. Widowhood is an example of the former, while age-derived personal changes are an example of the latter. Quality and quantity of relations, personal factors, cultural and situational elements, may all contribute to reducing or increasing loneliness. Perlman and Peplau claim that the discrepancy between real and desired relations is often viewed and labeled by people as loneliness, and that several factors affect ("modulate") such self-labeling (1981:45). Self-labeling as "lonely" may bring out in others a particular reaction. Finally, means of coping with loneliness includes changing the desired level of social contact, the actual level, or one's perception of the two together so that the gap between them is narrowed. Adaptation, task choice, changed standards, altering meaning, are all methods of coping with loneliness. This set of coping strategies is essentially similar to those listed by Clark and Anderson as pertinent to successful late-life adaptation in general.

There is little doubt that this approach is a powerful one. First, it casts a wide explanatory net. It not only deals with the variety of classifications which have been used in classifying the experience of loneliness, it also enlarges the notion to include all relational deficits. Second, and equally important, it deals with loneliness as a process with "antecedents," with a core experience, and with adaptation and adjustment.

In thinking about this view in terms of the old men we interviewed, a number of areas come to mind in which this approach needs clarification.

First, there is the area of self-labeling or self-attribution. Perlman and Peplau note that it is often difficult to decide if one is lonely or not, yet their definition of loneliness hinges on this: "As indicated earlier, the discrepancy between desired and achieved social relations is typically perceived by the individual and labelled as loneliness" (1981:46). Some individuals may steadfastly deny they are lonely, depending on a variety of psychological factors. For some, to think of one's self as lonely is stigmatic and may be avoided. While people may strongly deny their loneliness and even not be conscious of it, they may act in a way so that others may perceive them to be and believe them to be lonely. To be perceived as, treated as, and reacted to as if one is a lonely person may therefore be independent of one's belief that one is or is not lonely. This was the case with several men we interviewed and is one component in the disparity between our self-rated and observer-rated categories above. How does this system deal with such individuals who claim they are not lonely and never have been, but who give all the outward signs of being so?

Related to this is the notion of "need" as used in reference to the desired level of social activity. It is true that many people can think of "ideal" social situations and contrast these with a current real situation which satisfies some components of what is theoretically ideal, but not others. There may often be a discrepancy between what people conceive of and what they settle for. This might be especially marked in the case of widowhood, in which there may exist a model for a good relationship in what a person had had. People may settle for a new and somewhat satisfying relationship which only approximates the ideal.

Also, in the case of several of the widowers we interviewed, their marriage was viewed as ideal, this view possibly enhanced by retrospective sanctification. Loss of a spouse left a tremendous void. The ideal was not a theoretical ideal, but a real ideal, illuminated by a thousand specific details. Clearly, such an ideal can never be recovered unless the many details can be symbolically reduced into a replaceable, substitutable few. While Lopata (1979) suggests that retrospective sanctification is a mechanism which enables a person to psychologically disengage from another, for some men it sets up an ideal which is often unachievable. That retrospective sanctification is a mechanism of disengagement which presumably helps one overcome a loss does not square, of course, with the low remarriage rate after age 55. Thus "need" can be viewed as a function of an ideal as in the difference between "desired" and "actual" social relation, or it can be viewed as a more minimal and more minimally satisfying construct.

Problems with the issue of need and with the definition of "ideal" social relations lead us to another question. The system discussed above cannot really account for differences in the intensity of loneliness without reference, ultimately, to intrapsychic concerns. Perlman and Peplau distinguish between events that precipitate the onset of loneliness from those that predispose individuals to become lonely. Precipitators include changes in social relations, while predisposing factors include the normal quantity and quality of social relations and personality variables. The experience of the intensity of loneliness and consequently the mastering of it can only be viewed as directly related to one's personality, yet personality is not singled out by Perlman and Peplau as especially significant but is reformed as variables such as "shyness," "self-esteem," "social skills," all constructs which certainly have antecedent factors.

Finally, what does this system make of "cosmic" loneliness, the feeling of estrangement and alienation of person from some conceptualized world? Clearly, this exists and it exists as a relational deficit. Either person cannot be satisfied or world cannot be satisfying. Under the scheme of Perlman and Peplau, this type of "loneliness" would not be included since it does not involve "social relations." Or perhaps it could be subsumed as a deficit in the relationship between elements of self and other. One question we might raise in regard to cosmic loneliness concerns its occurrence over the life span. Would it occur more frequently among younger people who note a deficit between actual social relations and desired social relations which have not yet been experienced and are therefore prospective? Or would it be more characteristic of an older person's experiences in evaluating retrospectively the actuality of social relations in comparison with what should have been?

We must view this approach taken by Perlman and Peplau as a particularly valuable and complete analysis of loneliness, which sees only one "kind" of loneliness, that of a relational deficit. We have noted several areas in which the system could use clarification. We do agree, however, that the relational deficit approach does explain much of the loneliness experienced by the old men we interviewed.

Intensity

Loneliness may be felt more or less intensely. As an experience—as a captivating framework for living—or as an emotion, loneliness can absorb the entire person profoundly or it may lurk, most hidden, as a nagging reminder of a state of being a person wishes to forget or deny. One property of intense loneliness discussed by Weiss (1973:10) is that experiences of loneliness are often difficult or impossible to recall retrospectively (see also Sullivan 1953 and Fromm-Reichman 1959 for similar perspectives). One might assume, Weiss notes, that the frightening intensity of the pain of loneliness is difficult to recall because this difficulty must function as some sort of protective measure, an "active rejection" of or a defensive response to loneliness (1973:10). Loneliness "is so frightening and uncanny in character that they [those who have suffered loneliness] try to dissociate the memory of what it was like and even the fear of it" (Fromm-Reichman 1959:6, quoted in Weiss 1973:10).

According to Weiss, while people find loneliness difficult to recall, they also tend to dissociate periods of loneliness from their "actual" personality. Some of his subjects noted retrospectively that they were "not themselves" when they were lonely in the past. It would appear that intense loneliness can be so penetrating and so disrupting that the normal social self is transposed and disarranged. The loss of a loved one is felt inside as an internal loss (Parkes 1972), the pain of which is often observable on the outside through changes in demeanor, appearance, and other markers of the internal state. Associated, as Henry (1980) has pointed out, is extreme personal vulnerability; Henry concludes that loneliness and vulnerability are inseparable.

As such, a raw wound is open to self-scrutiny (self-awareness, pain, constant longing), and to the scrutiny of others (for sympathy, pity, or contempt). If, as George (1980), Weiss (1973), and Perlman and Peplau note, loneliness is a stigmatizing experience, such vulnerability may be especially crippling. Loneliness can be so gripping that one cannot hide one's emotions and vulnerability. The ability to control emotions and to not permit them to interfere with or "slop over" onto the normal, ongoing events is, of course, an important attribute of social life in American culture. Loneliness challenges normalcy. Loneliness can result in painful self-perception and self-awareness (Sadler and Johnson 1980). Intense loneliness tends to dichotomize the internal and external world as a person feels unable to respond to the demands of the outside world. But, at the same time, intense loneliness demonstrates the power of outside events (loss) to control or affect the events of the inner world. Indeed, Henry (1980) views vulnerability-through-loss as one important tool society has in order to "bring men to heel." Any illusions about an individual's power are shattered by loneliness and loss. Often, in situations of grief and loss, the theme of blame (Peplau and Caldwell 1978) or anger (Parkes 1972:78) emerges. At the very least, loneliness indicates to an individual the degree of his dependence on others.

While the above remarks concern primarily intense loneliness, the experience of the most intense loneliness, at least among those men we interviewed, is relatively rare. This brings us to an important point: it appears that the intensity of loneliness may be correlated with the duration of its experience. That is to say, those men who experienced loneliness "often" also experienced loneliness of greater intensity; those who experienced loneliness "sometimes" generally experienced it in moderate intensity; while the same trend extended to those who experienced it rarely or never. Here another dichotomous theme emerges; there is an essential difference between intense, oft-occurring loneliness, which is all-consuming and all-involving, and less intense, periodic loneliness, which is episodically *bracketed*. The former rarely permits life to continue as usual, while the latter may be managed so as to permit social life to go on.

The time factor is also significant in understanding the intensity of loneliness. If loneliness is, for example, induced through the loss of a loved one such as a spouse, the intensity of the loneliness may diminish with the passage of time. As we have mentioned, Bowlby (1980), in his study of loss, has isolated four phases in mourning the loss of a spouse. Characteristic of the latter phases are the persistence of the relationship in the mind and life of the survivor, the suffering of diminished physical and mental health, and "emotional loneliness" (according to Bowlby the equivalent of Weiss' [1973] loneliness of emotional isolation). Such loneliness is characterized by Bowlby as "deep and peristent" and difficult to mitigate. Reorganization, as part of the mourning process, may eventually lead to diminished loneliness. Townsend (1968:273) discusses two samples of widows (one British, one Danish) which demonstrate an initial drop in the number of widows who feel lonely "often" with the passage of time since the death of the spouse. (Responses were grouped at intervals from zero to four, five to nine, and ten to nineteen years after the death of a spouse.) Unfortunately, the living arrangements of the respondents were not given. Also, the data show an increase in the number of widows who feel lonely "often" with the passage of twenty years or more since the death of their husband. Moreover, there is no similar drop off for those who feel lonely "sometimes."

Among the men we interviewed, self-rated loneliness was also used by us as a significant indicator of successful or unsuccessful life reorganization. Men with the most intense experience of loneliness (generally those who experienced it most often) and whose loneliness was focused primarily around the deceased spouse were generally men whose life reorganization was least successful.

Persistent loneliness (either as currently intense or currently diminished) is one often-occurring feature of the loss of a spouse in old age. Intensely felt loneliness may diminish with the passage of time. Some of its meaning, the immediacy of the lost person about which the loneliness speaks, may be lost. The lost person may even be replaced by another, or the attachment may be diffused by its transference onto a specialized, deeply personalized environment such as a home. Nevertheless, it would appear that attachments to the lost loved one, now represented by memories, feelings, and objects will often become permanent fixtures within the life of the survivor, and such incorporation is part of reorganization after the death of a spouse.

Townsend elaborates upon one way in which the time factor is of crucial importance in the experience of loneliness. He notes,

> For younger persons time "heals" in the sense that there is a chance they will remarry or else replace the close relative or friend who has been lost with another relative in the extended family or with a new friend. For older persons this process of healing also occurs . . . but it is normally less rapid and substitutes tend to fall short of former intimates in the roles they play in the lives and affections of old people. (1968:275)

Range

The "range" of loneliness refers to the range of social situations in which loneliness is induced or experienced. As we have mentioned, loneliness may be experienced as continuous, as episodic, or as a rare event. Range is related to frequency and intensity, but both of these are characteristic of the experience of loneliness itself. Range, however, refers to those external situations or *settings* (Matthews 1979) which usually induce or trigger loneliness. Loneliness may therefore be said to occur over a *range* of significant settings.

There appears to be no literature on such a topic per se, although there is some on trigger mechanisms for grief and mourning.

Among the men we interviewed, the following events were listed as causes of loneliness, especially loneliness felt *for* a spouse or other departed relations.

1. Anniversaries, birthdays, special days.
2. Viewing photographs and personal possessions.
3. Coming home to an empty house.
4. "Moods," usually experienced at home (for several men, "moods" suddenly and inexplicably change, leading to loneliness).

5. "The realization that I am alone" (painful self-reflection).
6. Longing for or feeling the absence of children.
7. "Missing a warm body in bed."

Range and Isolation

While we have indicated that isolation and loneliness have little to do with one another, when loneliness is specific—the longing for a specific but unavailable person—it becomes closely tied to isolation. Events, procedures, and activities typically performed with someone else are now performed alone, and the self-awareness which accompanies such solitude is painful. The world is radically altered as the habitual is no longer so. Development of a new unself-conscious world of habit is necessary. It is isolation, often in the private domestic sphere, which induces loneliness. Outside, involved with others, a person may be absorbed and drawn out of his private world. "Coming home to an empty house" (often cited by men as an especially lonely experience) is said by some to shock them with the realization of who one is—that one is alone—and of who one once was—a member of a couple that no longer exists.

Though we know, then, that loneliness and isolation are not intrinsically intertwined, isolation can provoke loneliness when isolation is not seen as a habitual state of being and is painfully contrasted with one's current state. It is this comparison between the present and the past which is a central theme in the range of loneliness listed above. Depending on the individual, the range of situations which trigger loneliness is varied, and depends on each individual's meaning worlds. It appears to be the experience—alone—of habitual events once experienced in common that triggers loneliness.

All of the activities mentioned above are experienced individually and in private. As such, all are related to a temporary degree of isolation. The moods of loneliness acquired under isolated circumstances can carry over into social situations, but the men we interviewed rarely reported that "being with other people" made them lonely.

Loneliness Among the Elderly

"The elderly" have a stereotyped image of "being lonely." This image is highlighted by the findings of the Louis Harris survey on aging in America which found that while 12 percent of those in the 65 and older sample felt that loneliness was a "very serious" problem for them personally, 60 percent of the general, all-age sample felt loneliness to be a "very serious" problem for most elderly people (Louis Harris and Associates 1975; in the 1981 restudy these percentages were similar). While the popular image of old people as lonely is very persistent, many studies, including those of Louis Harris, have found that the elderly as a group do not seem to suffer overly from loneliness. Similarly, Townsend (1968) examined data concerning loneliness from three national surveys of the elderly. In the U.S. sample (N = 2,417), 9 percent were lonely "often," 21 percent "sometimes," and 70 percent "rarely or never." In a study of rural elderly, Kivett (1979) reported that 15.5 percent were "often," 41.8 percent were "sometimes," and 42.6 percent were "never" lonely. The question arises of how these figures might compare with those of loneliness experienced at other ages (cf. Revenson and Johnson 1984).

REASONS FOR LONELINESS AMONG OLDER MEN LIVING ALONE

The cause of loneliness experienced by the men we interviewed is, probably, the existence of relational deficits of various sorts. The predominant form of loneliness is that derived from the loss of a spouse. Other important causes are the loss of a parent, loneliness caused by a strained or altered relationship with a child, and, least frequently, a non-relation-specific, general feeling of estrangement, or "cosmic" loneliness.

Loss of a Spouse

The most important cause of loneliness for the men we interviewed was the loss of a spouse. This loneliness was especially characteristic of the 14 men who had unsuccessful life reorganization. This group of 14 tended to rate itself as lonely "often" (5 men) and "sometimes"

(8 men), rather than "never." The rating of loneliness by observers tended to agree with this evaluation with the exception that 2 men were evaluated upward (greater loneliness) and 1 downward.

Among these men, loneliness is an important theme which weaves itself through their lives. It is closely associated with bereavement. The intensity of loneliness can be great, as can the range of triggering situations. These men's descriptions of their bouts of loneliness were poignant. Despite this, some of these men had developed techniques to specifically combat loneliness. Most common was the attempt to get one's mind off loneliness through activity: walking, doing at-home projects, watching TV, or "getting out." Others used a will-power method, attempting to force themselves, internally, to control the overwhelming feeling. Interestingly, none of these solutions involved contact with specific others. That other individuals were not specifically sought out by lonely men is in line with the notion that bereaved attachment to the deceased spouse is a factor in the loneliness. Sometimes emotional outbursts—especially crying but also shaking and loss of control—were necessary to draw focus away from ongoing loneliness back to some "normal framework."

Among the 11 men who were judged to have successfully reorganized their lives, 4 rated themselves as lonely "sometimes" and 7 as lonely "rarely or never." Observer ratings agree with these evaluations in all but 3 cases, in which the perceived amount of loneliness was reevaluated upward. There, the lonely sought out particular individuals to help overcome their feelings.

Loss of a Parent

This was a theme which appeared almost exclusively among the never-married men, although it was mentioned by one divorced man as part of the cause of his loneliness.

Among the never-married men, 5 men rated themselves as lonely "sometimes" and 6 "rarely" or "never." Among the 5, loneliness was said to be due primarily to missing a parent, missing a pet, missing a friend, and missing a relative such as a sibling, but the first reason predominated.

Interestingly, among this group the shift between self-rated and observer-rated loneliness was greatest. Five never-married men were judged to be lonely "often," 2 "sometimes," and 4 "rarely or never."

This is accounted for by two things. As we indicated in our discussion above, a person may deny or not be conscious of loneliness but may give off to others the impression of being lonely. Such was the case for several of the men and led to changes in categories. Also, several men came, over time, to talk of the loneliness they felt. In one instance, a never-married man who was otherwise rather un-emotional and had revealed little of his loneliness said, revealingly, "Sometimes, I sit out on my front porch and cry because I miss my mother." This man, close to 80, rarely expressed any other positive affect.

Strained Relationship with a Child

Earlier we discussed strained relationships with children as related to life reorganization after widowhood. Three men who had not successfully reorganized their lives after their wife died mentioned experiencing "loneliness" due to the fact that they missed children or that they wished relations could be better.

Cosmic Loneliness

This was rare among the never-married men and the widowers but was voiced most commonly by divorced men. Of the 5 divorced men, 1 rated himself as experiencing loneliness "often," 3 "sometimes," and 1 "rarely." Observers rated the experience by all men of loneliness as "sometimes." The feeling or threat of estrangement was common to several of these men. For example, the man who rated himself as lonely "often" said of himself, "I am the loneliest person in the world. No one cares about me, I've been abandoned." This description of himself, although poignant, was somewhat theatrical. His living conditions were abysmal, and although he had an opportunity to change them, he did not. Yet one is forced to conclude that his sense of estrangement is fundamentally real.

CHAPTER 7

The Meaning of Living Alone

In this chapter we discuss the meaning of living alone to the men we interviewed. In doing this we are able to summarize and draw together a number of the concerns we have touched on in previous chapters. We discuss the meaning of living alone by making reference to a number of themes which appeared continually in the data we collected from our informants, some of which were explicitly stated and some of which were implicitly derived. We should note here, again, the living situation of our men. Forty-six out of the 47 lived alone at the time of the interview. One man—who had lived alone for several years in his 70s—currently lived with a sibling. Two men rented rooms in private dwellings, both maintaining that they "lived alone." Both were never-married men. Of the 47 men, we can rely on more complete data from 42 men, relatively incomplete data from 5 men.

OBJECTIVE LIVING CONDITIONS

Forty-six of the 47 men we interviewed actually currently resided alone in the sense that they maintained a household of one. The one exception was an 80-year-old man who resided with his sister for about three years. Prior to that, he lived alone after the death of his wife.

The basic residential patterns of the men we interviewed are listed in table 7.1 by type.

TABLE 7.1
Residential Patterns of Men in Sample

Type	Number of Residents in Sample
1. Mixed-age public housing (resident in excess of 10 years).	2
2. Senior-only housing (apartments only).	9
3. Resides in a home owned by self, resident at least 10 years, formerly shared house with now-deceased wife.	11
4. Resides in house owned by self, owned under 10 years, never shared residence with anyone else.	2
5. Resides in house owned by self, resident in excess of 10 years, never-married, house shared with parent.	1
6. Resides in rented house, resident for less than 10 years.	1
7. Rents apartment, resident in same apartment 10 years or more.	4
8. Rents apartment, resided there less than 10 years.	11
9. Rents a room	
a. Room has kitchen, but bathroom is down the hall.	1
b. With kitchen and bathroom privileges (in a house).	1
c. No kitchen or kitchen privileges, bathroom down the hall.	4

It should be pointed out that for all the men, aspects of their objective and subjectively perceived physical environment greatly influenced their lives. For example, the public-housing dwellers who reside in mixed-aged housing complained bitterly about aspects of their environment and pointed to environmental insults as reasons for aspects of their depressive or agitated states. Or many of the widowers who had shared a home for many years with a beloved wife pointed out the role of the home, and the continued presence of the spouse they felt there, in helping them to maintain themselves.

Two men resided in mixed-age public housing, each in a two-story, two-home unit. Both men had lived in different apartments in the same complex prior to moving to their current residence. Both men had numerous complaints about the condition of the apartments they lived in and about their ability to control their immediate environments. The apartment of one man had not been painted in years, and peeling paint was evident throughout. The other man had gone to the expense of having his apartment painted by a private contractor. Both men complained vigorously about noise and about safety problems. Both felt that the outside impinged on them, and that although they lived alone, they could not avoid feeling that unwanted others were pressing in on them. Both men were constantly aware of the outside world.

Nine men lived in apartments in "senior-only" housing units throughout the Philadelphia metropolitan area. These apartments are generally small (one room, kitchenette, bathroom) and are almost always recently built, and therefore for all men residence in them is a relatively recent event and has been of shortish duration (ten years or less). Senior-oriented services provided by the building management vary from a little (some help in organizing groups) to a lot (two meals a day and round-the-clock medical facilities). Rents vary too; some units have been built under federally mandated low-rent housing programs. In all cases the buildings are high-rise and have numerous residents and several public rooms and areas.

"Living alone" clearly has a special meaning here. This is for two reasons. First, regardless of the actual circumstances, all of the age-segregated residences come with an underlying ideological assumption that the building in some way represents a community. Residents are of a common age and generation. They often have common economic circumstances and may be members of a common ethnic or religious group. Implicit in such buildings is the notion that "we are all one." Second, there is an emphasis in all of these buildings on public space and public areas. Much of the ground floor in each, and other outside areas as well, have been turned over to general uses. Not only are there the standard areas such as the manager's desk or post boxes, but there are also large public sitting rooms, book rooms, lobbies, and meeting rooms which may be frequented by residents. The possibilities of measuring and controlling private and public space are more numerous and may take on finer shades of meaning here. Whereas the 2 men who lived in public housing clearly felt they lived alone and felt isolated in a hostile and capricious environment, in such senior-only units it is more difficult to feel totally alone.

Yet, given this orientation to public life, there was a wide range of opinions on to what degree people felt they lived alone. For example, 2 men who resided in age-segregated housing represented, more or less, extremes of opinions on this. One man who was outgoing and spent much of his time every day in public areas inside or immediately outside of his building said, "I don't really feel that I live alone. There's people all around." He was happy about these circumstances; it was his self-appointed task to spend much of the day speaking to others and trying to make them laugh. At times he also took pleasure in being able to close the door to his apartment, lean back in his recliner chair, and watch his television or listen to the radio. Nevertheless, his view of his apartment building was a communal one. He felt that the outside door was a door to his house and that the public areas of the building were his living areas.

Another man took an opposite point of view. Although he lived in a senior-only building, he felt that he lived very much alone. People almost never entered his apartment, he said. His apartment was a place which was very private, not something he wanted to share with anybody else. He viewed himself as an onlooker and was content, when he sat in public areas, to observe. His fellow residents were lonely, in his view, and somewhat wayward, and he claimed that he had little real interest in their affairs. The public areas of his building belonged to "others," not to him, and he approached them gingerly. The door to his own apartment carefully demarcated his own space. Nevertheless, he did spend time in public areas and he could point to people he knew in the building who had reputations of being even more isolated than himself.

In these situations, as in any, the degree to which one actually lives alone or feels oneself to be living alone depends on some subjective measurement of relatedness. While the degree to which communality and connectedness predominate depends on individual predilection, there appears to be a strong influence on the part of environment and ideology on these feelings.

Eleven of the men resided alone in a house which they owned and in which they had lived for at least ten years. Each of these men was a widower and each house had been shared with a wife who was now deceased. These were the homes in which the men's wives had taken ill and died. There was a lot of living that had been done in them.

Three of these eleven houses were single-family detached units, while the remainder were row houses. The feeling of absolute aloneness was easier to maintain inside of these homes than in the age-segregated units. In the latter even the individual who described himself as "a loner" was aware of the "community-oriented" nature of the residence and made ample use of the public areas of the building, adapting them to his own individual purposes. Among these widowers, however, there was rarely such a communal ideology (even in regard to the neighborhoods), and the division between public and private was more sharply focused. While a loner in the age-segregated units had to take note of public areas, a resident in a private home may more effectively cut himself off from others. He may not be a participant in a system colored by a communal ideology. He may live on a street or in a neighborhood where no one at all cares about him. If he leaves home, he will not pass through areas which necessarily belong to any group. He will pass through areas which will be more clearly labeled as "not his," since they belong to everyone in a *de facto* sense and there is no special ideology attached to them.

Individuals who in late life move together into a newly built age-segregated unit usually have little personal history in common (although they may share a common ethnic or religious heritage). They are, in a sense, starting out anew, moving into a "new neighborhood" or colonizing on new land. In some haphazard way, they may form a community. Or if a new community fails to develop, at the very least, new personal relationships are started. While in fact the past has been impermanent, causing people to make the move into a new home, the new life and the effects of varying sorts of communal ideology, may bring about a new feeling of future orientation, if not one of semipermanence, as expressed in the idea "I will be here a while." This is a new life in a sense.

However, for community residents, in their own homes, life in a particular house had generally been a long-term experience, and for many men there is a feeling of permanence attached to it ("I have been here a while"). But such permanence has had incorporated within it all manner of changes. While residence has been in one place, lots of things have come to pass: people have died, others have moved away, and the nature of a neighborhood may have changed.

For each of these 11 men, then, the home was a *central* environment and focus and had been for some time. Much had been experienced there, and as a result of interactions between an individual and his environment over time, a good deal of meaning, both implicit and explicit, had adhered to these homes. In this way, the home environment took on meanings closely tied to the core meanings of each individual resident's life.

Two men of the group lived in a house which each had bought within the last ten years. One of these men was a widower while the other had never married. Both men had never shared the residence with anyone since moving in. Both homes were row houses. While the never-married man had lived in the same neighborhood all his life, this new house represented a substantial change of residence for the widower, who moved closer to his relatives.

One bachelor continued to reside in the house he had shared with his mother. He had lived in the house for about twenty-five years; it was extraordinarily poorly maintained.

Another man resided in a house which he rented from his daughter who lived nearby. He said that he was offered a chance to live in the house for free, but insisted on paying rent. The upper floors of the house were closed off and the man lived exclusively on the ground floor.

Four men were renting apartments in which they had been residing for at least ten years (here we mean apartments in the community rather than apartments in age-segregated housing or public housing).

These apartments tended to be relatively inexpensive ($100 to $200 a month) and poorly maintained both by the apartment management and by the resident. In 2 cases, there was considerable emotional attachment to the apartments, although in 1 of these 2 cases, the thought of moving was also often uttered. Three of these 4 men were lifelong bachelors.

Eleven men currently lived in rented apartments and had lived in them for less than ten years. Seven of these men were widowers, 3 had been divorced, and 1 had never married. These apartments ran the gamut from the fancy to the modest, from a three-room apartment above a store to a large apartment in a modern apartment building. It is hard to draw a conclusion about life in these apartments, since the circumstances and conditions are so different. Each apartment represents a different experience of isolation and potential for isolation on the basis of its intrinsic features.

Finally, 6 men rented rooms. These were, in general, the least visually rich, expressive, and personalized apartments. Four of these 6 men were bachelors, while 1 man was widowed and 1 was divorced.

SUBJECTIVE ASPECTS

In reviewing what was communicated to us in interviews about the topics of "living," "living alone," "aloneness," and "daily existence," we are struck forcefully by two things. The first is the ease with which the men reflected on aspects of living. The second is the framework into which statements made about living and living alone fall.

By noting that the men reflected on living—and thereby living alone—with ease or naturally, we mean that discussion of these topics did not usually have to be prompted or pushed. Most men thought a good deal about what they were doing in life and why. Several domains of things—particularly some forms of activity—required few explanations; for other domains, men had evolved elaborate explanations, some highly rational, some deeply emotional, for what they were doing and why. In most cases, much of each man's current life-style was viewed both as *necessary* and as somehow satisfying for the most part. Given their particular constellation of needs and resources, most men felt they were living in a manner relatively satisfying, and at least relatively well understood.

Certainly one may argue that the use of natural explanations—explanations for events or doings which seem believable, plausible, generally seem to fit with the facts as they are understood by the user, and can be used as a kind of symbolic shorthand to communicate with others—is drawn out and emphasized in the interview situation. Undoubtedly this is true. But these are the same sorts of naturalistic explanations used by individuals, socially, to communicate with one another about themselves and used to rationalize one's behavior *to* oneself. Further, particular sorts of explanations for behavior and for activities may be used over and over during the course of an interview, thus demonstrating their naturalness to the user. We can also see the process of how such explanations are constructed. The discussion of how an individual behaved during a crisis, for example, may be given over and over, to help justify behavior, to give the behavior the status of an objective thing, an "official version" used to help the individual overcome internal conflicts over "what happened" and over his own role in the event.

Let us give an example of a naturalistic explanation of an activity. One man, who lived in a senior-only building and attended a local center about three to four days a week, was asked about the reasons he attended the center. He replied by saying, "It is my Activity." We render this here with a capital A, because it carries the sense and tone he used. By saying that center attendance is his "Activity," he threw into relief several important themes, some of which he was able to explain directly. He was a generally solitary and self-preoccupied man who believed himself to have few friends and who spent most of his time alone in his apartment. Attendance at the center—for about three hours a day, three or four times a week, was his one "submission" to a necessity which he grudgingly recognized—to see and interact with others. This man prided himself on his solitude and self-sufficiency. Since he had been living in his apartment, he said, only one building coresident had been in his apartment, and only once. He liked it that way. Although he attended the center several times a week, he said that he did not know center participants well, knew only a few by name, and never did more than chat about "nothing." Although he could be found sitting out on a public bench, he said that he rarely talked to others.

Nevertheless, he recognized the necessity for an "official" activity on a regular basis. It seems a bit like taking vitamins on a regular basis—one recognizes that it is a good thing to do, although one does not necessarily see the results until deprived. Clearly, he derived something positive from this activity, since he did it frequently. He recognized that it was better to have an activity than not, although by referring to it in such a way he not only honored it by signaling its importance but also spoke somewhat sarcastically about it: he was saying, "It's an activity, but not much of one."

Thus use of this naturalistic sort of explanation both encodes within it a variety of personal concerns and distills these into an essence. Naturalistic explanations are forms of themes, both a particular area of condensed meaning and a symbol for a variety of specific experiences (see appendix 1).

Such naturalistic sorts of explanations are only one of two kinds of explanatory statements informants made about themselves and their lives as a whole. Naturalistic explanations are heightened forms of statements about living and living alone, which by their very nature encode within themselves their own contrast. Thus statements such as "It is my Activity," "I never married because I was devoted to my mother," "I like Joe because he is someone to pass the time with," bring with them contradictory states: "I tend to be inactive," "Most people marry," "Maybe I have a problem with passing the time." At the very least, such naturalistic statements refer at some level to other possibilities, and may require further explanation.

The second sort of statement about living and living alone may be called an identity statement, one which pertains to certain guideposts of personal identity and does not beg further explanation or question. In identity statements meaning is usually self-evident, derived from the implicit meaningfulness of basic cultural entities and values such as "family," "spouse," "home," "the past," and "manhood." One does not usually have to justify or explain one's love for one's family because it is culturally "natural." And it is natural in a less conscious way than are the naturalistic explanations mentioned above.

This contrast in the form of meaning is useful in discussing the meaning of living alone. Meaning can be "naturalistic," implicitly contrastive, and require further explanation or expressive and non-contrastive as in identity statements. Statements concerning living alone—either the responses to specific questions or as this topic was discussed in more free-flowing ways—can be evaluated in terms of these two forms of meaning.

CONTRASTS

Feelings about living alone can be clarified on the basis of a series of contrasts, each pertaining to a specific important *issue* in the lives of the elderly men in the sample. The issues in which the contrasts are implicit or explicit are independence, connectedness, activities, time orientation, and the presence of others.

Independence vs. Being Tied Down

When asked what they liked about living alone, most men were fairly neutral about it or specifically disliked it. However, most men could single out the attribute of independence as a desirable aspect of living alone. They were able to make their own days and choose their own friends and associates. Here, there was a distinction on the basis of marital status. The never-married men are more completely emphatic in their insistence that independence is a desirable commodity. While the widowers in general agree to this proposition, they are generally less emphatic in their expressions. Several widowers, whose lives are unsuccessfully reorganized, dichotomize between practical independence, a desired state, and marital independence, not desired.

For most men, being independent has a value all its own despite its diffusion into different spheres of life. Independence is singled out as a significant concept in and of itself. Independence, as a positive attribute, is able to hide a myriad of unpleasant entities to "cover up" loneliness and anomie. Independence in living alone, however, can be punctuated by periods of intense longing and loneliness. Men can develop techniques to handle this. Independence gives one the freedom to avoid unwanted demands of others so that one can do all the things physically necessary to get by.

Independence is therefore a generally appreciated quality. Once acquired, it has enough of a value that it becomes difficult to think about giving up. Often, there is a considerable element of guilt involved in taking pleasure in independence, especially for some widowers. There may be guilt about surviving the wife, guilt about living off an income designed for two, guilt about enjoying independence. Rarely, however, is such independence fully joyous, although it can be. One never-married man described some private moments this way. "Here, I can close the door and shut out the world. . . . Sometimes, in the evenings, I'll take out my teeth, take off my shoes and trousers, take off my truss, put on some music, and lie down here on the sofa. I am in my own world then, fully content."

For the never married, independence is primarily conceptualized as the absence "of someone to tell me what to do" as well as the presence of an ability to make one's own schedule. For the widowers, the latter ability is more frequently stressed. Independence is closely tied to the need for control and to individualized self-expression. Situations are avoided in which the loss of independence is a possibility. It would appear that for many men social contacts remain peripheral because of a fear of dependency on others or of spending too much time in an undesired involvement.

One of the important things about independence is that many men separated it out as a unique and distinctive concern, a separate dimension of things, although analytically the notion of independence is clearly related to many other topics. Many men said directly, as a response or in passing, "My independence is important to me."

In terms of the contrast between "independence" and "being tied down," living alone clearly means independence, when independence is viewed as a valuable attribute or commodity in and of itself. Although some men were desperately unhappy, none complained a great deal about having "too much" independence; indeed, some looked to maximum independence as a necessary precondition to their adapting to and overcoming their great unhappiness. Yet the danger of having "too much" independence did occur to some men in particular ways. A handful mentioned the fear of dying alone and not being found in their homes for weeks after a solitary death. Several isolated men had taken precautions so that they would be checked on if they were not seen for a few days. The fear of loss of support and the fear of being unable to find support if needed were both articulated by several of these men. Yet such fears were discussed as if they were separate from "independence" per se.

Thus one generally positive attribute of living alone is the independence associated with it. Although for many, "independence" came about through unhappy circumstances, for most it was a relatively happy thing. This was stated in many ways: "I'm master of my own ship here," "A person needs my permission to enter," "I can do what I want," "I can live like I want."

Control or Lack of Control

The men we interviewed lived in a diversity of neighborhoods and situations and, despite this, generally felt themselves to have control over their own living environments. For most men, then, the meaning of living alone related to a feeling of personal control over their living spaces and the right to select elements which enter and intrude.

Interestingly, from the point of view of the general categories used by the men themselves to describe their lives, the notions of control over the environment and independence are unrelated. As we have mentioned, most men view "independence" as an important attribute in and of itself. Few, if any, think about something called "control over my environment" reflectively unless they are bedeviled by intrusions, and feel themselves unable to control what goes on inside their homes. Such confoundment is relatively rare, and its presence seems to be correlated with anxiety and other neurotic symptoms. For example, one man was constantly bothered by what he felt to be the specter of menacing neighbors; another slept with a baseball bat at hand for defense. A third man showed considerable symptoms of paranoia and felt outside noises were directed specifically at him. Other men who lived in the same neighborhoods (indeed, in 2 cases not 500 feet away) did not feel this way.

For most men, then, a degree of control over the environment can be a *de facto* attribute of living alone. It is only when intrusions occur that the living situation is related, in men's minds, to the lack of control. Such intrusions come in two varieties, those by strangers (as in the cases mentioned above), and those by familiars. Intrusions by familiars occur primarily through the symbolic presence of departed loved ones. Possessions, objects, etc., associated with others but still located in the home intrude on the consciousness of many men. Whereas intrusion by strangers is generally an unpleasant form of lack of control, intrusion by familiars is usually not unpleasant, although it can be when it provokes intolerable thoughts.

The quality of independence as conceptualized by these men refers to the ability to arrange one's own doings during a "day." Independence, in a sense, refers to one's ability to stay inside or leave a house. Control refers to one's ability to "shut out" the outside world, or to invite it in. One of the most important qualities cited by men is the ability "to close the door" when necessary, to filter out "the outside world." Although data were not collected on this theme systematically, it was mentioned by many of the men.

Social Equity or Inequity

For most of the men, living alone derives meaning from the notion of independence, and this notion is closely tied to that of social equity. By social equity we mean two things: first, that a person thinks of himself as "as good as" another person, and that, more specifically, he is able to contribute to the ongoing world of social usefulness in whatever ways he would, through interactions and the giving and receiving of tangibles and intangibles. For most men, social equity can at times subsume independence—"being able to do what I like with no one to boss me" as well as other emotions, for example, "helping out" or "doing things for others." The contrast between social equity and its opposite is quite marked. Being able to participate more or less fully in social affairs, to maintain an independent life-style, is clearly contrasted in the minds of most men with "becoming a burden." Becoming a burden, imaged as a feeble person in need of constant care, is considered the worst thing that can happen to a person. Several men, independently and without prompting, noted that if they were ever on a life-support system, for example, they would order "the plug pulled." The inconvenience to self and others is too great. One man put it this way: "You're just a vegetable . . . no good to yourself or anyone."

Living alone can represent a degree of personal solvency. It represents independence, the ability to conduct one's affairs on an equal footing, to engage in the give and take of which so much of everyday life consists. It stands in opposition to the debilitated and enfeebled state men fear, with "parts that don't work" or being "like a vegetable." Several of the men with children have standing offers to live with at least one of them, but still there is a desire to maintain one's own place. Living with children, although infinitely preferable to a "home," still can mean "being a burden." One man explained it this way: "I know that both of my children would want me to live with them, but you would have to think what it would be like . . . you couldn't help getting in their way. Suppose it's Saturday night and they wanted to go to the movies. You might honestly feel that it's fine for you to stay home alone, but they would always feel bad about leaving you and they would try to make you come, out of politeness or because they wanted you to come. So where would you be?" The chance for conflict, misunderstanding, or confusion is too large; the implicitly valued attribute of independence is threatened.

Activity or Inactivity

Depending on the activity orientation of an individual, his style of residence and the fact that he is living alone can have very different meanings.

We can explain this best by imagining a continuum on which the meaning of one's solitary existence and one's orientation to activities can be placed.

At one pole of the continuum the home is viewed as the base of activities, the place from which a person emerges in the morning to embark on a fully active "day." One is pulled outward by the force of social duties and connections. The orientation of life is external.

At the other pole the orientation is inward. Here, men are more isolated and the bonds of their social connection less strong. The home is the center and the strong bonds are there. A person is more attached to the solitary sociality of one's home and the meanings and associations it has.

Both images are rather simplified, of course, but they serve to emphasize certain features of the meaning of living alone as related to the array of activities and attachments a person has. Thus for those men who were most active (these men were, as we noted in chapter 5, men who have successfully reorganized their lives in widowhood and those never-married men whom we described as "sophisticates"), the meaning of living alone is strongly colored by an outward focus on daily activities. Certainly, these men consider themselves to be living alone, but they have strong social attachments and they feel themselves part of something on the outside. Each person is socially "located." Living alone does not intrinsically have an attached sense of aloneness. Indeed, some more active men look to home as a necessary refuge where they can escape from others when necessary.

For the less active and less well connected, the aloneness of living alone is more emphatic. The "pull" is not from outward attachments. For some of these men, the "pull" is inward, to memories of the past embodied in the home.

For still others, there is no pull inward or outward. Home has no special meaning, and it is "just a place."

For both groups of men, the relatively more active and attached and the relatively less, there is generally a distinct difference, as we have noted, between being at home alone during the day and the evening. Few men go out regularly at night unless it is to a specific place with specific means of getting there and returning. Most men rarely receive visitors at night. The transition between active day and inactive night can be especially difficult. Men from all levels of activity reported feeling sad about "coming home to an empty house." They generally felt less "alone" (as opposed to lonely) during the daytime.

The meaning of living alone, then, relates partly to the matrix of outside activities and one's subjective attachments to them. Activity can orient one outward, making a person's sense of aloneness and separateness disappear. One is "pulled" from a solitary space by social attachments. This is evidenced by the several men who made statements to the effect that "although I live alone, I keep busy." Here the implicit aloneness envisioned in "living alone" is defended against.

While most men like "independence," many do not especially like living alone, or are fairly neutral about it, evaluating it in a series of pluses and minuses. By being active, *if one can,* a person may generally shut out some of the impact of aloneness. Extended grief, however, can make it impossible for a person to be involved and drawn away by outside activities.

Familial Connectedness or Familial Apartness

Daily activities are usually undertaken by individual decision and commitment, although activities may appear to exert a pull which is external. Since many activities are performed together with other people, as we have noted, performance of an activity has an element of sociality as well. This is a separate issue from familial connectedness or apartness, from the relative degree *family* connections had by each of the men we interviewed. There are basically two issues here: whether or not one has family personnel to begin with, and the nature of each man's relations with family personnel. Among the men with children, the warmth of relations varies. Among those without children, the potential for help that children can offer must be acquired elsewhere if it can be had at all.

The meaning of living alone is therefore influenced by the factor of potential help. In determining this influence, the "rule" is that the men, in general, would prefer to maintain independence (which is usually viewed as maintaining one's own household, although several men were also clearly interested in the nonsolitary life). Beyond this (in general) the presence of supportive children with whom one has warm relations is important in maintaining an independent life-style in two ways. Children may voluntarily take over small chores and help with large ones, thus freeing an elder from a variety of tasks which may be difficult to manage and helping him to continue to live independently. Second, the presence of children acts, in general, as a security factor, that one will be looked after if there is a problem. For the men with children, then, if the relations with children are good, one can live independently but with an additional level of security.

Although some of the men with no children have achieved extensive support networks, many of these men articulated clearly the fear of what might be called "support failure." This will come about not necessarily through the character flaws of friends, but through the inability of friends, due to their own physical problems or familial involvements, to be able to help consistently if need be. In this respect, several men with no children (and one with insecure relations with stepchildren), who have relatively high incomes, made clear their interest in the possibility of nursing homes or life-care communities. For the others with smaller incomes and with no children, a retirement community was out of the question. Here a level of insecurity about the future was sometimes voiced, but usually not; rather, the need for independence was. One cannot help thinking that the voiced need for continuing independence is, at least in part, a denial of the fears about what will happen in the future.

Present and Past

Another important issue around which the meaning of living alone was played out was that of the relative value of the present and the past in current daily life. The home environment can represent the present-day evaluation of the past and the incorporation of the past into ongoing life. In living alone (and being elderly) most men sought to symbolically mark the past and to incorporate it in everyday life. Because a person was living alone, he had the full ability to construct his environment independent of the current needs of others and within his means. The meaning of living alone, therefore, was often tied to some incorporation of the past into present-day life. As we have noted (chapters 3 and 5), there was variation here. By not calling attention to the past, by not marking it, a person is generally making as strong a statement about his or her current life as a person who strongly marks the past.

NONCONTRASTS

This brings us to the second style of meaning relating to living alone, the noncontrastive. Contrastive meanings were issue-oriented. The issues were based on the common experiences of all or most men as they age. The meanings were derived from contrasts in possibilities: "I can be independent or I can be tied down," "I can have a value or I can be a burden." In general, men could *explain* what they meant by reference both to individual experience and to the set of contrasts.

Noncontrastive meaning is more expressive of unique individual experience and does not necessarily rely on contrastive sets. It deals more with basic issues of identity, "who I am and what happened to me."

Our conversations about living and living alone revealed several common areas of individual meaning attached to living alone. Although such expressive meaning was unique to the experiences of each individual, these can be grouped into common categories. These are family, spouse, home, past, and "the day."

Family

Living alone can rarely be divorced from the doings of current and former family members. In living alone, the psychic sense of connection to other people can be profound, as we have detailed above. While attachments to former residents, a spouse, in-laws, or children can be continual, regularly periodic, or episodic, it always provides a background reference point.

Consider the case of one man who had psychically "gotten over" the death of his wife, had successfully reorganized his life, and had close, subjectively significant relationships with a variety of people. Although he indicated in his responses to questions that he felt himself to be completely over his wife's loss, he said, "Everything I've said is like that [indicating that he had gotten over the loss "fully"] but it's not exactly true. There will always be something there." He will always have a feeling for his wife and live, in a way, under her influence, although things for him are not back to the way they were, but are different.

Spouse

As we have indicated again and again, the meaning of living alone for the widowers is closely tied, in a variety of ways, to the life led with the spouse.

Home

Various meanings attached to life are played out in the feeling and uses one makes of one's home. A great deal of one's sociopsychological identity is expressed in a home. This is where most of "living alone" is done.

Past

The meaning of living alone is closely tied up with the past in terms of real events and with the present-day evaluation of the past ("What am I going to let it mean to me?").

"The Day"

Some men indicated that they lived "one day at a time." When living alone, the working out of each day, the scheduling of events, of meetings, and of empty times, has a distinct flavor, since there is no one else within the household to orient one outward. Feelings about aloneness may further act as a force to repel individuals from the house during the day or, alternatively, to inhibit them from making contacts by staying at home.

Research Methods

In this appendix we outline in some more detail how informants were selected and interviewed, some of the theoretical approach which influenced our methods, and some general comments about the research site.

METHODS

Initially we recruited informants from senior-only housing projects well-known to us from previous research projects. A list of Philadelphia-area senior centers and housing units for the elderly provided us with additional potential sources. Letters or phone calls to unit or program supervisors enabled us to explain our project to them. Center program directors made announcements about our research to center attenders and thereby solicited participants, turning their names over to us. Initial contact with center attenders was most often made at a center. Housing unit residents were similarly approached, either by public announcements or individual solicitations by the unit manager. In all solicitations, the fact that we would pay twenty-five dollars to each participant was mentioned and served, no doubt, as an inducement in some instances. Eventually, we set up interviews with men in four housing units and six senior centers.

Locating isolates proved more difficult. Some were drawn from three Philadelphia-area in-home service programs, but only 1 man was currently receiving substantial formal services. Most recruited in this fashion received few or no services and were chosen from lists of former program clients living in the community. While 3 of the isolates chosen in this way were primarily homebound, most were fairly active. The remainder of the isolates were drawn through personal contacts of the center staff and through referrals from men who were already participating in the study. In all we interviewed 21 isolates.

While we had hoped to engage the participation of isolates through a "snowballing" method, asking the men participating in the project to refer us to other older men living alone they might know, we had little success with this method, but not for lack of trying. Either the men we interviewed had no friends with living circumstances similar to theirs and thus could refer us to no one; or the friends referred were of an overrepresented category (such as a nonisolate or overrepresented ethnic group); or friends or acquaintances were not known well enough to be recommended.

With the exception of the isolate and nonisolate categories, and with the general target number of 30 individuals of each type in mind, we did not have any hard and fast rules about who could participate. (In fact, we interviewed 1 elderly man who was living with a relative at the time of the interviews, but who had lived alone for much of his 70s.) We took no persons who were severely mentally impaired; all the men we interviewed could converse freely. Basically we took anyone we could get. However, as we went along we became aware that certain ethnic, religious, and economic groups were overrepresented or underrepresented, and we took steps to counter such disproportion by limiting some and seeking out others.

PHILADELPHIA AS A RESEARCH SITE

In many ways the Philadelphia area proved to be an ideal site in which to carry out this research. In 1980 the population of Philadelphia and the surrounding five counties (the total area from which our sample is drawn) was about 4.7 million, of whom about 1.7 million live in the City of Philadelphia (U.S. Department of Commerce 1981a, 1981b). In the City of Philadelphia, where most of the interviewing was done, the elderly made up about 14.1 percent of the total city population (Philadelphia City Planning Commission 1982), or some 237,000 persons. Approximately 25 percent of the households in the City of Philadelphia are headed by individuals age 65 or older (Shapiro 1982). This is a startling figure with profound implications for future city funding, for neighborhood life, and for the quality of the existing housing.

In 1978 there were approximately 15,000 one-person households with a male head age 65 or older in Philadelphia, while in the metropolitan area there were some 28,000 such households (U.S. Department of Commerce 1982). In the city, the population of older men living alone is about 6 or 7 percent of the total elderly population.

The particular history and character of the city and its suburbs strongly influence the daily lives of our informants. If anything, Philadelphia is a city of neighborhoods, each more or less named, bounded, subdivided, and generally ethnically identified. Associated with neighborhoods are particular parks and shopping areas, the latter often acting as "hangouts" for older men. Informants often talk about neighborhoods changing or remaining nice, despite change. In Philadelphia there is a more or less strict separation between white and black neighborhoods, although the boundaries between them are sometimes in flux.

For many of the men we interviewed, the fact that they lived in a particular neighborhood was of great personal importance to them. An association with a neighborhood helped define and place them. Even after moving away, some men return to the "old neighborhood" to visit or spend time. In all respects the qualities and significance of neighborhood and neighborhood life is not to be underestimated. Despite physical deterioration, the possibility of crime, and abandonment of buildings, neighborhoods continue to provide an important and vital *context* for experience for many of the men we interviewed.

Other assets of Philadelphia which were mentioned by our informants include the following.

1. An extensive network of senior centers. Funding for the centers is channeled from the federal government through the Philadelphia Corporation for the Aging, a semipublic body which functions as the local Area Agency on Aging. Each center is attuned to the

surrounding neighborhood and draws its clientele primarily from the neighborhood in which it is located. Centers are open from nine to four most weekdays of the year. Centers serve a variety of functions. Most have a daily activity program which involves various planned activities, announcements, lectures, informal socializing, and a noontime hot meal available for a small price. For some of the center-goers we interviewed, the inexpensive meal was a major attraction since they lived on a limited income. More informally the center provides a *context* and a *place* for doing things. Often these things amount to nothing more than talking, joking, or playing cards, but it is the special context of these events which is also important. Each center has a professional staff, and most provide door-to-door van service for persons who have trouble leaving their homes but who wish, nonetheless, to attend.

2. Transportation. Medicaid cards may be used by those over 65 to travel on a reduced fare basis on public transportation. Only 7 of the 47 men we interviewed currently own or drive their own car. The remainder either rely on friends or family for out-of-neighborhood transport or they use public transportation. Most public transportation is deemed safe to use in the daytime, but to be avoided at night.

3. Shopping streets and other public areas. Most neighborhood centers offer an array of stores, often gathered around one main avenue over the course of several streets. For many of the men we interviewed, going to a neighborhood center was a special event, marked as significant, which could require "dressing up." Stores in these areas are often small and intimate. Shopkeepers and other shoppers may be well known. Centers may be reached on foot or by public transportation. Neighborhood restaurants may also serve as "hangouts." Public libraries were also used by several men in the sample.

4. The city offers a growing network of information and services for the elderly. Newspapers and radio and television stations increasingly offer information for those over 65. Restaurants, supermarkets, and drugstores may offer discounts for "senior citizens." A number of medical and social service programs around the city are specifically geared to the needs of the elderly.

5. Recreation. The Philadelphia area offers a wide variety of recreational facilities, many of which were of interest to the men we interviewed. First and foremost, the professional sports teams were the object of considerable interest for some of the men, a vehicle for self-expression for others, while for some, sports provided "something to talk about." Also, there is easy access to the New Jersey Atlantic City casinos. The casinos sponsor specially discounted trips, targeted primarily at the elderly, so that the actual cost of transportation to the shore amounts to virtually nothing.

INTERVIEW PROCEDURE

Once contact was made and participation solicited and agreed to, an initial meeting between interviewer and informant was set up. While the interviews were conducted by four interviewers, a majority were conducted by me.

At an initial meeting, the aims and goals of the project were explained in detail to each informant. We further explained to each man our concern with and dedication to his rights of privacy and confidentiality. Each man was told that we intended to write up our findings, that all information we received from them would be treated with confidentiality, and that any information used in reports on our research would be significantly disguised so that real individuals and real situations could not be made out. Each man was told that he could refuse to answer any question for any reason at any time and that he could withdraw from participation in the research at any time for any reason. The men were told that they would receive twenty-five dollars for participation in the research and that a refusal to answer questions or a desire to discontinue participation would not jeopardize their receipt of the money.

The interview procedure was described. Each man was told that we would like to interview him about five times, at his home, at times which were convenient for him. Each man was encouraged to ask questions about the research project and the interviewer.

Thus it should be noted (again) that the accounts which have been presented above have been altered, in some cases substantially, so that the specifics of some incidents are not revealed. In no way, I believe, has the flavor or meaning of an event been altered, however.

The Anthropological Perspective

Interviews were carried out from an anthropological perspective. Our interviews had some characteristics of participant observation with an emphasis on "key-informant interviewing" (Pelto 1970). That is to say, while we did not reside with our informants, our interviews stressed seeing life in a naturalistic way as well as coming to understand each informant's personal meaning system, his own insider's point of view on life.

`Our attempt to get at a naturalistic setting dictated that our interviews take place at the home of each informant to whatever extent this was possible. In this we were mostly successful, interviewing 41 of the 47 men exclusively at their homes. Observing the content and layout of the home as well as using these as a basis for discussion added an important dimension to our interviews. In general, while homes are ruled by cultural (e.g., shared) principles of order, homes are also deeply personalized. They always say something important about their residents. They may contain memorabilia and other landmarks of a life. Often objects in the home are compact, tangible symbols: attached to them are deep meanings and memories. Seeing the object often makes the event, memory, or person which is attached to it easier to explain.

In the home it was easier to make an assessment of the activities and skills of the men we interviewed. For example, one anecdotal image of older men living alone is that they have failed to learn or prefer not to perform a variety of maintenance tasks such as cleaning, at least above a rudimentary level. Is this true? It would be difficult to inquire about this and get meaningful responses without actually seeing a lived-in environment. Further, we are able to get some sense of the intimate quality of life for each informant.

Findings of research indicate that older people spend a good deal of time at home (Hammer and Chapin 1972). As interested parties we are better able to understand how life is experienced by the elderly by coming to know what is seen through windows or from porches or backyards. We can appreciate how life is lived to some degree by seeing for ourselves which stores are on the street and the flow and feel of activity in the area.

THEORETICAL BACKGROUND

This brings us to another issue, specifically the theoretical concerns which colored the questions we asked in our interviews as well as our technique and style of interviewing. First and foremost, our interest, derived from anthropology, was in learning an individual's point of view (the insider's point of view) on his own life and the important things in it. Related to this is our second notion, that of individual as virtuoso, the notion that each individual plays an active part in the construction and maintenance of his life and self-identity. We will discuss each of these points in turn.

In general, anthropologists work in communities or with groups of some sort, be they residents of a village, hamlet, or island (traditional interests). While anthropology has had a long history of interests in individuals per se (witnessed by the many notable biographies of informants which have appeared), anthropology, nevertheless, has not done well in dealing with individuals. The most basic reason for this is that anthropology has emphasized culture in its sense of shared convention and has viewed meaning as derivative of shared symbols and the ordering of symbols. Emphasis on shared culture has led to the highlighting of various systemic components: kinship, social, economic, religious, and even symbolic *systems*. The emphasis on these is based on our own value-laden notion that such systems are necessarily distinctive and separable.

An interest in individuals and subjective meaning have for the most part been turned to the service of discovering and documenting cultural meaning. While the emphasis has been on systems, there has always been a background interest, both by necessity and theoretically in the individual.

In our attempt to understand the individual, we might make the analogy between each individual we interviewed and a particular culture. In an approach similar to that used by an anthropologist investigating another culture, we looked for in each individual patterns, meanings, and order. We tried to answer the questions, what are the major issues in this person's life? What is life like for him?

The second theoretical concern behind our research methodology was to treat each individual as a virtuoso, as an accomplished constructor of his own meaningful reality. It is only in this way that one can have an appreciation for what another has done in life, regardless of one's own values about how life should be led. Such an attitude helps suspend judgment about what another has done while always bringing to one's perception of another person a great deal of respect.

This approach may seem an unusual one to take with persons whose circumstances may be greatly influenced by social realities such as low income, poor health, declining physical abilities, etc. We did not neglect these influences on people's lives, however. We treated them in two ways. First, in our case material, we showed how negative social realities are perceived individually by each man. Also, wherever appropriate in our discussion of group trends, we attempted to correlate these with significant variables such as health, income, etc.

Our concern for the individual as virtuoso was dictated by several other ideas.

1. The focus on the individual does justice to the rather diverse group of people we interviewed. To the interviewer each person was unique, with a specific history and character. This view was enhanced by the manner in which the research was done. Interviewers saw informants several times, became somewhat immersed in their lives; the effort to gain information and understanding was collaborative (Frank 1979). Our approach was descriptive and interpretive rather than statistical and comparative. The focus was strongly on individuals, on individual motivations, on *individual interpretations of the events perceived as directing life,* and on processes of change and continuity.

2. The focus on the individual is in line with the interpretation that many of the men we saw had of their own lives. Despite the real deficits of aging (ill health, loss, etc.), many of the men we interviewed valued, first and foremost, their independence and their ability to decide for themselves what to do. In this regard most of the men saw themselves as relatively satisfied with life in general (despite a variety of specific unhappinesses) and often perceived themselves as in control of their fate (all of their inner and most of their outer fate), despite the ways the outside world constrained or molded behavior.

3. The focus on the individual is relevant for issues in personality and aging. In an important recent paper, Kaufman suggests that the ways in which events are interpreted by individuals have a great power to explain continuity and change in the adult personality. She suggests that continuity is created and maintained symbolically through the creation of *themes,* "cognitive areas of meaning," in the construction of older people's biographies which explain, unify, and give substance to their perceptions of who they are and how they see themselves participating in social life (1981:55). According to Kaufman, examples of themes are "My family is my life—I am nothing without them," and "I am a straw-in-the-wind, but I control my destiny." The meaning of themes to individuals depends on (a) their need for coherence and logic in defining and explaining life experiences; (b) the limitations and opportunities faced at different life periods due to social and historical circumstances; (c) the developmental tasks on which they currently focus; (d) their need for continuity across the life span; and (e) the interpretation of present circumstances, which include social settings, interaction patterns, and the impact of conceptions of the past on them (1981:56–57).

Kaufman's approach admits to and includes conflicts, and presents "themes" as one method of internalized conflict resolution by giving order to what would otherwise be disordered. In addition, we would suggest that many people carry within them a variety of conflicting themes which are "in play" at the same moment.

Also, the social context of a theme is a crucial element which is not clear from Kaufman's account. Themes seem to be reified or objectified pronouncements, fixed, repeated texts which operate in two directions. Themes are patterned "things" which individuals habitually "say" to others in order to create an identity in a social context; for example, "Things have always been good for me" or "I've always been a loner." However, themes are also things which one tells oneself. In both of these ways they are truly condensed, powerful, individualized, almost sacred symbols because they provide a kind of supraindividual framework for ordering meaning. Such thematic statements are brief condensations of a lifetime of experiences. The statement "I have always been a loner" may, for example, condense a lifetime of affect and a thousand experiences. In this way themes are somewhat like a cherished possession, something tangible which reminds one of a variety of experiences.

Themes then are the shapers of thought and experience. Thematic material tends to reproduce itself. Experience always yields to the shaping influence and logic of a theme, reified as a special "cognitive area of meaning." Memory too is subject to processes of recreation and editing (Langness and Frank 1981). Themes are thus "public" knowledge in two ways, as communicated to others and as conscious and therefore communicated to oneself.

We would suggest that there is also a more private part to themes. People hold dialogues with themselves the subject of which is not for "public" consumption. One property of reflexivity is the ability to question themes. Many of the men we saw mentioned at one time or another that they tell themselves things, although only a few volunteered specific—not general—examples. Is "telling oneself things" a special attribute of the elderly? We don't know.

We also use the notion of theme as a device of translation. In our discussions above we generalize themes from the experiences of several people. Such generalized themes represent the "lowest common denominator" of various individual experiences.

4. We view the use of themes in the manner described by Kaufman as part of a process of identity maintenance in old age. This is a key enterprise. The notion of an identity is made of two components. The first is the array of images a person has of herself. Such images are part of the natural way in which people experience things, part of the way in which a person uses internalized notions of self to sort, classify, and give meaning to experience. In such a way a person monitors and evaluates experience. Second, an identity includes those images and surfaces a person presents to the outside world. Both of these facets are part of one interconnected identity, and both are the subject of the same identity-maintaining enterprise.

Matthews (1979) describes aspects of identity maintenance among a group of older widowed women. She also describes the significance of settings in the maintenance of social identities in people's lives. Settings are defined as environments in which people lead their social lives. Settings usually come with a familiar cast of characters. Herein, the notion of a setting in the sense that it is an environment tailored to a particular individual is emphasized.

As we have noted, identities are often conceived of, represented, constructed, or thought about in forms such as themes, or in other patterned behavior or thought sets or in environments designed to express central identity components. Thematic material represents highly charged and condensed symbols of one's essential personhood, one's life and doings, and who one thinks one is. Themes and other such phenomena are the bridges between the entirely subjective realm and that which is entirely objective. Because themes are the things that *one tells oneself* as natural means of categorizing experience, they are also things one tells others about oneself and thus help determine the *social presentation of self.* In a manner similar to the seeming naturalness and effortlessness with which one experiences the everyday world, themes are "natural" or "naturally evolved" mental categories and explanatory vehicles.

TECHNIQUES

We concentrated on coming to understand individuals' lives as a whole in hopes of ascertaining something about different centers of meaning for each individual. Our interviews stressed a variety of different eliciting techniques and various levels of response. Of the 42 men we interviewed at length, most were interviewed from nine to twelve hours over the course of five or six sessions. Our target was approximately ten hours of interview time for each man. Men were interviewed most commonly once a week over a period of five to six weeks. This procedure enabled us to "check in" on a variety of ongoing activities, events, and relationships over a period of time.

In our initial contact we gathered general background data about each individual, including information on ethnic affiliation, health, income, family, occupation and residential histories, activities of daily living, religious affiliation, and some data on psychological state of being. Initially or subsequently we took an extensive genealogy in order to ascertain the possible extent of past and present kin ties, which kin ties were not currently in use and why, and the current kin network and its content. Similarly, we took profiles of past and present friends. The basic general questions used are detailed at the end of this appendix.

Initially, through the sessions with the first ten informants, sessions were tape-recorded and transcribed. Thereafter, as the procedure became standardized, handwritten notes were used. These were brought back to our offices for transcription and analysis.

In terms of length, our interviews were longer than standard, "structured" interviews, but far shorter than would be necessary for a full profile or life history. Once basic data was gathered we proceeded to what we conceived of as a series of directed "conversations," often facilitated by a group of general and specific questions, which were to aid in producing what we hoped would be a kind of open-ended, free-flowing discussion of the subject matter at hand (for example, an individual's former work mates, his relationships, marriage, activities, parents).

We used many, but not necessarily all, of the questions with each informant, as dictated by each research relationship, and the informant's and interviewer's characters. Questions were essentially used "to get the ball rolling" in the hope that a discussion of the topic would expand beyond the parameters of a minimal answer and lead to a reflective commentary on a topic by the informant.

Our hope that our conversations could produce subjectively meaningful material was generated by two notions. First, during the course of anthropological fieldwork there may develop a feeling of rapport and empathy between field-worker and informant. In a more traditional field situation (with a substantial difference in language and culture), such a relationship comes primarily after a considerable amount of interchange and derives from equivalence (gift giving, sharing of information, friendship). We hoped to some small extent to be able to achieve some kind of rapport with our informants so that their perception of us as outsider/interviewer became linked to a perception of us as person/sympathetic listener. We hoped for the achievement of a small degree of collaboration in which our purposes and goals would be the subject of mutual effort. Certainly, this was facilitated by our multiple visits.

We also hoped to achieve a mix of data reflective of responses to structured questions as well as derivative of each informant's subjective concerns, gathered from free-form, open-ended, or "stream-of-consciousness" material. In some sense, the search for such inner-derived material among individuals is akin to the search for core cultural values in field research in another culture. Our search for internal significance and internal ordering was aided by using at times a "blank screen" technique in interviewing—keeping responses to a minimum so as to encourage free, internally derived thoughts and ideas to surface.

We would like to be able to say that we were entirely successful in achieving a good degree of rapport with all of our informants in every way, but certainly this was not the case. In many instances there were obstacles. For some men, despite having volunteered for the project, we were viewed as an intrusion, and this could be seen in voiced impatience or in concern with finishing up. In all cases, our questions covered a great deal of personal and often painful material, and things did not always go smoothly. Some of the men were very hard to come to know. We did have some degree of success, however, and this is evidenced in the intimacy and reflectiveness of some of the data we gathered.

That our attempts were successful to any degree has to do with several factors. First, scheduling our interviews over a period of several weeks helped us to build up a certain momentum and trust. For several weeks, we became a regular feature in the lives of the men we interviewed. We always tried to take care in our interactions to be sensitive to painful and awkward topics. We tried to be friendly and cheerful, to carry out any requests which might be made to us.

We also tried to adopt a position of personal association by building a mental "scheme" of each informant and of the major events and persons in his life. Preparation time went into each interview in the form of reviewing notes of the prior interview, attempting to integrate into a mental picture the events and comments the informant had made, and thereby committing names and situations to memory. There is a great difference in results between asking a general question and being able to tailor the general question to very specific circumstances. Over time, as the "scheme" was filled in, knowledge could be reused to relate current events to past events. Similarly, as we gained more knowledge we could act as familiars with ongoing events.

Although some men had difficulty talking at times, our most important asset, certainly, was the willingness of the men to talk and to help us out with our project. We found in our initial contact with some men that they had, in fact, a profound need to talk, to describe some incident or some chain of incidents or painful experiences and to present and explain their current state in life by reference to a difficult past. In some men this need to speak was very great and we tried to respect it. Although we were concerned with conducting our interviews with some kind of order, we always tried to listen carefully to whatever was said, not only as a means to finding out more about an individual but also because it was clear that an important need was being met by our listening. Our "conversations" with our informants tapped into a generally large, preexisting load of feelings and ideas.

Basic Questions Used for the Interviews

Basic information:	Name; date and place of birth; marital status; children (name, residence, frequency of contact); years in current residence; ethnic identity; current and past occupation; income and its sources; health; education.
Genealogical data:	Names, life span, residence of: parents, siblings, children, children-in-law, and grandchildren; parents' siblings, children, and grandchildren; siblings' spouses and children; own spouse(s); spouse's parents; spouse's siblings and children. For each of the above: first name, living status, approximate age, location of residence, frequency and form of contact, nature of relationship (close or distant). For children: occupation.
Friends and acquaintances:	First names of "any close friends" or "other people you know" or "others who are important to you." For each: age, residence, frequency and form of contact, and nature and context of relationship.
Occupational history:	Outline of jobs held during adult life. Feelings about the jobs. Continuing contact with co-workers.

Basic Questions Used for the Interviews—*Continued*

Residential history:	Current and previous residences and their household members. Feelings about each place.
Loneliness:	Are you ever lonely? If so, how much? Would you say you are a loner? Who are you lonely for? When do you get lonely? When you do get lonely, what do you think about?
Activities:	What did you do yesterday? What are some of the things you like to do the best? What do you like at the senior center? When you do _____, do you like it?
Living alone:	What do you think about living alone? What is good for you about living alone? What do you dislike about living alone?
Problems and satisfactions:	If you had to make a list of problems or troubles in your life now, what would be on that list? What gives you the greatest satisfaction or pleasure in life now?
Spouse:	What kind of person was your wife? How did you meet?
Parents:	Tell me about your father (mother). What kind of person was he (she)?
Yesterday:	(asked in every interview session except the first): Let's go through your day from the time you got up in the morning. . . . What time did you get up? What did you do then . . .?
Marriage:	Have you ever thought about (re)marriage in recent years?
Morale:	Would you say that nowadays you are generally pretty happy?

These questions formed the bases around which conversations were held.

Recommendations for Service Providers

It is generally recognized by social service practitioners that it is difficult to interest older men in attending senior centers and that those men who do attend rarely become fully involved in center affairs. One major goal of our research was to explore activities of older men and the reasons they do or do not attend senior centers, and to offer a set of recommendations which might be useful to center staff in developing programs that capture and maintain the interest of men. In this appendix, we offer some suggestions on how center programming for men might be improved. First we focus on why men do and do not seem to attend centers. We then offer several specific suggestions for programs for men.

REASONS MEN ATTEND SENIOR CENTERS

Need for Structure, Companionship, and Belonging

Numerous cultural, social, and personal changes affect the lives of men as they age. Changing daily routines and associates may result in a conscious search for a more fixed structure and for the certainty of companionship provided by centers. This need for structure and companionship may subsume a variety of scenarios. Entry into the center is often begun after a man has gone through a particular transition or after he has "bottomed out" from a significant loss, commonly the death of his wife. Among those center attenders we interviewed, there was often a relatively lengthy period of time between an important life transition (retirement or widowhood) and entrance into a center. Thus in the case of the widowers we interviewed, there was generally a passage of time after the loss while the widower dealt with his grief, normalized his life to some extent, and commenced "building a new life" to the extent that he could. Part of building a new life was a search for new ways of filling in days and for a socially acceptable manner of meeting new people in a friendly environment.

The need for structure looms large for all men. Changes in structure and in group membership will often precipitate a search for replacements. Men need some way to "fill in a day" and to "pass the time." The specific form of the need depends on the personality and disposition of each man. A wide array of possible replacements are available at a center. Some men may desire and find a close intimacy, others merely surface companionship, someone "to pass the time with." Some men may fill in an hour or a morning while others may revolve their whole lives around the center, with entire days involved with center attendance and center friends.

If attendance at a center has come about in response to a major role transition, attendance can signify the reemergence of a man into the social world. This may be a difficult and dramatic step for many individuals. Attendance may be an attempt to put the past in the past, to respond to changes which have occurred, and to now live in the present. Attendance often involves a redefinition or a review of self-identity (see below).

Men who attend centers on a regular basis achieve a degree of regular scheduling in their lives. Having a regular schedule and relying on its certainty can be an important aspect of morale for many men. Acceptance, regularity, and "having a place" are important aspects of structure.

Functional Needs

Men with lower incomes stated clearly that one reason they attended a center was the low-cost meal provided daily. Each center which receives government funds can provide a fixed number of meals daily to center attenders, who must register for their meal upon their arrival at the center in the morning. A small payment (ten or twenty-five cents) may be required. The meal is served at noontime and may be the only low-cost, nutritious meal available daily for many older men. Since many men have never learned how to cook and may regularly eat at restaurants or skip meals to save money, the low-cost lunch at a center is a windfall.

The noontime meal is the "centerpiece" of the day at most centers. All activities stop while the meal is served. Public announcements are made to the group at large at that time. Many attenders leave the center for the day upon completion of the meal, their business at the center completed. Only a small percentage of regular attenders stay around for a full afternoon of activities.

Food is not the only functional need served by the centers. They may provide help with transportation to medical appointments and to shopping. They may help with solving housing problems, provide support in times of emergency, and are an able and ready source of information about services and benefits for older persons.

Nevertheless, of the older men living alone whom we interviewed for our project, it was quite clear that those center attenders who had the least amount of income relied on the meal they received at the center and viewed it as an important element in their day.

Ethnic and Cultural Appropriateness

The nature of the "others" who attend a center is very important to each individual who attends. Although federally funded centers are open to any older person, all public centers are located in particular neighborhoods, and most neighborhoods in Philadelphia or any other big city tend to be the province of one or another ethnic, religious, or racial group. Similarly, nonfederally funded centers, such as those attached to a church or retirement organizations sponsored by large corporations, tend, as well, to draw clientele with a mutuality of interests or a common background.

Men do not overtly state that they will attend a center only if there are "people like me" there. However, it is clear that this is a most significant consideration. Because centers are situated in and are associated with particular neighborhoods, "proximity" often includes "similarity."

In the most ethnically homogenous neighborhoods, centers rely on specific ethnic identity or ethnically appropriate actions (for example, men play *boccie* at a primarily Italian center). A feeling of ethnic or neighborhood cohesion is apparent at most centers.

Staff Support, Peer Friendship

Several men cited a specific friendship or supportive relationship with center staff as one important reason they continued to attend. In most cases reported, such a relationship was with a woman (most center staff are women). Similarly, an often-cited reason that men continued to attend a center was the quality of friends and acquaintances met there. Again, a man may pick from a variety of possible friendship roles, from a nonintimate same-sex relationship to a role as a "center of attention" from a group of older women.

Need to Achieve a Whole Life

Few of those men who were judged to be the most active attended a center, except in an executive or volunteer capacity. It appears that center attendance comes about primarily in order to assuage a particular need, to express individuality, and to achieve a sense of belonging. The reason that the most active men do not attend a center as a "regular" is that they have achieved these goals through some other means. Center regulars are trying to make whole lives for themselves.

Center attendance must entail an assessment of self-identity, an attempt which always must come to grips with the fact that to be old in America is a social stigma, with a low social evaluation and, often, a negative self-image. There is a loss of self-esteem for some men in associating with "all those old people" (as one man put it), but such a loss can be countered or offset when at least some needs are met.

Clearly, centers are not for everyone. There are many whose values and life-styles will remain at odds with those of centers and center attenders. Nevertheless, centers can be extraordinarily beneficial to older men.

REASONS MEN DO NOT ATTEND SENIOR CENTERS

Limited Knowledge

Centers do a very poor job of advertising themselves. Most center attenders noted that they heard about a center by word of mouth from a friend, child, or acquaintance.

It is unclear why centers do such a poor job of publicizing themselves; this is especially enigmatic because there is currently a great deal of interest on the part of the media in the affairs of older persons.

While people tend to know about "senior centers" as a generic entity, many remain ignorant of specific centers and their services in their own neighborhoods. Centers should do a much better job of stirring up interest and making themselves and their services known.

Busy Life

Some men say that they are "too busy" to attend a center. Some men may thus find a center to be superfluous; a busy life already exists. Being busy may be precisely that: existing obligations exclude the possibility of attendance. Or the statement that one is "too busy" may in fact disguise a "busy-ness" the purpose of which is to retain one's independence as it is idiosyncratically defined. Thus an ideology of self-sufficiency can cast doubt on the usefulness and appropriateness of center life.

Most men who attended centers did so for about three hours a day or less, a relatively small daily investment of time. Few men stayed on at the center after lunch. While many center attenders went five days a week, some did not. There was, further, variation in periods of attendance, and some men might miss for days or weeks at a time. Even for regular attenders, then, the investment of time could be rather minimal. Yet despite this, some felt themselves to be too busy to come. In many cases, then, "busy-ness" must in fact be something else.

Health

Perhaps the most serious problem in attendance is impaired health. Attenders may drift in and out of a center depending on the state of their health, and although they may want to continue full time. Individuals who are fully or partially homebound may not be able to attend. Fortunately many centers have a van service which can bring persons with a mobility problem to the center. Most centers are not designed with easy access in mind. Negotiating flights of stairs may be difficult for some. Noise is a problem in some centers; church basements and other such areas that now function as centers were never acoustically perfected and may be troublesome for individuals with reduced hearing capacity.

Involvement with One's Own Problems

One reason men reported that they do not attend centers or, indeed, seek many new situations at all is that their involvement with ongoing personal problems is too great and is viewed as preventing this. Depression and anxiety, after a loss or a role transition, have profound effects which must be worked through before a person can move on to new things.

Perception of the Center as Filled with Too Many "Others"

Perceived inappropriateness of one's presence at a center may be a detriment to continued attendance. While initially a man may "check out" a particular center to make sure that it is ethnically and generally appropriate, he may find, upon his continued attendance, that there are too many undesirable "others." For example, centers are often marked by a disproportion in the sexes which far exceeds that actual post-65 demographic disproportion. The general preponderance of older women is viewed by some men as alienating and isolating. This may be especially felt if a center has no concrete programs for men, since most regular programs (music, crafts, painting, etc.) tend to be dominated by women as well. Men need programs around which their participation can be focused. Also, class and educational distinctions may be operational. For example, older men with a blue-collar background may not be comfortable in an environment filled primarily with men with a white-collar background.

BECOMING A PART OF THE CENTER

While those men who join a center may view their lives at the center in a variety of ways, there is generally a period of transition—of socialization—to center life in which one's social identity is recast. The center may be viewed as a "last resort" in the minds of some men, the place where one turns when all other options have run out and the need to organize and fill in one's day is paramount. For other men, center life may be the continuation of a relatively stable and satisfying social life, especially if one is attending as part of a married couple.

The period of transition—the time of entry into center life—can be slow. If men hear of centers through friends and acquaintances, they may tend to "follow" those friends to particular centers and to participate as their friends participate. Men who walk in, without friends, may tend to be more hesitant in feeling at ease in the center. In both cases attendance at a center leads one to reflect on one's identity. Several men described a feeling of seeing "all those old people there" at the center. To be a center regular, then, one must internalize some aspects of a self-definition as "old." Now one attends a center and therefore must be one of those people who are marked as "old." Men often express the attitude that "I'm not old but those other people at the center are." This is one way of dealing with the negative self-attribute that attendance must provoke. Centers also try to counter the social stigma attached to being old through a kind of group-consciousness-raising (an attitude of "Old is beautiful") and an inversion of the popular stereotype of old (instead of the asexual, disengaged, rocking chair sitter, the flirting, laughing, highly active "doer").

When entering the senior milieu, men must therefore confront a self who is socially defined as old. Since this image is at odds with the dominant cultural image of men—that a man should be active, independent, and self-sufficient—a man who enters a center must confront these stereotypes, to the degree of his own reflectiveness. Men may decide that the center and self-image are at odds and therefore drop out and never return to the center. Others may adjust the sense of value dissonance, work through the transition period, and become a full participant. For some others, still, there may be no value dissonance to begin with. Nevertheless, for many men there is a process of taming which goes on during entry into center life, but the taming is rewarded within the framework of a new, positive set of values for an old age in which a good time is had and good friends are made.

The conflict between youth-oriented cultural values in defining masculinity and generally held negative stereotypes of old age, worked out in the mostly female center environment, is a fundamental problem in attracting and keeping male clientele. We address this problem below.

A new attender also faces several other problems of identity. First, he becomes involved in "something new" possibly for the first time in years. Men may go through the experience of spending several years in the daily care of a declining wife. After her death—and once the period of mourning is complete—attendance at a center may be a part of a general revitalization. The center may be viewed as a place full of possibilities. Further, over time, a man may believe himself to have found a significant place to which he now "belongs," where he has an identity and where he is known. While the degree of attachment to the center varies from person to person, most of the center attenders we talked to recognized a significant—if merely functional—tie.

Each man who continues to attend a center has confronted and dealt with, to a certain extent, the gender problems raised by the center: how does a man, socialized to particular values, get along in a center filled with women?

Whatever the identity conflicts provoked, for many men the benefits of center attendance outweigh the negatives. Thus although several regulars noted that the presence of so many women still bothered them, they had continued to attend the center for several years.

All individuals need to distinguish themselves from others, especially when they are part of a group. "Regulars" gradually carve out a place for themselves as they overcome the various problems of identity. While old age may have problems of loss, boredom, role changes, reduced income, and lowered self-worth associated with it, men may do away with some of them within the center.

SUGGESTIONS FOR CENTERS

The following is a list of several ideas which may be useful to center staffs in increasing the attractiveness of the center for male clientele and in providing services which we believe are necessary for men. While most centers are under severe financial stress and have limits on their space and on the staff they can hire, we make these suggestions with the knowledge that some are low cost and with the expectation that financial duress will not be permanent. Indeed, some of the suggestions relate specifically to ways in which the center can gain income.

Services Oriented Specifically to Men

Centers must provide more programs specifically for men if they are to attract men. The more resources allocated specifically for men, the larger the number of male attenders and the greater the likelihood of permanence in their attendance. This will be true not only if the men who attend are primarily unattached (widowers or bachelors) but also if they come as part of a married couple.

A special room or area for men is useful if there is space. Pool tables, card tables, and the like are uniformly regarded by men as pluses. If there is no space, a special period of time can be set aside during the week "for men only." Two weekday late afternoons, for example, might be set aside just for men. Such a practice might be attractive for those men who feel daunted by the dominance of women at centers.

Centers should be concerned about male staffing for such programs. It is unclear whether men would, in general, prefer male or female staff. But there should be some men available to work with men, on a full- or part-time basis. The reality is that, by and large, center staffs consist of women. Yet some men may find themselves more at ease with men.

The sex of a men's program director is much less of an issue than his personality and, of course, the existence and quality of the program itself. All centers can use a program for men, not only as an intrinsically beneficial thing, but also to counter the demographic and "cultural" imbalance at centers. A program for men must stress several things. It must have a special place or time in which men can separate themselves out from others. It must feature activities and events which are of interest to most men. It must remain neither too exclusivist nor too separate from center life as a whole, but it must allow men to fulfill their needs. With luck it will foster a spirit of comradeship and mutual support.

It is within the context of the men's program that the conflicts between widely held male values (independence and self-sufficiency, primarily) and the effects of stigma and negative and changing self-identity are most prominent. A men's program should be appealing to a wide variety of perspectives on what it is to be a man in late life. Those men who feel that a sense of independence may be threatened by participation in the center can have their feelings assuaged by the noncoercive nature of the variety of acceptable activities.

Publicity and Outreach

Centers must make an effort to extend themselves and to publicize their existence. To what extent this now occurs varies, of course, from center to center, but the rather haphazard and informal way in which men tend to hear about centers belies a failure to make known what centers are and what they do. Outreach should be a permanent feature of center life. Perhaps an open house may be held in which men who are regular attenders can act as hosts and sponsors for men who are contemplating attending. A lot more could be done with systematic advertising in the neighborhood, circulating fliers or mounting posters in local churches, clinics, businesses, and other gathering places.

Outreach to Those of Pre-Retirement Age

Centers could do more in public education of men and women in the 55-to-65 age range about the common experiences and problems of older people. While the goal of such outreach would be primarily educational, such programs could also serve to inform this age group of the existence and services of the center. In such a way a center could not only undertake the useful and necessary task of public education but it could also make contact with potential future attenders. An open public program, held once or twice a year and targeted to this age range, might be a useful format.

Funding and Community Support

A lack of funding for men's activities or for necessary equipment (a pool table, for instance) may be overcome by seeking the participation of local businesses, churches, and institutions in support of the activities of the center as a whole or of the men's program in particular. A great deal of positive feeling for older Americans exists, and it can be used when seeking the financial support of local businesses. Older persons can be the mainstay of so many local businesses, preferring the familiarity of neighborhood establishments over suburban malls and downtown as places of business. Local businesses may, in turn, be grateful and may be willing to help out centers with donations, particularly for specific, closed-ended projects.

A center wishing to staff a position as director of a men's program may similarly be able to do this on a low budget by specifically seeking a volunteer, for example, a social work student in need of a placement or a social science student with an interest in gerontology.

Employment Services

While it is true that men who retire do not often miss having to go to work, the opportunity to work, especially on a part-time basis, is often mentioned by men as something they would like to have. Some men have derived a lifelong identity from work and may wish to continue to work in retirement; others may wish to work to fill in "slack time" and to give some added structure to their days. Of course, the desire for added income may be the major motivating circumstance here.

While some may feel that it is not appropriate for a center to act as a job referral agency, there is no doubt that centers could act as a clearing house for information about informal and part-time jobs in the neighborhood, and due to the center's status it could act as a kind of "official" sponsor for its clientele.

More important, it is probable that public knowledge of the center's work-referral function would act as a further inducement for male clients.

Another related possibility is the establishment of a kind of work co-op under the auspices of the center. A good idea is a "fix-it service": a group of center men who fix small mechanical devices, repair pottery, radios, furniture, etc., not only for center clientele but also for any neighborhood residents. Such an enterprise would require a locked room at the center for storing items to be fixed and personally owned tools and materials. The specific insurance situation would vary from center to center, but the center could require a waiver if necessary. The co-op would require a center staff overseer. It could advertise by word of mouth, posters, and circulars. Any income could be split between the workers and the center. Since it is not uncommon for centers to sponsor sales of knitted items made by women attenders, and since men rarely participate in such activities nor do they have a similar outlet of their own, such a "fix-it service" might complement women's activities. And it would be undertaking work for which there is a real need. Since radios, clocks, porcelain items, furniture, and the like are constantly breaking, such a service may be truly useful instead of just "make-work." In fact there are very few places where one can get these things fixed. If services are priced inexpensively (ten or twenty-five cents to fix a plate, for example), if they are well publicized, and if they can draw noncenter clientele, they may be very successful.

It should be noted, again, that one of the most strongly voiced desires on the part of the men we interviewed was to have the opportunity to work part-time.

Mental Health Needs

The greatest need we perceived on the part of the men we interviewed and one which is implicitly addressed by the existence of centers is for mental health problems to be "treated." By mental health problems we do not necessarily mean "gross" clinical disorders, but rather some of the normal problems of "adjustment to change" in late life. Indeed, the very existence of "senior centers" is based on the idea that profound changes are frequent in late life and that a community based on the commonality of experiences can be built. In such a community, the senior center, the activity and sociality which occur tend to counteract the loss, loneliness, and anomie that can be part of old age. Implicitly, now, centers serve a "mental health" function.

But there is an area of need which must more specifically be met, the mental health problems of men. There is little doubt that men of the generations now age 65 and older have been socialized to contain their emotions and are less gregarious than older women. This does not mean that men do not experience emotions. They do, but they may not know how to handle them and may use patterns such as "denial" and "toughing it out" for emotions that are overwhelming and must be felt for relief to be had. Typically, an emotion that is overwhelming is the death of a man's wife. Similarly, a lack of gregariousness may be overcome and a man may feel "beaten down" if his wife dies or if his social networks are broken up due to deaths.

"Mental health" functions of centers must therefore address a possible lack of gregariousness and social skills on the part of men as a whole as well as the effects of specific incidents of loss and problems of adjustment in late life. Centers may offer professional counseling for more severe problems such as depression and anxiety; similarly, problems of adjustment on a daily basis are met by the very existence of the center: an attending individual is involved in some way in group activities that take him "outside of himself." It is the mid range of problems that must be met: the daily effects of loss, the discussion of options, questions of self-identity and adjustment, the meaning of the past, present, and future. Further, such mid-level problems must be dealt with, without an emphasis on the terms "mental health" or "adjustment," which may be frightening to some. Perhaps the best way to approach a number of "adjustment" or "mental health" issues is as something else. This can be in several ways.

1. The presence of a male staff member whose informal job it is "to get to know the men and how they're doing" may be useful in making men feel cared for. Inquiries about men should be made on an informal basis and should only proceed if a man seems to feel that such a contact is acceptable. Nevertheless, such inquiries should exhibit consistency, that is, they should occur on a regular basis, so that all men feel there is a "personal touch" on the part of the staff.

2. Talk groups. The use of talk groups is an important tool in aiding mental health. Three factors go into structuring a talk group. First, is it mixed sex or men (or women) only? Second, what is the nature and form of the topic? Third, how is it structured? (Is the burden of running it on a staff member? Is the membership closed

and attendance regular?) Such talk groups serve "mental health" functions without any pejorative connotations.

Whether a talk group should be men only or mixed sex depends on a number of factors, such as center resources, number of male attenders, and the topic. Nevertheless, since it is our view that in many centers men need specialized attention, the idea of attempting one regular men-only talk group should be examined. If a men-only talk group, once set up, fails, an attempt to "get one going" should be made on a regular basis, but with a change of topic and of structure.

There are numerous possible topics which may be of interest to men. We can mention a few here. *Current events and politics,* topics of common interest to most people, are the least personal subjects for many. A *sports reminiscence group* might discuss and "replay" specific seasons, baseball or football games, boxing matches of the past. Various *reminiscence groups* can discuss events of childhood, happy times of the past, etc. One which may be particularly interesting to some is a *neighborhood or local history project.* Such a project could be ongoing or seasonal, could involve remembrances or visiting specific places and discussing them, and could tie into a local university or county historical society. The most important thing is that such a project produce something tangible, that people's narrations and memories be written up, reproduced, and circulated, so that they and others may have copies. Finally, a *self-help or support group,* certainly the most intimate and difficult of these, could be formed to deal with specific or general adjustment and emotional issues and with specific adjustment and utility tasks which may be unfamiliar to men (cooking and marketing tasks, for example). Many men have specific utility deficits: many men may never have shopped in a supermarket, drawn up a household budget, ironed, cooked a chicken or frozen vegetables, or sewn on a button. All these may have been performed by wives. Yet some men may wish to learn in an environment in which they will not feel themselves to be ridiculed or stigmatized. There is a difference between "just coping" and "really living."

The success of these groups will have a lot to do with their leadership and organization.

A *current events and politics group* could be run informally, be open to both sexes or not, or rely on guest speakers or not. It would require some organization and leadership. A typical (weekly) program might consist of presentation of the week's news by the group leader (a staff member), perhaps an account of "this day in history," and an open discussion of some particular event ("the upcoming mayor's election"; "happenings in Central America"; "nuclear weapons").

A weekly *sports reminiscence group* would require more direct leadership and probably a "sports nut" as leader. A particular fight could be replayed from old newspaper accounts. A particular baseball season or World Series could be similarly replayed. Someone would have to gather and collate the material to be discussed prior to each session. Membership in the group could be restricted to men; regular attendance may or may not be required.

While such a group would clearly be fun for many men, it would also be competence-affirming, in that the memory of the details of specific events occurring in the past would be required and be renewed. It would be nonthreatening because sports is usually a topic of public discussion in which most fans have a degree of competency. Further, it would involve men together in a group and would perhaps be useful as a "stepping stone" to some involvement in another group.

A *reminiscence group* would also require strong leadership for continuity and focus, and to preserve equality among the participants (that the less loquacious be given a full chance to participate). Topics for such a group would depend to a large extent on the ethnic, experiential, and neighborhood background of the participants. Such a group might benefit from being mixed sex, particularly if it was regulated so that all participants had a full chance to speak (a certain period per session). While topics would be tailored for each group, types of topics which might be of interest are: how life elements such as work, family life, neighborhoods, technology, food, holidays, and politics were in the past. If there is any truth at all that some form of "life review" is beneficial to older individuals' sense of self and of unity, such a group may have benefits beyond the mere pleasure of discussing topics in an organized way.

Along this line, *a local or neighborhood history project* may be a means of involving older men in groups. There are several issues involved here. First, the goal of such a local history should be to record in a tangible way events which have occurred within the living memory of group participants in a particular neighborhood or area. In essence, this would consist of the collection of grounded oral history, a combination of personal recollection and remembrance in relation to specific locations in a neighborhood or city. The goal is to combine personal experience of each participant in all of his or her roles with a sense of specific historical era. A further goal would be to make a concrete written record of the results of the project: a publication or series of publications describing each event or occurrence studied in the history project. (For example, topics might be accounts of physical changes which have occurred in a particular street or area over time; factory or work life in the neighborhood in the past; changes in businesses; family life and routine; church life; entertainment; personal reminiscences of social support networks in the past.)

Clearly such a project will require considerable guidance; the recruitment of a suitable history teacher or professor and a center staff person as leader and organizer would be required. Meetings of the group would be fixed regularly.

Makeup of the group would of course depend on the interest shown by center members and the amount of enthusiasm on the part of the coordinators. It would appear that separate "task forces" for men and women might be a good idea, since much of life earlier in this century was experienced separately. Perhaps the groups of men and women could meet separately for a period of time and then join together once the program is under way. Nevertheless, a variety of methods may be in order: individual interviewing, group meetings, "walks" to view and discuss specific sites, and discussions of photo archival material and old newspaper accounts.

The end product of this group would be the production of one or two publications a year, on one or several topics.

There are numerous benefits from such a project. Functions such as "life review" and competence affirmation are obvious. Working in and relying on groups are also important here. Finally, there is the tangible product: the documentation of significant historical events and changes as personal experiences. Because life has changed so much, the documentation of such social history and of individual lives and experiences is an important goal.

A fifth type of group with mental health functions is a *men's support group*. This is envisioned as a men-only group which meets regularly to discuss specific age-related problems and experiences, for example, widowhood, loneliness, relations with women, family relations, adjustment problems, etc. This group, for mutual support and discussion, is the most overtly "mental health" oriented of the five we have listed here. As such, it may be the least successful group and the most difficult one to organize and sustain. This is because, as we have mentioned, older men may not at all be oriented to groups or to "mental health" issues as overtly stated. However, since the benefits of such a group may be great, an effort should be made, periodically, to organize and carry out such a group. It will be necessary for this group to have a center staff member as a facilitator and have a preferably male social worker as a group member.

In an era when center resources, indeed the whole senior center movement itself, is under serious attack, the situations and problems of some elderly may be forgotten in an attempt to adequately serve a majority. However, it is at just such times that the needs of minorities—in this case older men—so easily lost sight of, should be especially brought into view. Much of what we have suggested here is relatively low cost or self-funding. It mainly requires a sensitive commitment on the part of staff and a continued effort to interest and cultivate men in center life.

References

Arens, D. A. 1982. Widowhood and well-being: An examination of sex differences within a causal model. *Aging and Human Development*, 15:27–40.

Atchley, R. C. 1975. Dimensions of widowhood in later life. *Gerontologist*, 15:176–178.

Berardo, F. M. 1968. Widowhood status in the United States: Perspectives on a neglected aspect of the family life cycle. *Family Coordinator*, 17:191–203.

—— 1970. Survivorship and social isolation: The case of the aged widower. *Family Coordinator*, 19:11–25.

Bock, E. W. and I. L. Weber. 1972. Suicide among the elderly: Isolating widowhood and mitigating alternatives. *Journal of Marriage and the Family*, 34:24–31.

Bohannon, P. 1981. Food of old people in center-city hotels. In C. L. Fry, ed., *Dimensions: Aging, Culture and Health*. Brooklyn: J. F. Bergin.

Bowlby, J. 1980. *Loss: Sadness and Depression*. Vol. 3 of *Attachment and Loss*. New York: Basic Books.

Brody, E. M. 1981. "Women in the middle" and family help to older people. *Gerontologist*, 21:471–480.

Carey, R. G. 1979. Weathering widowhood. *Omega*, 10:163–174.

Clark, M. and B. G. Anderson. 1967. *Culture and Aging: An Anthropological Study of Older Americans*. Springfield, Ill.: C C Thomas.

Clayton, P. J. et al. 1973. Anticipatory grief and widowhood. *British Journal of Psychiatry*, 122:47–51.

Cleveland, W. P. and D. T. Gianturco. 1976. Remarriage probability after widowhood: A retrospective method. *Journal of Gerontology*, 31:99–103.

Cohen, C. I. and J. Sokolovsky. 1980. Social engagement versus isolation: The case of the aged in SRO hotels. *Gerontologist*, 20:36–44.

Cumming, E. and W. E. Henry. 1961. *Growing Old: The Process of Disengagement.* New York: Basic Books.

Eckert, J. K. 1980. *The Unseen Elderly: A Study of Marginally Subsistent Hotel Dwellers.* San Diego: Campanile Press, San Diego State University.

Ferraro, K. F. and C. M. Barresi. 1982. The impact of widowhood on the social relations of older persons. *Research on Aging,* 4:227–247.

Frank, G. 1979. Finding the common denominator: A phenomenological critique of the life history method. *Ethos,* 7:68–94.

Fromm-Reichman, F. 1959. Loneliness. *Psychiatry,* 22:1–15.

Gallagher, D. E., J. N. Breckenridge, L. W. Thompson, and J. A. Peterson. 1983. Effects of bereavement on indicators of mental health in elderly widows and widowers. *Journal of Gerontology,* 38:565–571.

Geertz, C. 1975. On the nature of anthropological understanding. *American Scientist,* 63:47–53.

George, L. K. 1980. *Role Transition in Later Life.* Monterey, Calif.: Brooks/Cole.

Gerber, I. et al. 1975. Anticipatory grief and aged widows and widowers. *Journal of Gerontology,* 30:225–229.

Glick, I. O., R. D. Weiss, and C. M. Parkes. 1974. *The First Year of Bereavement.* New York: John Wiley.

Gubrium, J. 1974. Marital desolation and the evaluation of everyday life in old age. *Journal of Marriage and the Family,* 36:107–113.

—— 1975. Being single in old age. *Aging and Human Development,* 6:29–41.

Hammer, P. G. and F. S. Chapin. 1972. *Human Time Allocation: A Case Study of Washington, D.C.* Chapel Hill: University of North Carolina, Center for Urban and Regional Studies.

Hartog, J. 1980. The anlage and ontogeny of loneliness. In J. Hartog, J. R. Audy, and Y. A. Cohen, eds., *The Anatomy of Loneliness.* New York: International Universities Press.

Harvey, C. D. and H. M. Bahr. 1974. Widowhood, morale and affiliation. *Journal of Marriage and the Family,* 36:97–106.

Havighurst, R. J. 1968. A social-psychological perspective on aging. *Gerontologist,* 8:67–71.

Helsing, K. J., M. Szklo, and G. W. Comstock. 1981. Factors associated with mortality after widowhood. *American Journal of Public Health,* 71:802–809.

Heltsley, M. E. and R. C. Powers. 1975. Social integration and perceived adequacy of interaction of the rural aged. *Gerontologist,* 15:533–536.

Henry, J. 1980. Loneliness and vulnerability. In J. Hartog, J. R. Audy, and Y. A. Cohen, eds., *The Anatomy of Loneliness.* New York: International Universities Press.

Heyman, D. K. and D. T. Gianturco. 1973. Long-term adaptation by the elderly to bereavement. *Journal of Gerontology,* 28:350–353.

Hutchinson, I. W. 1975. The significance of marital status for morale and life satisfaction among lower-income elderly. *Journal of Marriage and the Family,* 37:287–293.

Hyman, H. H. 1983. *Of Time and Widowhood: Nationwide Studies of Enduring Effects.* Durham, N.C.: Duke Press Policy Studies (Duke University Press).

Jacobs, B. 1974. *Involving Men: A Challenge for Senior Centers.* Washington, D.C.: National Council on the Aging.

Johnson, C. L. and D. J. Catalano. 1981. Childless elderly and their family supports. *Gerontologist,* 21:610–618.

Kaufman, S. 1981. Cultural components of identity in old age: A case study. *Ethos,* 9:51–87.

Kivett, V. R. 1979. Discriminators of loneliness among rural elderly: Implications for interventions. *Gerontologist,* 19:108–115.

Kuypers, J. A. and V. L. Bengtson. 1973. Social breakdown and competence. *Human Development,* 16:181–201.

Langness, L. and G. Frank. 1981. *Lives: An Anthropological Approach to Biography.* Novato, Calif.: Chandler and Sharp.

Lawton, M. P. N.d. Old men living alone. Research proposal. Philadelphia Geriatric Center.

—— 1981. An ecological view of living arrangements. *Gerontologist,* 21:59–66.

—— 1985. Activities and leisure. In M. P. Lawton and G. Maddox, eds., *Annual Review of Gerontology and Geriatrics.* New York: Springer.

Lemon, B. W., V. L. Bengtson, and J. A. Peterson. 1972. An exploration of the activity theory of aging. *Journal of Gerontology,* 27:511–523.

Lopata, H. Z. 1973a. *Widowhood in an American City.* Cambridge, Mass.: Schenkman.

—— 1973b. Loneliness: Forms and components. In R. S. Weiss, ed., *Loneliness: The Experience of Emotional and Social Isolation.* Cambridge, Mass.: MIT Press.

—— 1979. *Women as Widows,* New York: Elsevier.

Louis Harris and Associates. 1975. *The Myth and Reality of Aging in America.* Washington, D.C.: National Council on the Aging.

—— 1981. *Aging in the Eighties: America in Transition.* Washington, D.C.: National Council on the Aging.

Matthews, S. H. 1979. *The Social World of Old Women: Management of Self-Identity.* Beverly Hills: Sage (vol. 78, Sage Library of Social Research).

Morgan, L. 1976. A re-examination of widowhood and morale. *Journal of Gerontology,* 31:687–695.

Moss, M. S. and S. Z. Moss. 1980. The image of the deceased spouse in remarriages of elderly widow(er)s. *Journal of Gerontological Social Work,* 3:59–70.

—— 1984. Some aspects of the elderly widow(er)'s persistent tie with the deceased spouse. *Omega,* 15:195–206.

Moustakas, C. E. 1961. *Loneliness*. Englewood Cliffs, N.J.: Prentice-Hall.

National Council on the Aging. 1978. *Fact Book on Aging: A Profile of America's Older Population*. Washington, D.C.: National Council on the Aging.

Nydegger, C. 1980. Role and age transitions: A potpourri of ideas. In C. L. Fry and J. Keith, eds., *New Methods for Old Age Research*. Chicago: Loyola University, Center for Urban Policy.

Parkes, C. M. 1972. *Bereavement: Studies of Grief in Adult Life*. New York: International Universities Press.

Pelto, P. J. 1970. *Anthropological Research: The Structure of Inquiry*. New York: Harper and Row.

Peplau, L. A. and M. A. Caldwell. 1978. Loneliness: A cognitive analysis. *Essence*, 2:207–220.

Perlman, D. and L. A. Peplau. 1981. Towards a social psychology of loneliness. In S. Duck and R. Gilmour, eds., *Personal Relationships. 3: Personal Relationships in Disorder*. London: Academic Press.

—— 1982. Theoretical approaches to loneliness. In L. A. Peplau and D. Perlman, eds., *Loneliness: A Sourcebook of Current Theory, Research, and Therapy*. New York: Wiley-Interscience.

Philadelphia City Planning Commission. May 1982. Highlights of the 1980 Census for Philadelphia. Technical Information Paper.

Pihlblad, C. T. and D. L. Adams. 1972. Widowhood, social participation and life satisfaction. *Aging and Human Development*, 3:323–330.

Reichard, S. K., F. Livson, and P. G. Peterson. 1980. *Aging and Personality: A Study of Eighty-Seven Older Men*. New York: Arno Press. Reprint of the 1962 edition.

Revenson, T. A. and J. L. Johnson. 1984. Social and demographic correlates of loneliness in late life. *American Journal of Community Psychology*, 12:71–85.

Riesman, D., N. Glazer, and R. Denney. 1961. *The Lonely Crowd: A Study of the Changing American Character*. New Haven, Conn.: Yale University Press.

Rosow, I. 1974. *Socialization to Old Age*. Berkeley and Los Angeles: University of California Press.

Rowles, G. D. 1978. *Prisoners of Space? Exploring the Geographical Experience of Older People*. Boulder, Colo.: Westview Press.

Rubenstein, C. and P. Shaver. 1980. Loneliness in two northeastern cities. In J. Hartog, J. R. Audy, and Y. A. Cohen, eds., *The Anatomy of Loneliness*. New York: International Universities Press.

—— 1982. The experience of loneliness. In L. A. Peplau and D. Perlman, eds., *Loneliness: A Sourcebook of Current Theory, Research and Therapy*. New York: Wiley-Interscience.

Rubinstein, R. L. In press. The construction of a day by elderly widowers. *Aging and Human Development*.

Sadler, W. A. and T. B. Johnson, Jr. 1980. From loneliness to anomia. In J. Hartog, J. R. Audy, and Y. A. Cohen, eds., *The Anatomy of Loneliness.* New York: International Universities Press.

Shanas, E. 1979a. Social myth as hypothesis: The case of the family relations of old people. *Gerontologist,* 19:3–9.

—— 1979b. The family as a social support system in old age. *Gerontologist,* 19:169–174.

Shapiro, H. S. 1982. Census data tracks a graying of Phila. *Philadelphia Inquirer,* June 14, 1982, p. 1.

Sullivan, H. S. 1953. *The Interpersonal Theory of Psychiatry.* New York: Norton.

Townsend, P. 1957. *The Family Life of Old People.* London: Routledge and Kegan Paul.

—— 1968. Isolation, desolation and loneliness. In E. Shanas et al., eds. *Old People in Three Industrial Societies.* New York: Atherton Press.

Treas, J. and A. Van Helst. 1976. Marriage and remarriage rates among older Americans. *Gerontologist,* 16:132–136.

Tunstall, J. 1965. *Old and Alone: A Sociological Study of Old People.* London: Routledge and Kegan Paul.

U.S. Department of Commerce, Bureau of the Census. 1982. *Current housing reports.* H-170-78-33. Philadelphia, PA-NJ SMSA. Housing characteristics for selected metropolitan areas. Annual Housing Survey, 1978. Washington, D.C.: GPO.

U.S. Department of Commerce. 1979. *Statistical Abstract of the United States: 1979.* Washington, D.C.

—— 1981a. *Advance Reports: 1980 Census of the Population and Housing.* PHC-80-v-40. Pennsylvania. Final population and housing units count. Issued March 1981. Washington, D.C.

—— 1981b. *Advance Reports: 1980 Census of the Population and Housing.* PHC-80-v-32. New Jersey. Final population and housing units count. Issued March 1981. Washington, D.C.

U.S. Senate. 1982. Special Committee on Aging. *Developments in Aging: 1981,* vol. 1 (Senate Report 97–314). Washington, D.C.: GPO.

Von Witzleben, H. D. 1958. On loneliness. *Psychiatry,* 21:37–43.

Ward, R. A. 1979. The never married in later life. *Journal of Gerontology,* 34:861–869.

Weiss, R. S. 1973. *Loneliness: The Experience of Emotional and Social Isolation.* Cambridge, Mass.: MIT Press.

Index